ZYGMUNT BAUMAN AND THE THEORY OF CULTURE

ZYGMUNT BAUMAN AND THE THEORY OF CULTURE

Dariusz Brzeziński

Translated by Katarzyna Bartoszyńska

McGill-Queen's University Press
Montreal & Kingston • London • Chicago

ISBN 978-0-2280-1396-9 (cloth)
ISBN 978-0-2280-1397-6 (paper)
ISBN 978-0-2280-1490-4 (ePDF)
ISBN 978-0-2280-1491-1 (ePUB)

Legal deposit fourth quarter 2022
Bibliothèque nationale du Québec

Printed in Canada on acid-free paper that is 100% ancient forest free (100% post-consumer recycled), processed chlorine free

This publication was written at the Institute of Philosophy and Sociology of the Polish Academy of Sciences, which also co-financed its translation.

This research was funded by the National Science Centre in Poland on the basis of the grant awarded after obtaining a doctoral degree, based on the decision no. DEC-2014/12/S/HS2/00391.

LIBRARY AND ARCHIVES CANADA CATALOGUING IN PUBLICATION

Title: Zygmunt Bauman and the theory of culture / Dariusz Brzeziński ; translated by Katarzyna Bartoszyńska.
Other titles: Twórczość Zygmunta Baumana w kontekście współczesnych teorii kultury. English.
Names: Brzeziński, Dariusz, author. | Bartoszynska, Katarzyna, translator.
Description: Translation of: Twórczość Zygmunta Baumana w kontekście współczesnych teorii kultury. | Includes bibliographical references and index.
Identifiers: Canadiana (print) 20220391947 | Canadiana (ebook) 20220391971 | ISBN 9780228013976 (paper) | ISBN 9780228013969 (cloth) | ISBN 9780228014904 (ePDF) | ISBN 9780228014911 (ePUB)
Subjects: LCSH: Bauman, Zygmunt, 1925-2017. | LCSH: Culture—Philosophy. | LCSH: Sociology—Philosophy.
Classification: LCC HM479.B39 B7913 2022 | DDC 301.092—dc23

Contents

Acknowledgments

This book is a revised and modified version of a work originally published in Polish as a result of a research project financed with the support of the National Science Centre in Poland (Grant no. 2014/12/S/HS2/00391). I am very grateful to Professor Joanna Kurczewska, the director of the Department of Theoretical Sociology of the Institute of Philosophy and Sociology of the Polish Academy of Sciences, for creating excellent working conditions for my research. I also owe a debt of gratitude to Professor Mark Davis, Dr Thomas Campbell, and Dr Jack Palmer from the Bauman Institute at the University of Leeds, with whom I not only consulted on my research but also started working on other projects related to Zygmunt Bauman's thought (e.g., Palmer and Brzeziński 2022b; Brzeziński et al. 2021; Palmer, Brzeziński, and Campbell 2020). Some of them have emerged from materials in the Special Collections of the University of Leeds Library, where the Janina and Zygmunt Bauman Archive is based. I am very grateful to Professor Mark Davis, the founding director of the Bauman Institute, and Timothy Procter, the collections and engagement manager at the University of Leeds Library, for allowing me to conduct the research in the archive and for all of their assistance in the process.

Portions of this book have been presented at numerous conferences and seminars at, for example, University of Oxford, Imperial College in London, University of Leeds, Jagiellonian University in Kraków, University of Warsaw, Adam Mickiewicz University, University of Wrocław, University of Lodz, University of Gdańsk, the Polish Academy of Learning, and the Polish Academy of Sciences. The feedback I received from audiences was crucial to my work. I also wish to sincerely thank the early readers of this book – or its various fragments – for their observations and comments, with special gratitude to Professor Aleksandra Jasińska-Kania, Professor Izabela Wagner, and Dr Jack Palmer. Of course, all responsibility for the analyses and opinions expressed here is mine alone. Two sections of this book were previously published in scientific journals in slightly modified forms: the first chapter was published in 2020 as "From Revisionism to Retrotopia: Stability and Variability in Zygmunt Bauman's Theory of Culture," in *European Journal of Social Theory* 23 (4): 459–76; and a part of the second chapter was published in 2017 in Polish as "Redukcja i proliferacja ambiwalencji: Teoria kultury Zygmunta Baumana w polskim okresie jego twórczości," in *Studia Socjologiczne* 1 (224): 29–57.

I would like to express my gratitude to Dr Katarzyna Bartoszyńska, the translator of the book, for her excellent co-operation. My thanks are also due to Professor Magdalena Szczyrbak, the translator of the first chapter, which was published in 2020 in the *European Journal of Social Theory.* I also express my gratitude to those who decided to financially support the translation of this book: Professor Andrzej Rychard, director of the Institute of Philosophy and Sociology of the Polish Academy of Sciences; Professor Adrien Favell, director of the Bauman Institute at the University of Leeds; and Irena Bauman, the daughter of Zygmunt Bauman, who supported this initiative on behalf of the Bauman Estate. I also wish to sincerely thank the editors at McGill-Queen's University Press, with whom I had the pleasure of working on this project, especially Richard Baggaley, the UK editor, for his help and understanding, and Angela Wingfield for her excellent copy-editing work.

Finally, I would like to thank my wife, Karolina, for her love and continuous support.

ZYGMUNT BAUMAN AND THE THEORY OF CULTURE

Introduction

THE MEANING OF THE THEORY OF CULTURE IN THE WORK OF ZYGMUNT BAUMAN

Zygmunt Bauman (1925–2017) was one of the greatest intellectuals of the twentieth and early twenty-first centuries, recognized by numerous prestigious awards and accolades, and the author of works that are valued both by scholars in the humanities and social sciences and by a broader public. During the more than six decades of his academic career he wrote over seventy books and dozens of academic articles, as well as numerous essays and feuilletons (Palmer, Brzeziński, and Campbell 2020). In them he examined a remarkably broad range of issues, including social theory and methodology, the human condition, and social, cultural, political, and economic transformations. What is more, it was not uncommon for him to connect all the various dimensions of these reflections, which gave many of his works an eclectic character. It is worth mentioning in this context that Bauman defined *sociology* quite broadly. In a conversation with Keith Tester he asserted that the discipline "is porous on all sides and is notorious for its enormous, insatiable absorptive power," and also that "it comes nearer than any other academic discipline to embracing human experience in its entirety" (Bauman and Tester 2001, 40). This conviction was reflected in his frequent references to the work of historians, political scientists, philosophers, economists, psychologists, and literary theorists. His work is multidisciplinary and has a multiplicity of different threads running through it, as well as featuring multiple paradigms. From the period beginning in the 1950s, when he wrote his works in a Marxist-Leninist vein, to the second decade of the twenty-first century, when he developed his idea of liquid modernity, he used a variety of theoretical approaches in his work. Some of them he also, to a significant degree, co-created.

Despite such significant variety in the studies he conducted, some common points can be identified. Three decades ago, Bauman named two of them: the problem of suffering and the question of culture (Bauman 1992a, 206, 207). In my opinion, his observations from that time period apply to all of his work, including the papers that he wrote in the late twentieth century and in the twenty-first century. As far as the issue of suffering is concerned, Bauman identified it at the beginning of his academic work with the situation of the working class, but in later years he extended his analysis to many other groups experiencing injustice, exclusion, or violence (see, for example, Bauman 2016b, 2004c, 1989c). He not only analyzed the condition of the downtrodden but also pointed to the need to undertake actions aimed at changing their situation. However much the methods he proposed for carrying out these transformations varied over time, the very idea of transcending existing reality remained an unchanging feature of his sociology (Jacobsen 2007). The second point outlined by Bauman – which is the subject of the considerations in this book – concerns the theory of culture. My analysis will be situated in the context of schools of thought developed in the second half of the twentieth century and the beginning of the twenty-first, primarily featuring Marxism-Leninism, humanistic psychology, Marxist revisionism, functionalism, structuralism, ethnomethodology, critical theory, existentialism, hermeneutics, post-structuralism, postmodernity, and reflections on globalization. On the one hand, I will explain how Bauman's work was inspired by the work of representatives of these orientations, and, on the other, I will describe the importance of his work for the development of all these intellectual currents. The diachronic and comparative perspective that I will apply in my analyses will serve as a basis for more general reflections on contemporary transformations in the humanities and social sciences.

Among the great variety of sociological reflections on culture, two opposing types are often distinguished, which will be described here as "systemic" and "repertoire"[1] (see, for example, Griswold 2013; Sewell [1999] 2005, 152–74; Swidler 1986). According to the first, culture is a collection of norms, patterns, or meanings creating a coherent whole that is internalized during the process of socialization and reflected in practices undertaken within a given collective. The opposite perspective assumes that culture comprises a loosely integrated collection of heterogeneous elements, providing individuals with the means to act in concrete situations. Reflections on both ways of defining culture were also undertaken by Zygmunt Bauman ([2017a] 2018; 1999, vii–lv; 1997b, 127–40). Of the first of these, he said: "[T]he ultimate state that culture was envisaged as attaining was that of a *system*, in which every element has a function to perform, in which nothing is left to chance, no element is left alone, but dovetails, gears and co-operates with the other; in which a clash between the elements may come solely from an error in design or build, from neglect or deficiency; and which has room solely for such rules of conduct as perform a useful function in supporting the envisaged model of order" (Bauman 1997b, 129). The second he described in the same text in the following way: "a vision of culture starkly different from the one ossified in the orthodox paradigm: a vision of a perpetually restless, unruly and rebellious action, ordering yet itself not ordered, blasphemously disregarding the sacrosanct distinction between the substantive and the marginal, the necessary and the accidental (a mind-boggling attitude, if seen from the order-installing perspective)" (133). In Bauman's view the main direction of the evolution of a theory of culture was demarcated in the last few decades by the shift from its systemic forms to its repertoire ones. Both ways of understanding culture were, however, consistently present in his work, though at different phases of his career one of them would move to the forefront. Bauman made many attempts – with varying degrees of success – to connect both of them within the framework of a single theory of culture.

Although the problem of culture was the central question throughout all of Bauman's work, previous studies have not included a holistic or comparative approach to the subject. Referring to the first of these issues, it is worth pointing out at the outset that a portion of the monographs devoted to an examination of his work is focused above all on his analyses of the transformations of modernity (e.g., Rattansi 2017; Blackshaw 2005). Even the books whose authors went beyond this issue (e.g., Tester 2004; Smith 1999) contain very few references to his analyses from the fifteen-year period of his work at the University of Warsaw. Meanwhile – as I will demonstrate – many of the texts that are only available in

Polish have significant meaning for understanding Bauman's later work. This pertains especially to his theory of culture. Referring to the second of the issues, I would like to observe that scholars of Bauman's work rarely locate it in a larger context of the transformations taking place in the theory of culture. They use a comparative approach above all in reference to his theories of modernity (e.g., Jacobsen 2017; Elliott 2007). The question of the relationship between his visions of culture and the work of representatives of such schools of thought as revisionist Marxism, neo-evolutionism, or ethnomethodology, for example, is rarely the subject of their analysis. Thus, the originality of this book is based on its holistic analysis of all of Bauman's work on culture in the context of a broad spectrum of theoretical frameworks developed in the social sciences and humanities in the second half of the twentieth century and the beginning of the twenty-first. In this context, the critical dimension of the analyses presented in this book should also be emphasized, as many of the monographs on Bauman's work are clearly written in a more descriptive vein (e.g., Tester 2004; Beilharz 2000; Smith 1999).

The analyses have been organized as follows. In the first chapter I describe the constitutive features of Bauman's theory of culture and sketch out the main paths of its evolution. I point out four continuous elements of his reflections on the subject. I also distinguish four major phases in the development of his theory of culture, each lasting approximately fifteen years; they are analyzed in the subsequent chapters. In the second chapter I focus on Bauman's theory of culture in the years 1953–1968. I demonstrate that during this entire time, reflections on culture played an essential role in his work, and in the 1960s they moved to the forefront. At the time, he problematized this category in two ways. On the one hand, he identified it as a mechanism to reduce ambivalence, and, on the other, he offered the opposite image, as a proliferation of ambivalence. In the third chapter I analyze Bauman's work from the time of his forced emigration out of Poland to the beginning of the 1980s. I argue that of primary importance to his theory of culture from that period was the idea of *praxis*, adopted from Antonio Gramsci. He initially identified this term primarily with the tendency to structure social reality, in order to then direct particular attention to the process of its transformation. The fourth chapter is devoted to a reflection on the relationship between Bauman's theory of culture and his perspective on the issue of the transformation of society: from modern to postmodern. In the first part of this chapter I undertake a critical analysis of his perspective on culture as a disciplinary mechanism, and in the following portion I point to the understanding of this category as a "flexible repertoire of interpretive resources" (Kempny 1995, 188). I emphasize that these two levels of reflection were clearly interconnected. The fifth chapter contains an analysis of Bauman's work in the twenty-first century, within the framework of liquid modernity. I concentrate on two particular dimensions of his analysis of culture from that period: individualization and globalization. I refer to his reflections on the process of the "liquification" of structures, institutions, and norms but also point out that with the passing of time he emphasized ever more clearly the opposite processes. In the concluding portion I lay out the aspects of Bauman's theory of culture that to the greatest degree penetrated into the social sciences and humanities.

Finally, I would like to highlight three particularly important events that took place in the course of writing this book. Firstly, I discovered the editorial copy of Bauman's book *Sketches in the Theory of Culture*, previously considered to be irretrievably lost. It was supposed to have been published in 1968, but the political situation in Poland at the time and the severe repression of the author (Wagner 2020, 258–86) made this impossible. The proofs were lost, and Bauman's manuscript was confiscated by border agents when he and his family embarked on their forced emigration to Israel (Brzeziński [2017] 2018, vii–xxv). Studying that book – published first in Polish in 2017 and then in English in 2018 – allowed for the illumination of previously unknown aspects of Bauman's theory of culture. Secondly, in February 2016 I spoke with Zygmunt Bauman about the evolution of his theory of culture in his home in Leeds. I was also the beneficiary of numerous instances of kindness from him and his second wife, Aleksandra Jasińska-Kania. Throughout the later months I remained in contact with Zygmunt Bauman via email, primarily in relation to the publication of *Sketches in the Theory of Culture*. In the last letter I received from him – on 23 December 2016 – he expressed his joy that the book was being published. This is connected to the third event: Bauman's death at the beginning of 2017. I would like to express here the personal aspect of this loss. For me it meant the departure of an author whose works had significantly shaped my own sociological imagination. Bauman's theory of culture has also defined, to a great extent, my interests in sociology. I hope to continue to develop them further, with many thanks to the professor for illuminating this fascinating path.

1

CONTINUITIES AND CHANGES IN ZYGMUNT BAUMAN'S THEORY OF CULTURE

INTRODUCTION

Published posthumously, Zygmunt Bauman's book *Retrotopia* begins with a reference to Walter Benjamin's commentary on Paul Klee's watercolour, painted in 1920 and entitled *Angelus Novus* (Bauman 2017c, 1–2). In his ninth thesis on the philosophy of history, Benjamin suggested that the figure depicted in the painting could be compared to the "angel of history." He stated that the angel was heading towards the future, even though he had his back turned. The figure was looking at past events, which he saw as "one single catastrophe which keeps piling wreckage upon wreckage, and hurls it in front of his feet" (Benjamin [1940] 1969, 249). Referring to this interpretation, Bauman ignored its religious and mystical dimension and focused only on the relationship between the fear of the past and the rush towards the future. In this context he referred to the time when this work of art was created, shortly after the end of the First World War. Bauman also argued that the watercolour – subject to reinterpretation – remained a useful illustration of ongoing changes in the twenty-first century. In his view, the angel of history should be seen today as looking fearfully, not at the past but at the future. He argued that the latter remains increasingly uncertain and, what is more, is filled with a growing number of threats. At the same time, the past – subjected to mythologization – appears more and more often as an oasis of safety and calm. To describe this turn toward the past – symbolized by the 180° rotation of the angel of history – Bauman used the concept of retrotopia (Bauman 2017c).

I have described both interpretations of Paul Klee's painting because they allow me to outline the analytical framework of Bauman's sociological work. Although his reflections on the consequences of the growing fear of the future served as the closure to his sociological work, its beginning was related to the analysis of a reality in which the fear of the past clearly affected social life. Bauman started his academic career eight years after the end of the Second World War, and, on the one hand, his earliest texts include references to not-so-distant tragic events, while, on the other, they testify to his belief in an imminent entry into the "kingdom of liberty" (Bauman 1955; Bauman and Wiatr 1953; see Walicki 1997). Over the course of the more than six decades of sociological work – ranging from a future-oriented Marxism-Leninism to the analyses of "retrotopic" tendencies in liquid modernity – Bauman continuously voiced his thoughts on cultural transformations as well as engaging in theoretical reflections related to them. What is more, he carefully followed related investigations carried out in the humanities and social sciences. He assessed new concepts and not infrequently incorporated elements of them into his own analyses. These are, accordingly, characterized by a significant dynamism, manifested through numerous turning points and reassessments. However, one may also see elements of continuity and stability in them. Bauman referred to this in the following manner: "I was seeking for an answer to the same questions all along, and if I didn't find it, I moped elsewhere. But I took my questions with me" (Bauman 1992a, 207). Were we to use the metaphorical language so close to his heart, and to compare the subsequent stages of the development of his theory of culture to the rings of a growing tree, the problems that troubled him – and to which he referred in this utterance – would constitute its core.

This chapter seeks to demonstrate the continuities and changes in Bauman's work on culture. The reflections will form a foundation for analyses presented in later chapters. In the first section I highlight the fact that many of the concepts developed by Bauman during his early career continued to determine his way of thinking about culture in subsequent years. This applies in particular to *the critical dimension* of his thought, *the combination of synchronic and diachronic analyses, the constant references to social structure*, and, finally, to the striving for *a balance between agency and structure.* In the second section I outline major directions in the evolution of Bauman's theory of culture over six decades. They were based, above all, on a shift away from identifying the functionality of culture as vital for the stability of the social system toward emphasizing its changeable and dynamic nature. They were also related to Bauman's development of reflections on the genesis and rise of modernity. In this context he stressed the rise of disciplinary mechanisms during modernity alongside the growing importance of ambivalence, pluralism, and individuation in contemporary condition. The book *Retrotopia* marks yet another reassessment in his theory, pictured as the angel of history turning his face towards the future, while heading towards the past.

CONSTITUTIVE ELEMENTS OF ZYGMUNT BAUMAN'S THEORY OF CULTURE

In the conversation that Keith Tester conducted with Bauman at the beginning of the current century, the latter pointed out that theoretical reflections on culture should correspond to its nature. This nature, in turn, he argued, remained "a permanent revolution" or a rebellion against any attempts at a permanent ordering of social reality. He noted: "If ... we agree to use the concept of culture in the way here suggested, then theory which takes culture seriously, as the specifically human mode of being, cannot but be a 'critical' theory ... Once you accept culture with its endemic restlessness and its inborn inclination to transcendence as the foundational characteristic of the human mode-of-being, the idea of 'critical theory' appears pleonastic, like 'buttery butter' or 'metallic iron'" (Bauman and Tester 2001, 33). The conviction presented here was one of the constitutive features of Bauman's theory of culture throughout most of his academic career (except its beginning, discussed later in the chapter). On the one hand, he made efforts to develop a theoretical apparatus that would allow him to capture the essence of culture, and, on the other, he intentionally shaped it to inspire opposition to the processes that he described using this framework. Towards this end, he relied on many rhetorical strategies, including the hyperbolizing of specific trends. This method was used in his analysis of the modern "garden" culture (Bauman 1987), the culture of individualism (Bauman 2001d), the cultural dimensions of globalization (Bauman 2011a), and so forth. However, the best way to present it is to show how it was applied in Bauman's analyses of consumer culture, because it remained a constant object of his scholarly inquiry over more than six decades.

It is worthwhile in this context to compare Bauman's texts from different stages of his scientific career. In 1966, he published the book *Culture and Society: Preliminaries*,[1] in which – alongside many other threads – he painted a picture of a socially and culturally heterogeneous community (he called it "Htht").[2] He claimed that in the absence, or as a result of a substantial weakening, of other elements holding this society together, market mechanisms were increasingly gaining in importance (Bauman 1966a, 420–50). They played, as he believed, the most significant role in the formation of individual motivations, and they were reflected in all the dimensions of collective life. Among the exemplifications of this phenomena he listed the reification of interpersonal relationships,[3] the commodification of the axiological sphere, and so on.[4] These analyses were to a large extent convergent with the studies that Bauman carried out several decades later, which were devoted to the role and the meaning of "consumerist syndrome"[5] (Bauman 2007a). Both in the 1960s and in the current century, he focused exclusively on the negative consequences of the development of consumerism, and in his descriptions of them he relied on hyperbolizing. While this type of sociological discourse may give rise to reasonable doubts – which will be discussed further in the book – what is worth noting is the intention underlying such discourse. It was his ambition to break through the barrier of common-sense thought and to plant seeds of critical thinking.

The critical dimension of Bauman's theory of culture always went along with another constitutive element of his analysis in this area, namely, the combination of synchronic and diachronic perspectives. To start with, it is worth mentioning that his model of a socially and culturally heterogeneous community ("Htht") was part of a diachronic typology[6] (Bauman 1966a). It was inspired just as much by the Marxist philosophy (Marx and Engels [1932] 1970) of history as by neo-evolutionary approaches (White 1959; Steward 1955). In *Culture and Society* Bauman distinguished four types of communities, taking into account the heterogeneity and homogeneity of their social and cultural dimensions. He analyzed the processes that took place in the second half of the twentieth century within the Htht communities in the context of phenomena that occurred in former types of societies.

A similar combination of synchronic and diachronic reflections was typical of his studies on culture in subsequent years. For instance, in one of the chapters of his book *Culture as Praxis*, published in 1973, he highlighted the transformations taking place in the Western world in terms of how ambiguity was approached (Bauman 1973b, 120–57). The transition from the Middle Ages to modernity was, in his view, marked by the following property: "The orderliness of the human world, far from being automatically assured, now became a matter of continuous and active concern" (134–5). The processes that were then set in motion resulted, he argued, in the striving for the elimination of all forms of ambivalence. However, Bauman's analyses of the social reality of the second half of the twentieth century convinced him that this trend was then reversed, which, he believed, could mean that "human culture will face a revolution unmatched by the most drastic upheavals of the past' (157). These analyses anticipated his subsequent studies related to the genesis and the transformation of modernity.

In the late 1980s and in the 1990s, Bauman carried out analyses based on a diachronic model in which he distinguished traditional, modern, and postmodern societies (Bauman 1987). Even though, with the passage of time, he devoted increasingly more attention to the condition of culture in postmodern society, in his analyses he almost always referred to earlier centuries (e.g., Bauman 1997b, 1992b, 1991a). In the twenty-first century the co-existence of the diachronic and synchronic dimensions in Bauman's studies was, in turn, manifested through the juxtaposition of "solid" and "liquid" modernity (e.g., Bauman 2000c). Bauman argued that – despite the two conditions being united by a thirst for "creative destruction" – in each of them this desire was realized differently. In the case of solid modernity, it was linked to the striving for the formation of structures unaffected by time, while, at present, it takes the form of a never-ending chain of changes subject to constant acceleration. It is worth stressing, however, that some of the processes he described in the context of postmodernity and liquid modernity were very much in keeping with his reflections dating back to the 1960s and the 1970s. At that time he also wrote about ongoing heterogenization, the proliferation of ambivalence, appreciation of individualism, and so forth (Bauman [1968c] 2018, 1966a). What is more, both at the beginning and at the end of his work, Bauman used the notions of "liquidity" and "amorphousness" in descriptions of contemporary culture (Bauman [1968c] 2018, 117, 118, 149, 150, 163, 164; see Brzeziński [2017] 2018).

A statement from the very beginning of *Culture and Society* serves as an excellent introduction to the discussion of another constitutive feature of Bauman's theory of culture: "Human life is happening between two powers. One of them is everything a human being wants – or, to be more precise, what he or she perceives, defines and classifies in his or her vision of life as 'wanting' ... The second power is everything a human being must – or, to be more precise, what he or she perceives, defines and classifies in his or her vision of life as 'necessity' ... The dissimilarity between the perceptions of the two types of signals are referred to by people as the difference between 'subject' and 'object'" (Bauman 1966a, 7). These words refer to the conflict between a set of human desires motivated by external factors and individuals' ability to realize them, resulting from existing circumstances. Bauman then labelled the former as "culture," and the latter as "society." Using a Marxist framework, he claimed that, with time, their interdependence decreased, which de facto meant that structural conditions ossify the difficulties pertaining to the materialization of socially desirable goals. The essence of Bauman's analyses of the transition from societies that were socially and culturally homogeneous to those that were socially and culturally heterogeneous was to indicate both the causes and the consequences of these processes. At the same time, in accordance with the strategy resulting from the engaged nature of his work, he stressed strongly the negative consequences of this stratification.

Although in subsequent years his understanding of culture differed in some respect from the one just described (as an opposition to society), Bauman invariably referred to social structure in his later reflections on culture. This is clearly visible in his works related to the strengthening of existing divisions in the contemporary world and the emergence of new ones. In the manner so typical of him – which Mark Davis calls a "will to dualism" (2008b, 103–8) – Bauman presented them as binary oppositions. He wrote about "tourists" and "vagabonds" (Bauman 1997b); groups subject to "globalization" and "localization" (Bauman, 1998c); or "seduced" and "repressed" consumers (Bauman 2007a). All of these oppositions may be described using the words found in *Legislators and Interpreters*: "Our society consists again of two nations. Only ours are nations of the seduced and the repressed; of those free to follow their needs and those forced to comply with the norms" (Bauman 1987, 169). Both in his reflections from the 1960s on socially and culturally heterogeneous communities and in his work on liquid modernity, Bauman argued that the most important factor determining social divisions in the contemporary world was the scope of the ability of individuals to achieve socially desired goals. Richard Kilminster and Ian Varcoe, who scrutinized this aspect of his work, wrote that, in his view, "culture is linked inextricably with power because some people are able to structure the world more than others, and they do so for others" (1996, 217). It should be noted that Bauman did not content himself with a mere description of this phenomenon but made attempts to demonstrate the need to implement changes within the existing condition.

Last but not least, it should be emphasized that Bauman's conceptualization of culture as a mechanism affecting human motivations was almost always accompanied by his emphasis on the role of human volition. During his academic work at the University of Warsaw his theory of culture was largely consistent with the positivist tradition (Bauman [1966b] 2021, 1966). However, he also started to stress the active role of the human in the shaping of reality, arguing that it did have a changeable, dynamic form ([1967] 2021, 1965). Over the next few years – when Bauman was affiliated with the universities of Tel Aviv and Leeds – he tried to merge these two visions of culture into one complex theory. In 1973 he wrote: "Being structured and being capable of structuring seem to be the twin-kernels of the human way of life, known as culture" (1973b, 51). In subsequent years Bauman wrote more and more on the changing balance between structure and agency in his diachronic studies of culture as well. He claimed, for example, that in modernity culture had the form of a "disciplinary mechanism," whereas in postmodernity it took on the form of a "repertoire" (1997b, 1991a). In the twenty-first century Bauman continued these reflections but also examined issues related to the proliferation and reduction of ambivalence in a different sense. On the one hand, he stressed the "liquefaction" of social reality, manifested in the processes of individualization and globalization (2011a, 2001d). On the other hand, during the last years of his life he examined the return to the formation of strong cultural identities, which became visible, *inter alia*, in the development of nationalist movements (2017c, 2016b).

Bauman's reflections on structure and agency were inspired by a variety of theories, but he always emphasized the substantial role of Marxism and structuralism. As regards the influence that the revisionist version of Marxism exerted on his oeuvre, he said at the beginning of the twenty-first century: "From Gramsci I learned about culture being a thorn in the side of 'society' rather than a handmaiden of its monotonous order-reproducing routine; an adamantly and indefatigably mutinous agent, culture as propulsion to oppose and disrupt, a sharp edge pressed obstinately against what-already-is" (cited in Tester and Jacobsen 2005, 147). In the afterword to *Sketches in the Theory of Culture*, written in 2016, Bauman retrospectively contemplated his inspiration by structuralism: "I took the work of Lévi-Strauss as – in grasping culture and in studies of it – a path from utopia to practice, concretely and more specifically, from 'structure' to 'structurization.' The obsessive, compulsive rush to structurization (organizing, ordering, rendering intelligible) of human ways of being-in-the-world appeared to be, from then on, a way of being for cultural phenomena – and this quality did not render culture homeostatic, or a force for entrenching the 'system,' but quite the opposite: a tool of constantly, insistently, obtrusively, and irrevocably dynamizing the human condition" (Bauman [2017a] 2018, 253). It should, however, be emphasized that the influence of these two traditions on Bauman's theory of culture changed over time. I will refer to this issue in the next part of this chapter, where I also present the other inspirations on his work. This introductory analysis of the evolution of Bauman's theory of culture will be accompanied by a discussion of the influence that he had on contemporary theories of culture.

THE MAIN TRENDS IN THE EVOLUTION OF ZYGMUNT BAUMAN'S THEORY OF CULTURE

In the conversation between Zygmunt Bauman and Keith Tester, in which Bauman described culture as a "permanent revolution," he stressed that such an approach clearly differed from classic conceptualizations. He noted: "[A]ll too often 'culture' (particularly in its classical anthropological uses) stood for a *soi-distant* service station of structure, an instrument of continuity, reproduction of sameness and resistance to change ... 'Culture' in that context stood for inertia, not movement and change, and was practically synonymous with 'habit,' 'routine,' absence of reflection, bias, prejudice" (Bauman and Tester 2001, 32). It was in opposition to this approach to culture – continually criticized by Bauman since the late 1960s (see, for example, Bauman 1973b, 157–78) – that he formed his later theory.

In the 1950s and early 1960s, however, he regarded culture as a property of social reality, whose role was to ensure its durability and stability ([1966b] 2021). He equated it with norms, values, and goals that were passed on from generation to generation and which endowed the members of a given community with a well-defined identity. Adopting such a perspective, Bauman held that individuals were to a large extent passive recipients of cultural content, which, in turn, affected their perception of reality as well as the activities they pursued. In *Culture and Society* he wrote: "[A] distinguishing property of phenomena analysed as part of the notion of 'culture' is to be seen in … their capacity for interiorisation. The term 'interiorisation' may, of course, refer only to these phenomena which were first external to the individual who interiorises them. It is thanks to their primitive 'externality' that they are also compelling and that they are experienced as pressure or coercion" (1966a, 14). This understanding of culture strikingly resembled Émile Durkheim's concept of "social fact" (Durkheim [1895] 1982). And it is worth noting that it was this very concept that Bauman was repeatedly opposed to in his later publications (e.g., Bauman 1976d).

Bauman's critique in that area was formed on two planes: the metatheoretical plane and the plane deriving from the engaged nature of his work. First, Bauman highlighted the reductionist nature of the classical concept of culture (1973b, 157–65). He argued that the emphasis put on the domination of structures over agency resulted in the misconception of culture as "second nature," that is, a sphere in which human volition becomes appropriated (1976e, 1–42). Likewise, such an approach, in his view, gave no sound foundation for the explication of the transformations occurring in the realm of norms and values. In the afterword to *Sketches in the Theory of Culture* Bauman described it in the following way: "The functional cohesion of the system rendered cultural change (it was not possible to ignore that it was taking place, or to deny its banality) a puzzle, demanding to be solved with the help of specific – rare or even unique – circumstances: to put it one way, a remarkable accident" ([2017a] 2018, 252). Second, Bauman discerned the correspondence between (to use his wording) the "positivist" understanding of culture and the phenomenon of alienation in Western modern society (1973b, 157–78). The emphasis on the subordination of individuals to specific models, norms, and rules – so typical of most of the schools in classical sociology – was interpreted by him in terms of the legitimization and, at the same time, of the petrification of existing social configurations.[7]

It should be noted, however, that in this context he also criticized conceptualizations of culture that were informed by an "anti-positivist programme" (1976e, 43–70; 1973c). Bauman maintained that even though studies grounded in phenomenology, ethnomethodology, or existentialism appreciated the importance of human volition, they did not form an appropriate basis for critical thought. He substantiated this by claiming in *Culture as Praxis*: "Not only does the trend under discussion remain silent as to the virtues or vices of our, or any other, society, but it deprives itself of the intellectual means which would enable it to incorporate, as its legitimate component, any statement to this effect. Owing to the purely formal, substance-free nature of its basic categories, it can produce no fulcrum strong enough to carry an indictment of the shape historically assumed by any human society, and no yardstick one can wield to gauge a society's qualities" (1973b, 166).

Bauman's subsequent reflections on culture opposed both the positivist and the anti-positivist theory. He strived for the development of an understanding of culture that would properly weigh both structural determination and human agency. On the one hand, this approach was to make possible an explanation of the fact of the persistence of some norms and values, but, on the other, it was conceived as a foundation for reflection on cultural change. Coming before both Pierre Bourdieu's ([1979] 1984) concept of structural constructivism and Anthony Giddens's (1984) theory of structuration, Bauman presented the concept of "culture as praxis" (1973b). The notion of praxis, borrowed from Antonio Gramsci ([1948–51] 1971), was understood by Bauman in two ways. First, he linked it to activities aimed at structuration of social reality, clearly noting at the same time that they were of a continual, processual nature.

Second, he used it to refer to the inherently human ability to question the status quo and pursue alternatives to it. Both poles of human praxis – structuration and transformation – formed the basis for his innovative, complex, and non-reductionist theory of culture (Bauman 1973b; see Tester 2004, 69–71). What is more, it fit squarely within the underpinnings of critical thought, as plainly attested by Bauman's following words: "Human culture, far from being the art of adaptation, is the most audacious of all attempts to scrap the fetters of adaptation as the paramount hindrance to the full unfolding of human creativity. Culture, which is synonymous with the specifically human existence, is a daring dash for freedom *from* necessity and freedom *to* create" (1973b, 172).

The role that Bauman ascribed to social transformations was reflected in his subsequent interest in utopia (Jacobsen 2008, 2007; Bauman 1976d). Inspired by works focusing on this subject matter – written by intellectuals such as Herbert Marcuse (1972), Ernst Bloch ([1954–59] 1986), and Karl Mannheim ([1929] 1954) – he decided that this notion was to be understood as an "aspect of culture," within which one relativized existing reality and showed its possible extrapolations. However, he did not equate these with pipe dreams or illusions; rather, he argued to the contrary that they had an exceptional influence on the course of historical events. Bauman wrote: "Utopias share with the totality of culture the quality – to paraphrase Santayana – of a knife with the edge pressed against the future. They constantly cause the reaction of the future with the present, and thereby produce the compound known as human history" (1976d, 12). Here, it should be pointed out that – in line with his critique of alienation – Bauman opposed any types of utopian visions that entailed the strict subordination of individuals to prescribed models and rules. In accordance with the concept of "permanent revolution" (Bauman and Tester 2001, 32), he recommended that utopias be endowed with a processual form (Bauman 1976d, 133–41).

Closely related to this approach to transformation was also the perspective from which he analyzed hermeneutic theories in the second half of the 1970s (1978). Bauman believed that reflection informed by these theories made it possible to lay bare the assumptions adopted within common-sense thinking and, at the same time, to pave the way to their replacement with ideas formulated in the process of reflection on the essence of human existence. However, Bauman did not give them the status of invariable truths, nor did he maintain that they should be developed solely by intellectuals. What he claimed was that the role of these theories was to stimulate dialogue on socially relevant issues, as well as to monitor this discourse itself. In this regard, he found Jürgen Habermas's concept of "communicative action," which he interpreted in the context of utopian thought, especially valuable (Bauman 1978, 239–46; Habermas [1968] 1971).

Although in the 1970s Bauman's theory of culture was concentrated mainly on the synchronous relation between structure and agency, in the two subsequent decades he focused on how each of the two came to dominate Western civilization at various stages of its development. His diachronic studies of this issue were of a binary nature, and they were based on a comparative analysis of modern and postmodern conditions.

In accordance with the perspective he adopted – inspired, among others, by the works of Michel Foucault ([1975] 1977) and Max Horkheimer and Theodor Adorno ([1947] 1972), as well as Max Weber ([1922] 1968) – he regarded the desire for the subordination of the human world to the primacy of reason as the constitutive feature of modernity (Bauman 1987). He stressed that the blueprints that were conceived at that time – based on the concept of "garden cultures" (Gellner 1983) – offered new structural, institutional, and normative solutions that were to ensure the stable and harmonious existence of human societies. Bauman wrote: "We can think of modernity as of a time when order – of the world, of the human habitat, of the human self, and of the connection between all three – is reflected upon; a matter of thought, of concern, of a practice that is aware of itself, conscious of being a conscious practice and wary of the void it would leave were it to halt or merely relent" (1991a, 5). The adoption of this perspective lay at the core of Bauman's conviction that the theory of culture of the modern period must concentrate above all on the issue of order-making. He claimed that even though modernity was based on emancipatory movements, it resulted in the enslavement of the individual, perfectly illustrated by Foucault's concept of panopticism (Bentham [1791] 2017). His analyses on the consequences of this process can be effectively illustrated by the words of Shigalev, the hero of one of Dostoevsky's novels: "Starting from unlimited freedom, I conclude with unlimited despotism" (Dostoevsky [1872] 2000, 402).

What is more, Bauman argued that the subjugation of human agency following the implementation of blueprint aspirations was reflected in adiaphorization, that is, in the departure from the moral evaluation of an individual's activities (1993). All these aspects of culture in the modern era were subject to Bauman's criticism, as running counter to his critical thought (Bauman 1991a, 1989c, 1987).

The ever more dynamic and multidirectional transformations taking place in the Western world in the second half of the twentieth century, coupled with reflection on the tragic consequences of modern aspirations, were – in Bauman's view – the foundation for the formation of a completely new condition.[8] From the 1980s onwards, he labelled it – in keeping with the trend in the humanities and sciences that was dominant at the time – postmodernity (Bauman 1997b, 1991a, 1987). His theory of culture focusing on this formation was taking shape in opposition to the previously mentioned studies of modernity. First, although earlier efforts had been made to reduce any ambivalence, in the postmodern condition ambiguity came to be the constitutive feature of cultural reality. Second, the disciplinary mechanisms so typical of modernity were replaced by a growing appreciation of human volition. Third, modernity was characterized by teleological thinking with a finalistic orientation, whereas, in the contemporary formation, changes are of a rhizomatic nature (Deleuze and Guattari 1987, 1983). It should be stressed that Bauman's own evaluation of these transformations was marked by ambivalence. On the one hand, he positively assessed the liberation of individuals from structural and normative determinism. Here, he accentuated the opportunities that this situation created for the development of the moral self (Bauman 1993). On the other hand, he argued that the form of individualism of the time remained at the other end of the continuum with regard to the efforts aimed at the assumption of responsibility for the Other. He called this process "postmodern adiaphorization," simultaneously demonstrating that its consequences may resemble those seen during the period of modernity (2000b, 95).

Many of the theoretical discussions on culture in which Bauman was engaged in the current century were a follow-up to his analyses grounded in postmodern thought. However, in the year 2000, Bauman dissociated himself from this orientation[9] and offered a theory of liquid modernity instead (Bauman 2000c). At its core was the conviction that the process of modernization constituted, continually for centuries, the *signum specificum* of the Western world. Its current form differed, however, from the one that had taken shape during the Enlightenment. This is because transformations today have an autotelic nature, and their driving forces are not the institutions of authority but concrete individuals. Describing the impact of these transformations on culture, Bauman wrote: "Released from the obligations imposed on it by its creators and operators, obligations consequent upon their initially missionary and later homeostatic role in society, culture is now able to focus on fulfilling individual needs, solving individual problems and struggles with the challenges and troubles of personal lives" (2011b, 12). From the perspective of this "individualized" or "privatized" modernity, Bauman scrutinized transformations taking place in various walks of social life, focusing on the fragility of the conditions existing in them. He paid special attention to the issue of the "liquefaction" of identity narratives (2005), human relations (2003), and community ties (2001a).

The evolution of Bauman's theory of culture in the twenty-first century was also a consequence of his engagement in the debate on globalization (Bauman 2011a, 2008b). His reflections on this issue were framed by the conviction that the process of globalization was unfolding in a disjunctive manner (Appadurai 1996). Bauman argued that there was no correspondence between the intensification of the flow of capital, information, and technology, on the one hand, and the abandonment of political institutions and structures within national states, on the other. He described this situation using the term *interregnum*, which he borrowed from Antonio Gramsci (Bauman 2016a, 2010b; see Bordoni 2016). As regards cross-cultural issues in the time of the intensification of global interdependencies, Bauman focused on the juxtaposition of two approaches: multiculturalism and communitarianism (2011b). He claimed that the former one raised cultural diversity to the rank of the highest value without accentuating the need to face other global challenges. As for the latter, he criticized it for its "smothering of difference and effacing ambivalence of cultural choices in order to create an imagined totality capable of resolving the thorny issues of social identity" (1999, xli). As far as Bauman was concerned, it was necessary to find the right path between Scylla of the apologia of diversity and Charybdis of the manifestation of difference. He advocated for politics based on dialogue, as part of which new institutional and normative solutions could be developed on the supranational level (e.g., Bauman 2017c; see Brzeziński 2020).

In his last publications Bauman remained faithful to this approach, though he also noted that its materialization encountered ever more serious obstacles (Bauman 2017c). These, he believed, resulted from the development of the policy of securitization as well as the strengthening of populist and nationalist movements (2016b). These processes were interpreted by Bauman as a return to the concept of culture that characterized solid modernity. It was in this context that he wrote about the increasing entanglement of the present in the mythologized picture of the past, and he described the trend using the concept of retrotopia (2017c).

CONCLUSION

To conclude, I refer to Bauman's introduction to the second edition of his *Culture as Praxis*, published in 1999, in which he retrospectively assessed his earlier studies of culture. He said: "When read thirty years after it was written, the book seems to pass well the test of 'truth.' It fares somewhat less well in the test of 'nothing but the truth.' And it fails rather abominably the test of 'the whole truth'" (1999, vii). These words were written when Bauman was creating his theory of liquid modernity. Seen from this perspective, many of his reflections from the 1960s and 1970s remained – as he concluded – valid. In this chapter I have demonstrated the legitimacy of his claim. I have shown that the constitutive features of Bauman's reflections on culture include their compliance with the spirit of engaged sociology, a combination of synchronic and diachronic perspectives, the inclusion of the context of the social structure, as well as references to both structure and agency. I have compared these aspects of Bauman's work to the core of a tree trunk, around which new rings appear with the passage of time. I have demonstrated that the growth of the rings was linked chiefly to the social transformations taking place in the second half of the twentieth century and at the beginning of the twenty-first century. In this context Bauman focused in particular on such phenomena as the proliferation of ambiguity and the appreciation of individualism, as well as the continual acceleration of change. In parallel, he investigated culture as part of the modern formation; he brought to light its systemic nature, reflected in the order-making and disciplinary practices.

Bauman's theory of culture always had both a descriptive and a conative function (Jakobson 1960). He paid attention to present and future risks and threats and encouraged the invention and implementation of new, alternative solutions. In other words, the idea of utopian thinking permeated his vision of culture as a "permanent revolution." It is also clearly visible in his last book, *Retrotopia*, in which Bauman tried to make readers aware of the necessity of thinking in terms of responsibility for the condition of the contemporary world. It is worth quoting here his last statement in the book: "In this one case – in opposition to the cases to which Margaret Thatcher used to impute it – the verdict 'there is no alternative' will hold fast, with no likelihood of appeal. More than any other time, we – human inhabitants of the Earth – are in the either/or situation: we face joining either hands, or common graves" (Bauman 2017c, 167).

2

THEORY OF CULTURE IN THE POLISH PERIOD OF ZYGMUNT BAUMAN'S WORK

INTRODUCTION

In Zygmunt Bauman's work prior to 1968 two significant phases can be distinguished. In the first, lasting until the beginning of the 1960s, the main subject of his research was sociology of politics. Joining the research program introduced by Julian Hochfeld (Hochfeld 1958), Bauman conducted studies on political systems in socialist and capitalist countries. He studied the British labour movement (Bauman [1960a] 1972a; 1959), analyzed political life in Poland (1962a, 1962c), and reflected on Marxism in its "mechanistic" and "activistic" versions[1] (1964b, 546–9). The dissonance, growing year to year, between Bauman's vision of socialism and the situation in Poland played a role in lessening his research productivity in the sociology of politics.[2] It was systematically displaced by the theory of culture.[3] This change was reflected in the research profile of the Department of General Sociology of the University of Warsaw; Bauman became chair of the department after Hochfeld left for a post in UNESCO in Paris.[4] Elżbieta Tarkowska[5] remembers this period as follows: "The transition from the previous research problematic of the Department, namely, the sociology of political relations, towards an anthropology of Polish society, took place gradually: from a revision of Marxism (in the case of Zygmunt Bauman, the works of Antonio Gramsci played a particular role, especially *The Prison Notebooks*), through the theories of social change, to the anthropological theories of culture. Already in the second half of 1963, and definitely in 1964, a shift in Zygmunt Bauman's interest became clear, from studying problems of politics to analyzing issues of culture" (Tarkowska 1995a, 11). The institutional dimension of this transition was Bauman's founding, in 1967, of the Laboratory of Anthropology of the People's Poland as a part of the Department of General Sociology. A wide variety of research was planned under this unit, but its functioning ended shortly after Bauman was expelled from the university in March 1968.

Bauman's research on culture during the Polish period of his work were in line with a broader trend that appeared in Polish sociology at that time. Paweł Łuczeczko (2011, 65) wrote on the issue as follows: "Practically from the beginning of the 60s, the younger generation of researchers expressed their disagreement with the dominating current of studies that examined participation in cultural life; they outright criticized the then-current model of the study of culture, either postulating the application of an anthropological approach, or making connections to cultural anthropology and indicating the advantages it offered for a sociologist of culture." The characteristic lineaments of this new research approach included an emphasis on the theoretical analyses of culture and a focus on the cultural transformations of that time (Czerwiński 1965; Kłoskowska 1964; Mokrzycki 1964). Joining in this tendency and simultaneously, to a significant degree, co-creating it, Bauman published in the 1960s a dozen or so articles in Polish and English that were devoted to the issue of culture. He also wrote two books: one of them, *Culture and Society: Preliminaries*, was published in 1966; however, the publication of the second one, *Sketches in the Theory of Culture*, was halted as a result of the 1968 Polish political crisis.[6] This latter book, for many years believed to be irretrievably lost, has survived in one, incomplete editorial manuscript. Its recent discovery, reconstruction, and publication[7] (Bauman [1968c] 2018) allows us to fully map out Bauman's theory of culture in the Polish period of his writings.

During this time it is possible to distinguish two different ways in which Bauman theorized culture. In one, culture is grasped as external to individuals and as exerting a compelling influence on them. Its function consists of "reducing the uncertainties of the world" (Bauman [1968c] 2018, 27), that is, indicating certain choices as proper and "obvious." In this way culture contributes to the maintenance of social order. In some of Bauman's works from this period, however, he clearly departed from this concept. He asserted, for instance, that in the second half of the twentieth century culture ceased to be a "system" and became a "loose collection of not necessarily coherent collections and meanings" (1966a, 433). Bauman assumed that this change would require working out an entirely new way of theorizing culture ([1968c] 2018, 116–18). Many of his reflections on this subject at the time were very innovative. From today's perspective some of them can be also seen as a presaging his theory of culture at the end of the twentieth century and the beginning of the twenty-first century (e.g., Bauman 2011b, 1997b, 1991a). The opposing ways of grasping culture mentioned here will be the subject of a detailed analysis in the second and third parts of this chapter. First, however, I turn my attention to acquainting the reader with Bauman's reflections on culture during the time that his research interests were directed toward the sociology of politics. I will illuminate how the evolution of his thought from Marxism-Leninism to revisionism changed his view on the cultural dimension of society.

THE THEORY OF CULTURE AND SOCIOLOGY OF POLITICS

At the beginning of Bauman's academic career his reflections on culture were consistent with the following conviction expressed by Karl Marx and Friedrich Engels in *The German Ideology*: "Morality, religion, metaphysics, all the rest of ideology and their corresponding forms of consciousness, thus no longer retain the semblance of independence. They have no history, no development; but men, developing their material production and their material intercourse, alter, along with this their real existence, their thinking and the products of their thinking. Life is not determined by consciousness, but consciousness by life" (Marx and Engels [1932] 1970, 47). In accordance with this approach, Bauman argued in the 1950s that culture depended on the economic base, and its transformations derived from changes in both the ownership of the means of production and the relations of production. He claimed that the main function of culture was the legitimation and petrification of the existing socio-economic order, with which it formed a coherent whole (see, for example, Bauman and Wiatr 1953). From this materialistic perspective Bauman criticized theories that emphasized the role of individuals in the process of creating culture. He referred to the theories as "bourgeois." For example, in 1953 he wrote, on the humanistic sociology of Florian Znaniecki (1952, 1919): "The starting point for both the historical process, and for an understanding of it, is for Znaniecki the creative act of an individual, that is undetermined and undefined, without any cause. This is an extremely subjective position. There is no place for the masses as a creative force of history in this concept" (Bauman and Wiatr 1953, 80).[8] *Ergo*, Bauman assumed the existence of a one-sided relationship between culture and the individual. He focused attention solely on the way in which individuals are shaped by culture within a specific social order.

It should be emphasized, however, that according to the Bauman's belief at the time, cultural conditioning could be maintained longer than economic realities. The transformation of means of production and relations of production did not produce an automatic transformation of norms and values; they could persist for some time, working as "a clot of historical experiences" (Bauman 1962b, 19). This belief was reflected in his emphasis on the need to facilitate the formation of specific dispositions proper to socialist formations. In this context he wrote about the importance of equal educational opportunities, the development of literacy, the breaking down of barriers in assessing managerial positions, and so forth (Bauman and Wiatr 1953). Bauman assigned an essential role in this process to the corresponding formation of relations between the directors and the workers in factories, which were de facto to recreate model relations between the party and the people. "Our factories 'produce' socialist people," he wrote. "There, in productive work, the consciousness and character of the citizen and host of the socialist homeland should be formed" (Bauman 1962b, 40). The goal of all these efforts was intended to create a new cultural reality, corresponding to the Marxist premises. The Polish philosopher Jerzy Kossak presented these premises as follows: "The new quality of socialist community appears to Marx as a new culture, where man returns to his species life – to the collective, conscious, creative transformation of the world. He returns to the culture of social life, where joy and the need for creative activity bloom again. A new system of values is created here based on a bold materialistic world view, a sense of internationalism, and a sense of common responsibility for both the people's republic and a new work ethos" (Kossak 1987, 16).

Bauman in essence expected the rebirth of the creative and social properties of individuals, which had been suppressed for centuries by the class organization of society.[9] In his analyses of the situation in post-war Poland, written during the 1950s, he described a significant advance in the work of – as he called it – "cultural revolution" (Bauman and Wiatr 1953, 91–3). However, he simultaneously pointed to the obstacles standing in its way, among which he especially emphasized the process of acculturation of Western cultural patterns in socialist societies, such as individualism, consumerism, or materialistic aspirations. In a book *Career: Four Sociological Sketches* he assessed the reality in then contemporary Poland as follows: "[W]e are a hundred years behind America and a hundred years ahead of America. Behind – in terms of technical and economic development. Ahead – in terms of human relations, organized in a new, more perfect way, which in America is only a glimmering of the future" (Bauman 1960b, 87). He also issued the following warning, however: "The passive-consumer model of life comes to us at a time when the imperative of an ant's diligence and almost hamster-like precaution is still longed for and incredibly needed" (85, 86). In accordance with these words, Bauman appreciated the attitude founded on both the acceptance of a perspectivist orientation and an evaluation of efforts undertaken from the point of view of an expected future. In the context of his works that came a quarter of a century later and referred to the modern condition, this attitude could be called "a pilgrimage" (Bauman 1996).

From the perspective of Bauman's later theory of culture it is worth making two other observations here. Firstly, he grasped the acculturation of Western models in the framework of socialist societies as an exemplification of a global process of the flow of values and ideas. Among the factors underlying this process he listed, first of all, the development of means of mass communication. Bauman wrote: "We live in an era in which, as never before, the history of the world is world history, and the culture of the world is world culture. The world market for the exchange of commodities, the international exchange of literature and the press, films, radio and television programs, mass tourist travels on huge routes – all of this contributes to blurring the edges of national cultures, to their merging into one world civilization with regional-national variants" (1960b, 84). These reflections can be interpreted as the nucleus of his analyses of the relationship between globalization and culture that he conducted in the last decades of his life (see, for example, Bauman 2011b, 1998a). Secondly, it is worth emphasizing – as mentioned already in the first chapter – the continuities between the analysis and the critique in Bauman's theory of culture. In the 1950s, and later, a significant part of his work was devoted to indicating the negative consequences of an unhampered development of the market. Throughout all of his work he also negatively assessed the focus on individualistic aspirations, which he perceived as discouraging from interest in social issues. Bauman always contrasted the culture of individualism with a vision of social relations founded on the concern for the common good (Brzeziński 2018).

Bauman analyzed the issue of the acculturation of capitalist norms and values into socialist structures and institution in the 1950s, in the context of not only the Eastern bloc but also the Western bloc. In 1957 an award by the Ford Foundation enabled him to spend most of a year as a visiting scholar at the London School of Economics (see Wagner 2020, 205–12). Under the supervision of Robert McKenzie he conducted research on the evolution of the British labour movement.[10] The results of these analyses were presented in his habilitation thesis, originally published in Poland in 1960 and then translated into English (Bauman [1960] 1972a). One of the most significant conclusions presented in this book was that rather than overturning the existing order, the British labour movement had been embedded into the structures of British capitalism. "If the working class," he wrote, "has not actually become established on the socio-economic status level which it has already reached, it has, at all events, accepted the contemporary hierarchy of which this level is a part" (258, 259).

These transformations were accompanied by relevant changes in the realm of the organized labour movement and its elite leadership. Bauman described the process of the bureaucratization of the former. As to the latter, he indicated that the charisma and determination, which had previously distinguished the leaders of the labour movement, had been replaced by conservative attitudes. Peter Beilharz wrote on this issue: "While Bauman does not labour the early Marxian theme of alienation in this text, he does work the idea that it is the integration of the working class into capitalist society which changes its nature, making of it a systemic actor rather than the negation of the negation, the denial of everything capitalism stands for" (2000, 13). Bauman finally claimed that the radicalization of the British labour movement would be possible only and exclusively under the influence of external factors, such as, for example, the change in the balance of political powers in the world.

The phenomenon of the gradual departure from socialist values was also demonstrated by the empirical research conducted by Bauman in Poland (Bauman 1962a, 1962d).[11] In this context, it is especially worth referring to the research on Warsaw youth that he conducted at the beginning of the 1960s (1962d). The premise of the research was to indicate the frequency of one of the four following types of career pattern: first, aimed at financial success; second, characterized by a stable, risk-free life of limited aspirations; third, socially oriented; fourth, based on an independent, bohemian lifestyle. The respondents, men aged eighteen to twenty-four, were raised in post-war Poland in a system of education rooted in socialist values. In accordance with Marxist assumptions it should have been expected that they would perceive their careers first and foremost through the lens of engagement in the name of collective good. But, as the results of the study showed, this approach characterized only a small group of young men, who came primarily from the intelligentsia and had high levels of education. A slender percentage identified themselves with the nonconformist position. Respondents most frequently embraced the two models of career that were first mentioned. Bauman described the first one as a combination of Western ideas and the bourgeois tradition, and the second as a composition of values characteristic of the middle class and the mass society. Also worth emphasizing is that both types of career were characterized by a strong focus on consumption. The studies of Warsaw youth served as a refutation of Bauman's expectations as to the systematic spread of socialist values in Poland. In an interview with Keith Tester and Michael Hviid Jacobsen in 2005, he said: "Looking back, I suspect that the outcome of our research into the attitudes of Polish youth marked, perhaps not the first, but certainly the most profound, of my disenchantments" (cited in Tester and Jacobsen 2005, 44).

Bauman's disappointment was closely related to the political situation in Poland at that time, and specifically to his unfulfilled hopes raised by the Polish October 1956 events (Wagner 2020, 190–6; Tester 2004, 43–6). This so-called Polish thaw was a time in which the reformist faction led by Władysław Gomułka[12] began a process of de-Stalinization, a partial democratization and liberalization of Polish society.[13] Bauman's strong support of these reforms was most fully expressed in his first published book, *The Problems of Democratic Centralization in Lenin's Works* (1957c). On the one hand, he criticized the Stalinist perversions of Marxism-Leninism, with special emphasis on the alienation of the party. On the other hand, he presented his belief that the reforms introduced then in Poland were going in the right direction. Bauman made an attempt to argue that under the right leadership of the Polish United Workers' Party it would be possible to reconcile democracy and centralism, individualism and submissiveness, and criticism and discipline. He wrote: "The party has undertaken the work of a great repair, but the success of its struggle depends on whether it is able to gather masses of workers, peasants and intelligentsia around itself, or whether it manages to mobilize the forces in the minds and hearts of working people – forces that have been dormant for a long time, but which under a refreshing breath of democratization awaken to active life." (1957c, 3). Bauman's condition for the success of the reforms initiated in October 1956 was not fulfilled, however. On the contrary, the Polish United Workers' Party began a systematic retreat from the gains of the Polish thaw.

Therefore, as time passed, Bauman became increasingly critical of the political situation in Poland.[14] This process was accompanied by significant changes in his theorization of culture. An analysis of this issue requires a discussion of Bauman's inspirations in the late 1950s and early 1960s. First, I will analyze the influence that his intellectual masters at the University of Warsaw, that is Julian Hochfeld and Stanisław Ossowski, had on his work (see Wagner 2020, 171–90; Tester 2004, 34–43). Next, I will present how Bauman's social thought was shaped by both Albert Camus's ([1951] 1953) vision of "the rebel" and Antonio Gramsci's ([1948–51] 1971) philosophy of praxis. It was to the works of all these intellectuals that Bauman most often referred in his retrospective statements on the evolution of his sociology during that time (see, for example, Bauman 2008a; Bauman and Tester 2001, 19–22; Bauman 1972a).

Bauman talked about Julian Hochfeld in his inaugural lecture delivered at the University of Leeds on 7 February 1972: "Incisive, at times virulent, always a passionate fighter for what was to him the supreme sense of his being-in-the-world – free, wholesome, multi-faceted, his was the authentic life of struggle in which ideas are constantly put to the test of the possible and the possible is perpetually checked against the ideal" (Bauman 1972a, 186). Bauman was first a student of Hochfeld, next an employee of his department at the University of Warsaw, and finally his successor as head of the department.[15] The research conducted by Bauman in Poland and Great Britain, discussed earlier in this chapter, was in line with the research program formulated by Hochfeld (1958).

In the contexts of Bauman's revisionist and cultural turns discussed here, it is of particular importance that after October 1956 he became an adherent of Hochfeld's idea of "Open Marxism" (see, for example, Hochfeld [1957] 1982). This concept – developed on the basis of the vision of Kazimierz Kelles-Krauz (2018; see Snyder 1997) – assumed that Marxism should remain in dialogue with other theories, including "bourgeois" ones. "By its very nature," wrote Izabela Wagner, "Hochfeld believed, Marxism had to be open to analyses of a changing world and non-Marxist social theories. This idea inescapably favors a democratic and pluralist culture" (2020, 181). The influence of Open Marxism was very present in Bauman's papers written after the Polish October, such as "Tractate on Bureaucracy" (Bauman 1957b)[16] and "Marxism and Contemporary Sociology" (Bauman and Wiatr 1957). In these works he postulated continued progress in the field of the democratization of social life and also claimed that the political discussions should be open to the public and engage a wide range of people. Compared to his earlier reflections on culture, these texts draw attention to the agency of individuals in terms of social and cultural changes. What is more, inspired by Hochfeld's claim that Marxist assumptions should be verified by empirical research, Bauman pointed to the need for a sociological analysis of the party, as is evidenced in his paper "On the Need for a Sociology of the Party" (1957a).

Stanisław Ossowski was characterized in Bauman's aforementioned inaugural lecture at Leeds in the following way: "His mission – because sociology was the mission of his life – was to hand on the torch of knowledge – pure, intransigent and unblemished – with which to dissipate the gloom of unreason and deceit, ignorance and illusion" (Bauman 1972a, 185). The relationship between Bauman and Ossowski was of a different nature than that with Hochfeld. When Bauman was a student at the University of Warsaw, Ossowski, a staunch critic of Stalinism, was banned from both teaching and publishing. In 1956 he was reinstated in his post on the wave of the Polish October, and a year later he took over as chair of Sociology.[17] Ossowski developed and propagated interdisciplinary humanistic sociology (Ossowski 1962; see Chałubiński 2006; Kurczewski 1988). Although the research profile of the department[18] in which Bauman worked at that time was of a different nature than the humanistic sociology, he was strongly influenced by Ossowski's concepts, including his theory of culture.[19]

The first article by Ossowski, published after a break of several years caused by the publication ban,[20] was *Tactics and Culture* (Ossowski [1956] 2016).[21] This widely commented-on paper was devoted to the freedom of science and its relationship with culture. Ossowski argued that the intellectual must be independent from all dogmas in his research, or, in other words, "disobedient in thinking." He associated the freedom of science not only with the right, but also with the duty, to oppose the status quo. The paper reads: "Ever since the origins of culture, there has been a front struggle for truth – truth consecrated neither by church authorities, nor by political authorities, nor by economic authorities. Those conquered in the scale of days or years win in the scale of eons and the words 'E pur si muove!' continue to resound in the ears of generations" (1998 [1956], 94). As time passed, the model of the intellectual postulated by Ossowski was increasingly reflected in Bauman's work. Bauman was becoming more and more critical not only of the political situation in Poland but also of the ideology officially adopted by the authorities. Culture, which he previously perceived as subordinate to the economic and political system, was becoming for him an increasingly autonomous – or even subversive – sphere (see, for example, Bauman 1963).

In his retrospective statements Bauman indicated that despite the many differences in Hochfeld's and Ossowski's approaches to sociology, their works were similar in the sense that they were "inspired by ethical motives" (Bauman and Tester 2001, 21). They both believed that sociologists should be sensitive to human suffering and strive to reduce it. In the opening words of this book I emphasized that this conviction was also the *signum specificum* of the whole of Bauman's sociology. One of the issues analyzed in this and the following chapters will be the influence of this assumption on Bauman's theory of culture at various stages of its evolution.

An important source of inspiration for Bauman's social thought in the period discussed here was also *The Rebel* by Albert Camus ([1951] 1953). Bauman read this book in the late 1950s,[22] never returning to it again, but years later he remembered it as one of those readings that most shaped his sociological imagination (Bauman 2008a). During this period, when the main area of his research was the sociology of politics, *The Rebel* significantly influenced his revisionist thought, and, both then and later, it contributed to shaping his view on the transformative role of culture (see Tester 2002, 62–7). As for his revisionist thought, it should be noted that in the late 1950s and early 1960s Bauman's position resembled that of the man depicted in the early pages of Camus's essay. It reads: "What is a rebel? A man who says no: but whose refusal does not imply a renunciation. He is also a man who says yes as soon as he begins to think for himself" (Camus 1953, 46). With reference to these words, it can be said that Bauman's then contemporary criticism of the Polish United Workers' Party did not lead to him abandoning his identification with Marxism. Instead, it constituted the basis for his search for alternative interpretations of it.[23]

As to the long-term impact of *The Rebel* on Bauman's sociology, it should be noted that this book contributed to the formation of his belief that the role of culture was to constantly develop a critical attitude towards reality. In the book *Culture as Praxis*, published in 1973, Bauman wrote on that matter: "Through culture man is in a state of constant revolt, in which, as Albert Camus would say, he simultaneously fulfils and creates his own values, the revolt being not an intellectual invention, but a human experience and action" (1973b, 178). The seeds of such a theory of culture are already visible in Bauman's works from the beginning of the 1960s. A significant role in forming them was played by his being inspired by the philosophy of Antonio Gramsci, interpreted through the prism of the Camus's thought. In 2008 Bauman claimed in this regard: "Gramsci translated to me Camus's philosophy of human condition into a philosophy of human practice" (2008a, 233).

In considering this issue, it is worth pointing out, first, that Gramsci's *Prison Notebooks* ([1948–51] 1971)[24] strongly affected the further evolution of Bauman's revisionist Marxism,[25] which had been initiated earlier by the influence of the thought of Julian Hochfeld and Stanisław Ossowski. In light of Gramsci's philosophy, Bauman ultimately rejected the idea of historical determinism and argued that history was only and exclusively a product of human praxis. In line with this assumption he also emphasized the fundamental role of the creative, active, and critical attitude of individuals in the process of social change (see, for example, Bauman 1967a, 1963). In an article written in 1963 he acknowledged that Gramsci provided the reader with "the most optimistic vision of the human world of those promoted today, imbued with faith in the creative forces of the human being and constructed with the sole purpose of developing these forces and stimulating them to act" (1963, 34). As far as the issue of culture is concerned, it should be remembered that according to Antonio Gramsci the proletariat would not be able to overturn the existing socio-economic formation if it could not first emancipate itself from the cultural hegemony of the ruling class. This meant both the necessity of opposing existing norms and values, and the creation and spreading of a new culture.

Inspired by this concept, Bauman began to develop his reflections on culture in two opposing directions. On the one hand – making reference to Gramsci's idea of "cultural hegemony" – he pointed to the structuring properties of culture, that is, to the role that it plays in legitimizing the existing order. He applied these reflections at that time largely, though implicitly, to the dominant role of the Polish United Workers' Party in shaping cultural reality in Poland. In later years he devoted much attention to the way in which common-sense thinking was shaped by many other factors as well (see, for example, Bauman 1976e). On the other hand, he argued that culture was the aspect of reality that makes possible a critique of the status quo, and it might also simultaneously lead to an establishment of an alternative order in its place. As I pointed out in the first chapter of this book, he shaped much of his later theory of culture on the basis of this belief.

I will summarize the analyses presented in this section of the chapter by referring to the typology of the two versions of Marxism that Bauman presented in his book *Outline of the Marxist Theory of Society*, published in Polish in 1964 (Bauman 1964b, 546–9). As far as I am concerned, the former one, "mechanistic," effectively describes Bauman's approach to Marxism at the very beginning of his academic career (Bauman and

Wiatr 1953), while the latter, "activistic," is an excellent illustration of his revisionist Marxism a decade later (Bauman 1963). The evolution of his thought during this period included, firstly, the rejection of the belief in objective historical laws and pointed to the fundamental role of human praxis in the process of social transformation. Secondly, it was connected to the departure from demonstrating the necessity of an unambiguous subordination to the Polish United Workers' Party, for the sake of emphasizing a critical attitude toward the world. Thirdly, it was characterized by a turn from a Manichean perception of reality through the prism of ideological divisions to an increasing appreciation of axiological pluralism. This evolution was also reflected in the transformation of Bauman's theory of culture. He ceased to understand culture as dependent on a socio-economic base and began to focus on the role of individuals in the process of cultural change. As time passed, he also focused more and more on the transformative function of culture, rather than on its role in stabilizing the existing socio-economic order. This did not mean, however, a straightforward replacement of one way of grasping culture by another, but rather an attempt to combine the two. Both perspectives were consistently present in Bauman's later work, but the emphasis that he placed on each of them was constantly changing. In the following two parts of this chapter I will concentrate on how the inspiration from various orientations within the humanities and social sciences during the years before his forced emigration was reflected in the development of his theory of culture in each of these directions. One of them I describe as a reduction of ambivalence, and the other as a proliferation of ambivalence.

CULTURE AS REDUCTION OF AMBIVALENCE

The classic work of Alfred Kroeber and Clyde Kluckhohn, *Culture: A Critical Review of Concepts and Definitions* (1952), will be the framework for the analyses developed in this part of the chapter. This use does not result from the conviction that Bauman's theory of culture from the 1960s can be inscribed within one of the ways of defining *culture* that were listed by the two anthropologists, that is, as "descriptive," "historical," "normative," "psychological," "structural," and "genetic."[26] Bauman's multidimensional analyses elude this classification. I will, however, use this typology as an analytic tool to structure my reflections regarding Bauman's vision of culture as a mechanism to reduce ambivalence. He presented the main assumptions of this approach to culture as follows: "From the perspective of an activist and materialist Marxist philosophy, the function of culture is based on reducing the uncertainties of the world. Culture (much like – according to Pierre Boulez[27] – all creation) is based on the transformation of the unpredictable into the necessary" (Bauman [1968c] 2018, 27). In the analyses that follow I will point out the sources from which Bauman drew inspiration, developing his theory of culture in this direction, and I will also evaluate the theory.

The *descriptive* understanding of culture derives from classical anthropology (see, for example, Malinowski 1944; Benedict 1934; Tylor 1871). It assumes that culture is a set of values, meanings, habits, models of behaviour, and any other – material and non-material – traits that are characteristic of a given society and determine the life of its members (Kroeber and Kluckhohn 1952, 43–6). For example, Bronisław Malinowski wrote that culture "obviously is the integral whole consisting of implements and consumers' goods, of constitutional charters for the various social groupings, of human ideas and crafts, beliefs and customs" (1944, 36). Ruth Benedict stated that "culture is that complex whole which includes all the habits acquired by man as a member of society" ([1929] 1931, 806). Both these concepts were referred to by Zygmunt Bauman in his first chapter of *Sketches in the Theory of Culture*, titled "The Origins of the Semiotic Theory of Culture, or the Crisis of Cultural Anthropology" ([1968c] 2018, 7–30]. On the one hand, Bauman pointed to the value of the concept, especially when compared to classical evolutionist visions. On the other hand, he argued that, in line with this understanding of culture, the focus of anthropologists on cultural differences closes the way to reflection on the common attributes of the human. Searching for a golden mean between – as he put it in another book (1966a) – "distributive" and "attributive" understandings of culture,[28] Bauman turned to the anthropology of Claude Lévi-Strauss. "If ethnography is a description of customs and institutions, anthropology is not the study of institutions, customs, but the structure of human thought that is manifested in them," Bauman claimed ([1968c] 2018, 24]. The complicated relationship between the theories of both intellectuals will be the subject of further detailed analyses throughout this book.

The *historical* way of understanding culture, distinguished by Kroeber and Kluckhohn, is focused on issues of "social heritage" or "social tradition" (Kroeber and Kluckhohn 1952, 47–9). The following words by Bauman are a perfect illustration of this understanding of culture: "Culture is the creation of the accumulated experiences of life processes of many generations, and simultaneously 'serves' those processes" (Bauman [1968c] 2018, 232). It should be stressed, however, that he associated the strength of the influence of tradition with the level of social development. Inspired by the neo-evolutionism of Leslie A. White (1959) and Julian Steward (1955), Bauman concluded in his Polish article "Two Opposite Approaches to Cultural Analysis" that the only objective and universal criterion for this development was the level of advancement of technology. He wrote: "[W]hen using such a measure, two major types of cultures can be distinguished: (a) stable cultures, requiring a constant amount of energy and preventing its increase; (b) developmental cultures, requiring increasing amounts of energy and stimulating an increase in its absorption" (1964a, 59).

His further analysis of both types of formations was founded in large part on the issue of the role of tradition. Bauman argued that for the stable cultures, tradition would be a point of departure for all undertaken regulations. He claimed that in their case there was no room for any kind of innovation.[29] These recognitions were part of the widely accepted, at that time – and systematically criticized for the last few decades (see, for example, Carrithers 1992; Wolf 1982) – "achronic" perspective on studying culture. I will analyze this issue in my fourth chapter. For Bauman, the exact opposite of stable formations were the "developmental" cultures that he presented as widely open to continuous change, innovation, and growth. In their case, he wrote that "'past' and 'tradition' lose their guiding role in real life" (1964a, 67). In his publication *Culture and Society* two years later, Bauman described them as socially and culturally heterogeneous community ("Htht") (1966a). Although this model of culture will be the subject of my further analyses, it is worth noting here that in its case the proliferation of ambivalence completely replaced its reduction.

The *normative* sphere (Kroeber and Kluckhohn 1952, 50–4) was also particularly important in Bauman's theory of culture in the 1960s, Inspired by the functionalist approach in sociology (Parsons [1951] 1991)[30] and anthropology (Malinowski 1944), and the culture and personality approach (Linton 1945; Benedict 1934), he argued that within every culture there occurs a selection of particular norms, which makes the activities undertaken by its members to some extent predictable. Bauman wrote: "Culture transforms amorphous chaos into a system of probabilities that simultaneously is predictable and can be manipulated – predictable precisely because it can be manipulated. The chaos of experience transforms into a consistent system of meanings, and the collection of individuals into a social system with a stable structure. Culture is the liquidation of the indeterminacy of the human situation (or, at the very least, its reduction) by eliminating some possibilities for the sake of others. The basic tool for realizing this elementary function of culture is the model of behaviour" ([1968c] 2018, 58).

The emphasis on the normative understanding of culture did not decrease with Bauman's inspiration from structural semiotics. He then drew attention to the informational load of signs, serving to transmit the values constitutive for a given group. In a paper, "Towards a Semiotic Theory of Culture," he equated culture to a "system" operating on the principle of unconscious infrastructure (similarly to *langue*) and forming a frame of reference for individual behaviour (analogously to *parole*) (Bauman [1968c] 2018, 59–61).[31]

These analyses are closely related to the *psychological* understanding of culture that focuses on the issue of the internalization of norms and values. "What is actually stressed is the acquisition of habits by individuals and why they retain or change habits," wrote Kroeber and Kluckhohn (1952, 50–4) on this understanding of culture. Earlier in this chapter I emphasized that at the very beginning of Bauman's academic career he only analyzed one side of the relationship between cultural patterns and the lives of individuals: the influence of the former on the latter. Years later, he recalled his view of the matter as follows: "Society is like a billiard table and humans are like billiard balls, they move where they are pushed. The direction in which they move and the speed of movement is determined by the fashion of pushing, and that fashion in turn depends on people with cues – legislators and teachers" (Tester and Jacobsen 2005, 89). Although in the following years of Bauman's work in Poland his view of this issue ceased to be so unequivocal, he still paid great attention to the issue of the assimilation of cultural patterns.

He agreed with Talcott Parsons that "[l]earning ... means the incorporation of cultural patterns into the action-system of individual actors" (Parsons [1951] 1991, 9).[32] In line with the author of *The Social System*, Bauman analyzed how the norms and values were internalized by individuals through the institutions of socialization and control. A very interesting example of his perspective on this issue is his belief at the time that conscience was a "social product" (Bauman 1962b, 45). By this, he meant that it is society that equips the individual with a collection of norms and values. He argued that without them, the individual would not become a moral subject.[33] Foreshadowing the later analysis in this book, it is worth stressing that this belief stands in stark contrast to Bauman's reflections on morality in the late twentieth and twenty-first centuries (2008b, 1993). At the time, he indicated that morality "resists codification, formalization, socialization, universalization" (1993, 54).

Culture understood as a mechanism of reduction of ambivalence is also an excellent example of a *structuralist* understanding of this term. "The definitions in this group," wrote Kroeber and Kluckhohn, "tend to be remote from the overt, observable uniformities of behavior. Culture is a design or system of designs for living; it is a plan, not the living itself; it is that which selectively channels men's reactions, it is not the reactions themselves" (1952, 61, 62). Bauman's structural understanding of culture is mostly related to the inspiration he drew from Claude Lévi-Strauss. This influence was so significant that he retrospectively called the period of his work in the years 1965–70 "Lévi-Straussian" (Bauman [2017a] 2018, 251). Structuralism would also become one of the foundations of the research program implemented by the Laboratory of Anthropology of the People's Poland, chaired by Bauman at the University of Warsaw. Bauman's interpretation of the structural anthropology was, however, far from a conventional one. He claimed: "I took the work of Lévi-Strauss as – in grasping culture and in studies of it – a path from utopia to practice: concretely and more specifically, from 'structure' to 'structurization'" ([2017a] 2018, 253). Bauman stated that under the influence of Lévi-Strauss he began to recognize that culture fulfilled two complementary functions. On the one hand, it provided a certain kind of stability and repeatability that he considered a *sine qua non* requirement for human beings and, in general, all living creatures.[34] On the other hand, he argued that culture could not renounce its structuring properties, which meant it remained in a state of "permanent revolution" (Bauman and Tester 2001, 33). Bauman therefore considered the role of culture in reducing ambivalence to be a permanent, never-ending process. This concept was the foundation of his 1970s theory of "culture as praxis" (Bauman 1973b) that will be analyzed in my third chapter.

Here it is also worthwhile mentioning that Bauman's interpretation of Levi-Strauss's thought at the time was most likely, to some extent, inspired by Max Gluckman and the Manchester School he founded (Evens and Handelman 2006). Bauman was a Simon fellow in the Department of Anthropology of the University of Manchester in 1966 (Wagner 2020, 222–5). And one of the department's hallmarks was an attempt to move from a structural to a processual understanding of culture.

On the *genetic* understanding of culture, Kroeber and Kluckhohn wrote that it was "focus upon the question: how has culture come to be? What are the factors that have made culture possible or caused it to come into existence" (1952, 65). They distinguished the subsets of this approach to culture that were oriented toward artifacts, ideas, and symbols.[35] This division resulted from the fact that some of the researchers sought the origins of culture in the active role of humans in producing material goods, others in their intellectual creativity, and others in the fact of their making use of symbols. Bauman's perspective on this issue during the 1960s cannot be clearly categorized within any of these three groups. In the text entitled "Man and Sign" ([1968c] 2018, 62–93), Bauman distinguished two dimensions that were especially important to the process of phylogenesis: mastering the external environment and perfecting communication skills. He wrote: "The solution to the first task is technology; the second, models of behaviour. Both tools for organizing the world collectively comprise culture" (86). Culture understood as a way through which it becomes possible to impose a structure on external reality, created, in Bauman's view, an environment in which the development of a human being could take place. As a consequence, "Adapting biologically to the cultural world, the human became a slave of culture. It is the limitation that humans imposed on themselves, in placing it on their world" (87). His view on phylogenesis at the time was inspired by both historical materialism and structuralism. Bauman aspired to unite these two perspectives, also grasping them in a framework derived from revisionism. He argued: "[T]ools, much like the signs, are two signs of human praxis that cannot exist without each other. This praxis is the true distinguishing feature of the human species" (91). Directing his attention to this issue, he aimed to show that culture was not only a restriction imposed on humans but also a structure that allowed them to transform their inner worlds, which in turn would contribute to changing the world itself.

The analyses in this part of the chapter, based on the typology of Kroeber and Kluckohohn, have allowed me to demonstrate the multidimensionality of Bauman's approach to culture in the 1960s. The various sources of inspiration from which he drew (such as functionalism, the culture and personality approach, neo-evolutionism, structuralism, and revisionist Marxism) – frequently in a critical or selective way – allowed him to build a very innovative theoretical framework.[36] What united all of Bauman's aforementioned views on culture at the time was the conviction that it comprised a mechanism of the reduction of ambivalence. This meant that culture would provide collectives with a coherent identity, allowing them to undertake organized activities, and also contribute to the maintenance of social order. It is not difficult, however, to perceive certain weaknesses in this understanding of culture. Above all, it is worth emphasizing a certain discrepancy between Bauman's views on the primacy of culture in guaranteeing social stability and his reflections on the mutability of history. His synchronic and diachronic analyses were conducted to a large degree independently of each other, and all efforts to unite them did not take any kind of coherent form. Secondly, he referred to many different ways of understanding culture, and they were not always consistent with each other. For example, his statement in the book *Culture and Society* that culture consists of elements that can be internalized (Bauman 1966a, 14) is difficult to reconcile with his position expressed elsewhere that the only objective measure of cultural development is technological progress (1964a, 53–9). There were many more such inaccuracies in his theory of culture from that time, which makes it difficult to treat it as a coherent one. Thirdly, the ideas referred to here had a decidedly conflating character, to use Margaret Archer's term (1988). Bauman directed his attention to the question of the regulative role of culture, leaving very little space for the active role of the human in the process of transforming social reality. It is difficult to reconcile this view with the emphasis that he placed in his revisionist view of Marxism on the category of *praxis* (Bauman 1967a) and also with the discussion devoted to the "humanistic vision of the human," to be analyzed in the following portion of this chapter.

CULTURE AS PROLIFERATION OF AMBIVALENCE

To a large extent, irrespective of the aforementioned reflections, in the 1960s Bauman also theorized culture in the context of the process of proliferation of ambivalence. Four levels of his analysis devoted to this issue can be distinguished. The first concerns his *critique of the positivist concept of identity* (e.g., Bauman [1967b] 2021); the second relates to the *limitations of the structuring properties of culture* (e.g., [1968c] 2018, 94–118); the third addresses the issue of *the progressive separation between culture and society* (e.g., 1966a); and finally the fourth relates to *the development of consumerist culture* (1966a, 374–450). Taking all of these into account, Bauman claimed that the cultural reality of the second half of the twentieth century was characterized primarily not by the reduction but by the proliferation of ambivalence. In *Sketches in the Theory of Culture* he wrote on this isssue: "[W]e live in an age, that seems, for the first time in human history, to acknowledge cultural multiplicity as an innate and fixed feature of the world – one which gives rise to new forms of identity that are at ease with plurality, like a fish in water – and even boasts of the fact that it not only discovered, but even accepted as a truly human state and mode of being both noble and dignified, this indeterminacy of the human condition as humanity's calling" ([1968c] 2018, 117). In this part of the chapter I will analyze Bauman's findings on the origins and consequences of the revolutionary cultural transformations mentioned here, and then I will assess his reflections on the matter.

With regard to the first of the aforementioned levels of analysis, it should be noted that in many papers written by Bauman in the second part of the 1960s (e.g., [1968c] 2018, 167–71; [1967b] 2021; 1965) he strongly opposed the positivist concept of identity according to which human behaviour is determined largely by external forces. An analysis of individual motivations from the stimulus-response perspective was, in his opinion at that time – as opposed to his earlier thoughts – an unjustified simplification. He noted: "The presence of a creative act in every human event means that it evades the positivistic perspective – that it can only be partially contained in a schema with a finite number of measurable variables. That which remains beyond the limits of the positivist schema is a fighting and active human, endlessly engaged in choosing, evaluating, organizing the world. Who is not only an endpoint of energy vectors but also a point of departure" ([1968c] 2018, 171). Thus, without questioning the significance of the structural and institutional determinants of human action, Bauman strived to juxtapose their analysis with a reflection on individual creativity and agency. Among the sources of his reflections in this regard, two that deserve particular mention are revisionist Marxism and humanistic psychology.

At the time discussed here, Bauman continued to develop his revisionist thought, independent of, and even in opposition to, Marxism-Leninism. It was most fully expressed in his article "Modern Times, Modern Marxism" (1967a). In it, Bauman criticized the belief that Marxism was founded on the premise of economic determinism. In his opinion, such an approach not only contradicted the assumptions of Marx's philosophical anthropology but also could be used to legitimize practices aimed at subordinating the life of individuals to the goals set independently of their will. He claimed: "What is of primary concern is how to adjust society to individual needs, not the reverse; how to extend the range of freedom of individual choice; how to provide room enough for individual initiative and non-conformity" (404, 405). According to this – quite revolutionary – approach, the emancipatory role of Marxism should be realized first in the individual sphere and then in the social sphere. It was not the emphasis on the external conditions of individual choices but the release from such pressures that, according to Bauman, would open the way to the realization of the axiological potential of Marxism. *Ergo*, the role of the Marxist intellectual should be not to present ready-made solutions but to encourage their development by individuals, as well as to seek ways of implementing them.

In the second half of the 1960s, Bauman was also very influenced by humanistic psychology (see, for example, Bauman 1965). As far as this approach is concerned, external reality is no longer understood as a source of stimuli (as in behaviorism) or as control mechanisms (as in psychoanalysis) but as a space for creative expression (see Maslow 1962).

In the context of the vision of an autonomous entity, Bauman wrote: "'Duty' ceases to be external to the personal 'reality'; it begins to emerge directly from this reality, merges with it into one. The phrases 'human personality is like this' and 'human personality should be like this' are becoming synonymous" (1965, 225). This vision can be interpreted as a harbinger of his later concept of postmodern ethics (1993). An important inspiration for Bauman was also Abraham Maslow's concept of the hierarchy of needs (Maslow 1943). Bauman interpreted it in the context of the Marxist assumptions and ideas. He argued, following Maslow, that the realization of the need for self-actualization was possible only after satisfying the needs of a lower order. And for this to happen – Bauman claimed – an appropriate social organization was necessary (1965, 232, 233). In the context of Bauman's inspiration by humanistic psychology, it should also be pointed out that it had a significant impact on his beginning to analyze the emotional, spiritual, and corporeal aspect of human life. It is especially evident in his article "Notes beyond Time," published in Polish in 1967 ([1967b] 2021). This paper begins with a critique of the reductionist image of the human being in contemporary sociology. In the following parts of this text, Bauman draws attention to the holistic nature of identity, referring to humanistic psychology. This approach is reflected in his analyses of the relationship between love and fear, as well as love and sex.

In the second part of the 1960s Bauman also analyzed the issue of the proliferation of ambivalence with regard to the obstacles to the realization of the structuring properties of culture. In the paper "The Problem of Universals and the Semiotic Theory of Culture" ([1968c] 2018, 94–118), published as a part of his *Sketches in the Theory of Culture*, he developed Edmund Leach's (1964) analysis of the phenomena that are not classified by culture. Bauman distinguished two of their types: those that lack culturally assigned meanings and those characterized by an excess of them. The former, described by him as the "blank spots" on the cultural map of the world, are those aspects of reality that are beyond the scope of current human comprehension. On the one hand, they very often cause anxiety, but, on the other, they are the subject of the constant efforts to understand their nature. These blank spots are usually incorporated into the order of the structured world over time. In contrast to them, phenomena belonging to the latter type elude unequivocal classification. Bauman called them the "undemarcated margins" and wrote that they are characterized by a variety of meanings. In response to their special status, these aspects of reality are often made taboo, repressed, or physically annihilated. Bauman analyzed these processes using the example of the relationship between "familiarity" and "strangeness." In much the same way as Simmel did ([1908] 1921), he argued that groups or individuals characterized by cultural ambiguity are often subjected to various forms of ostracism, solely because they do not fit into the cultural patterns characteristic of the majority of society (Bauman [1968c] 2018, 112–16). It is worthwhile to stress that these reflections were developed by him until the end of his life (e.g., 2016b, 2011a, 1991a), and their analysis is one of the leitmotifs of this book.

At the end of the discussed paper "The Problem of Universals and the Semiotic Theory of Culture," Bauman argued that ambivalence ceased to be "marginal" in the cultural condition of that time, de facto becoming its constitutive feature. "I would not hesitate to acknowledge this problem as the most important riddle for the diagnosis of our times – as the *sine qua non* condition of all future efforts, and all efforts connected to the future," he wrote ([1968c] 2018, 117, 118). Bauman was not convinced then as to whether this change had a stable and irreversible character. In the following years, however, ambivalence became one of the most important analytical frameworks in his sociology (Junge 2008).

The aforementioned analyses of Bauman were conducted during the time that the assumptions of post-structuralism were being formed. His reflections on the limits of the structuralist method, as well as his emphasis on the growing significance of cultural ambiguity, fit into that intellectual climate of the second part of the 1960s,[37] shaped by the works of Jacques Derrida ([1967] 1976), Roland Barthes ([1967] 1977), Julia Kristeva ([1969] 1980), and Michel Foucault ([1969] 1972). It is not certain to what extent he was inspired by their work at the time, but, as the correspondence collected in the Zygmunt and Janina Bauman Archive at the University of Leeds has revealed, Julia Kristeva was among the intellectuals with whom he was in contact before his forced emigration from Poland.[38] In any case, his thoughts on the irreducible complexity of the world are one of many examples of the very innovative nature of the theory of culture that he developed in the Polish period of his work.

The third plane on which Bauman analyzed the issue of proliferation of ambivalence in the second part of the 1960s concerned the progressive disjunction of culture and society (Bauman 1966a). In the first chapter of this book I pointed out that the analytical separation of these categories was based on Bauman's argument that while culture shapes individual motivations, the social system determines whether they can be realized. "The system of social dependencies is functional with regards to culture when it makes possible for people the acquisition of goods, which culture causes them to desire," wrote Bauman ([1966b] 2021, 28). Then he added: "And there are at least as many non-functional societies and aspects of social structures as there are non-functional cultures and cultural elements." The issue of the emergence and development of "non-functionality" was analyzed by Bauman in detail in his book *Culture and Society*. In it, he presented a vision of the evolution of societies from being socially and culturally homogeneous (he called them "Hmhm") to being heterogeneous in both of these planes ("Htht"). This concept developed and extended his typology of the "stable" and "developmental" cultures that was discussed earlier in the chapter (1964a).

According to Bauman, Hmhm societies are characterized by "syngenism" (see Gumplowicz 1899) at the level of culture, and "synergy" in relation to society. It means that a sense of brotherhood is created between the members of this formation, and its social institutions are oriented toward achieving the common good (Bauman 1966a, 186–204). However, both these properties are systematically weakening with the heterogenization – and at the same time emancipation – of society and culture, claimed Bauman. On the one hand, growing social stratification makes it more and more difficult for many individuals to achieve culturally desirable goods. Therefore, the phenomenon of syngenism is systematically replaced by the mechanism of schismogenesis, by which Bauman understood – following Gregory Bateson ([1935] 1972) – to be the formation of a competitive attitude between individuals and groups. On the other hand, culture is losing its structuring properties as a result of its growing diversity. "The culture of a society in which various cognitive and evaluative perspectives intersect ceases to be a system. It becomes a loose set of not necessarily coherent patterns and meanings. It becomes a mass culture. It becomes an accidental multiplicity of unique cultural contacts," wrote Bauman (1966a, 433). With regard to Htht societies,

Bauman used terms, well known from his later publications, such as "liquidity," "variability," and "amorphousness" ([1968c] 2018, 149, 163). He thereby highlighted an inadequacy of the then current analytical framework in relation to the changes in the human condition of the time, and also the need to work out new ways of describing it.

In his analyses of Htht formations Bauman devoted much attention to the issue of the consequences of the heterogenization of culture for individual identities. He claimed that this new cultural condition forced individuals to develop new skills that would enable them to navigate a world of multiplicity, complexity, and the contradiction of values. He wrote: "Individuals and groups are within the influence of many systems at once ... and in many situations they are doomed to choose between competing patterns of behaviour, between the greater and lesser evil, between good from one point of view and good from another point of view" (1966a, 166). Similarly to what he wrote a few decades later about identity changes in the context of the postmodern and liquid modern condition (e.g., 2004b, 2001d, 1997b), already in the 1960s Bauman had indicated that flexibility was becoming a more and more important feature for individuals. The liquidity of the world obliged them to constantly re-evaluate their life goals, while making them fully responsible for their choices.

These reflections also led Bauman to the conviction that the Htht condition required far-reaching changes in regards to pedagogy ([1968c] 2018, 216–30). He argued that educational activities should focus no longer on instilling a specific axiological system but on transmitting the so-called metanorms that would equip individuals to choose among competing values. "The new opportunity," he wrote, "is a creative, innovative personality, a strength of consciousness that is self-reliant, and is far better equipped to confront disillusionment and cynicism, insured against a frustrated escape to a small private world. This opportunity is attractive enough to justify taking on these new tasks, although they will require great effort" (230). The changes in education postulated by Bauman were, therefore, fully consistent with his humanistic vision of an individual that was discussed earlier in the chapter ([1967b] 2021, 1965).[39]

At that time Bauman also rejected the assumption about the existence of an isomorphism between cultural and geographical boundaries.

Continuing and developing his earlier thoughts on the global flow of values and ideas that were discussed in the first part of this chapter, a few years later Bauman analyzed the course and the consequences of the increasing importance of intercultural relations. For example, in a paper entitled "Cultural and Extra-Cultural Organization of Society," published as a part of *Sketches in the Theory of Culture*, he wrote: "The goods created by humans are now reckoned in a global scale, and access to goods is now determined by relationship going far beyond the boundaries of one nation … The modern world is … the arena of chronic and many-sided cultural contacts, an endless reshuffling of the boundaries of energy and information systems, and a notorious discrepancy between the sphere of information and the sphere of energy" ([1968c] 2018, 164). In this context, Bauman also pointed to the emergence of a new institution of global "cultural brokers," specializing in the transmission of information, as well as related values and norms, across national borders. *Ergo*, in his opinion, the process of cultural heterogenization was not completely spontaneous, because it was, to some extent, directed by actors operating on a global scale (see also Bauman 1998a).

Last but not least, the fourth level of Bauman's analyses of proliferation of ambivalence in the 1960s concerned the market and consumption. He indicated that they played a central role in the cultural reality subjected to the process of heterogenization. In 1966 Bauman explained the genesis of this phenomena as follows: "The role of the market … is based on the fact that in the absence of other connections, typical of traditional societies – such as blood ties, relationships of personal dependence, ties created by non-economic violence — the market becomes in fact the only intermediary between the diversified and mutually independent fragments of society, the only keystone of the broken-up social structure" (1966a, 420). From one point of view, it can be said that the market and the consumer culture contributed to the proliferation of ambivalence because they encouraged people to constantly reach for new goods and services. From a different point of view, however, it can be said that they played an integrative function because they promoted the coherent set of values, based on the acquisition of goods. It is worth emphasizing that, in accordance with Marxist premises, Bauman assessed the relationship between the axiological sphere and market mechanisms very negatively (420–50). In this context, he pointed to the developing phenomenon of the "mercantilization" of interpersonal relations. He also argued that, as part of the consumer culture, individuals defined themselves mainly through the prism of the goods they purchased. Finally, he claimed that although the market created the illusion of freedom, its mechanisms in fact appropriated human subjectivity.[40] All the processes listed here were interpreted by Bauman as manifestations of the mechanism of alienation. This dependence, it should be noted, was perceived by him as carried out not through repression but through seduction. In many of his publications from the late twentieth and the twenty-first century he described this process as the constitutive feature of consumerist culture (2007a, 1987).

The influence of Marxism on Bauman's theory of heterogeneous culture manifested not only on the denotative but also on the conative plane (see Jakobson 1960). He clearly pointed to the necessity of a critical re-evaluation of the situation in which things exercised power over man. Referring to the thought of Antonio Gramsci, Bauman considered consumer culture as a hegemonic culture, while demonstrating the need to oppose it with another, competing proposal. For example, in the paper "Masses, Classes, Elites: Semiotics and the Re-imagination of the Sociological Function of Culture," he argued: "If we do not accept uncritically the values that existing culture is adapted to creating and spreading, when we perceive the essential flaws in the dissemination of values that a given culture adheres to in its ideology, we have the right to subject the dominant system of culture to critical analysis and offer a counter-proposition of another system. If the proposed system has better odds of serving already-existing needs, or evoking the needs that are stifled by the actually existing system, it is historically rational and adequate; the proposed idea then has the chance of concentrating social energies, sufficient to become a factor shaping social reality" ([1968c] 2018, 244). Pointing to the need to create a "counter-proposition to the system," Bauman did not strive to clearly outline the properties it should have. In this context, he listed only a few of the most important postulates, which he derived from both revisionist thought and the humanistic vision of an individual. These included the phenomena already discussed in this part of the chapter, such as syngenism, synergistic institutions, and the expansion of the scope of individual freedom. If this concept were to be treated as an exemplification of utopian thought, then it should be stated – in relation to Russell Jacoby's works, which Bauman appreciated (Bauman and Rovirosa-Madrazo 2010, 51, 52; Jacoby 2005) – that it was definitely more iconoclastic than blueprint. *Eo ipso*, Bauman argued for the need to relativize the status quo, as well as to develop alternative thinking, noting that specific solutions should be developed through dialogue and co-operation (1966a, 453–64).

In this part of the chapter I have highlighted four dimensions within which Bauman analyzed the process of the proliferation of ambivalence in the culture of the time during the 1960s: the humanistic vision of the individual, the growing complexity of cultural reality, the progressive separation of culture and society, and consumerist culture. In the case of each of these planes of analysis, I indicated the many inspirations from which he drew. I also emphasized that Bauman not only creatively developed these concepts but also proposed very innovative ways of problematizing culture. Many of his ideas at the time – such as the vision of a growing cultural ambivalence, the theory of consumer culture, or the concept of cultural globalization – would be fully developed in his later works. It should be noted, however, that his analyses of the proliferation of ambivalence were dispersed in various of his works and did not together form a comprehensive, coherent theory. Additionally, some of these concepts were presented in the same works in which Bauman developed the vision of culture as a mechanism for reducing ambivalence. This often gives the reader the impression that there are numerous tensions or even contradictions between his works of that period. However, all these inconsistencies may also be considered as a manifestation of the liminal nature of Bauman's work in the 1960s. Moreover, I would claim that the coexistence of the vision of the reduction of ambivalence and the vision of the proliferation of ambivalence in his works seems to reflect the liminality of the social, cultural, and political reality of the late 1960s.

CONCLUSION

During the fifteen years of Zygmunt Bauman's academic work in Poland before March 1968, both his political views and his scientific interests changed significantly. Firstly, Bauman was initially an ardent follower of communist rule, who become a revisionist faithful to Marxism-Leninism, and then abandoned the latter in favour of his model of revisionism that was inspired, *inter alia*, by the philosophy of Antonio Gramsci. Secondly, although he started his academic career as a sociologist specializing in political research, he began to devote more and more attention to culture, becoming in a very short time an outstanding specialist in its theorization. Thirdly, as time passed, Bauman abandoned the positivist vision of the human being and developed its humanistic dimension, drawing inspiration from a whole range of orientations in the social sciences and humanities that were newly emerging at the time.

All these changes were accompanied by a significant re-evaluation of his theory of culture. There was a turn in Bauman's sociology from pointing to the dependence of culture on the economic base, to emphasizing its active and creative role in shaping social reality. In the 1960s he developed two – both opposite and complementary – understandings of culture: one related to the process of reducing ambivalence, and the other to its proliferation. On the one hand, Bauman perceived culture as a sphere of norms, values, or meanings proper to a given society that significantly influenced the lives of its members. On the other hand, it was for him a constantly expanding repertoire of various cultural elements from which an individual could freely draw. Referring to both Marxism and structuralism, Bauman made efforts to combine the two aforementioned ways of understanding culture, which, however, did not lead to the creation of a coherent theory. However, the innovativeness of his research from this period is evidenced by the fact that he repeatedly referred to them in his later work.

Bauman's analysis of the reduction and proliferation of ambivalence, dating back half a century, is a useful interpretative framework for analyzing the events taking place in Poland at that time. In the paper "The Problem of Universals and the Semiotic Theory of Culture," published in *Sketches in the Theory of Culture*, he distinguished the means by which homogeneity-oriented systems strive to eliminate the phenomena that are considered a threat to their stability. In his opinion, in certain situations these phenomena are subjected to "cultural repression or physical annihilation" ([1968c] 2018, 116). He wrote: "The concept of 'enemy' elicits our hatred; the concept of 'traitor' – also our loathing … The slogan 'who is not with us, is against us' has its deep justifications, as does the amount of energy released by this slogan: it is only necessary to prove, and maybe even to cause as a result of some action, the singular meaning of the situation that is postulated by this slogan" (113, 114). At the time that these analyses were being prepared for publication, the authorities were campaigning in Poland against "Israeli Zionists" and "West German revisionists," presenting them as "enemies" and "traitors" to the nation (Eisler 1998). These efforts took on strength, especially during the Polish 1968 political crisis. Those who were considered "strangers" were fired from their jobs, subjected to a smear campaign, and eventually forced to leave the country. A victim of these activities was also Zygmunt Bauman, who was fired from his job at the University of Warsaw and shortly thereafter left Poland in the post-March emigration (Stola 2017; Bauman 1969a). Due to the censorship record, sociologists in Poland could not cite his works for two decades. His *Sketches in the Theory of Culture* was sentenced by the authorities to never see the light of day. It was published in Polish at the very beginning of 2017, shortly before Bauman's death.

3

TWO FACES OF PRAXIS: STRUCTURATION AND TRANSFORMATION

INTRODUCTION

After leaving Poland in 1968, Bauman went to Israel, where he was appointed professor ordinarius at Tel Aviv University and guest professor ordinarius at Haifa University College (Wagner 2020, 287–313). Then, in 1971, after short stays in Canada, the United States, and Australia, he moved to Great Britain and became the director of the Department of Sociology at the University of Leeds. He occupied this post until his retirement in 1990 (Wagner 2020, 314–33; Campbell, Davis, and Palmer 2018, 353, 354). In his work spanning the period beginning with his emigration from Poland to the early years of the 1980s – when his interests began to be concentrated mainly on the issue of modernity – three major topics can be distinguished (Smith 1999, 77). The first one was the theory of culture. Bauman devoted a book entitled *Culture as Praxis* (1973b) to this issue and also engaged this problematic in other papers written at that time (e.g., 1973c, 1972a). The second area comprised sociology and the philosophy of science. Not only did Bauman analyze many theoretical and methodological concepts in this area, but he also promoted his own vision of critical sociology (e.g., 1978, [1976b] 2021, 1976d, 1973c, 1972b, 1971c). The third topic that drew his attention was power and social change. He studied the political situation on both sides of the Berlin Wall and reflected on the possibility of their revolutionary transformation (e.g., 1982, 1981, 1976a, 1976c, 1974, 1972c, 1971a, 1971b). The development of Bauman's theory of culture was closely tied with analyses conducted in the framework of the second and third areas of research.

Among the materials acquired by the University of Leeds after Bauman's death and housed in the Special Collections of the university's library are documents pertaining to research initiatives in the theory of culture that he was aiming to complete in Israel. One of them is a preliminary research project proposal entitled "Cultural Focus and Semiotic Density" (Bauman ca. 1970). Its goal was to analyze the significance of cognitive anthropology for a general theory of social systems. Bauman wanted to use this framework to create a centre of cultural semiotics at Tel Aviv University. The documents reads: "It goes without saying that the proposed research to bring conclusive results has to be complex, multi-faceted and relatively prolonged. It requires enlisting and instructing a small but high-class staff of relatively independent investigators, preparing a full record of findings of the rapidly developing discipline, an up-to-date card index, designing relatively complex research devices etc. This amounts, in other words, to creating in the Tel-Aviv University the first in Israel and one of the first in Israel and one of the very few in the world centre for cultural semiotics" (3). For the time, it was an ambitious and innovative research initiative. But due to Bauman's departure for the UK it could not be realized. Although most of his papers from the period in Israel are devoted to the sociology of power and social change, some of them contain implicit references to theorizations of culture. This applies, for example, to the texts in which he considered the issue of the relationship between structural constraints and human praxis (1971b, 1971c, 1969a).

On the subject of the situation of British sociology in the early 1970s, Richard Kilminster and Ian Varcoe wrote the following: "The 'orthodox consensus' (Giddens) consisting of the Anglo-American tradition of the structural functionalism of Talcott Parsons and Robert K. Merton, which was committed to promoting sociology as science, testing theories and building up empirical findings, was under fire. This was a highly politicized period, both inside and outside of sociology. Rival paradigm-communities, schools and factions (such as ethnomethodology, Althusserian Marxism, critical theory, structuralism, feminism, phenomenology, 'theorizing,' existential sociology) competed fiercely to be heard in the sociological marketplace" (1996, 2). The situation described here found its reflection in the theory of culture. It was increasingly common to go beyond the understanding of culture that was characteristic of functionalism (Parsons 1972). For example, the University of Birmingham's Centre for Contemporary Cultural Studies, founded in 1964, developed left-oriented analyses of popular culture, media, and hegemonic power relations (e.g., Hall and Jefferson 1976; Hoggart 1969; Williams 1966). A significant change was taking place in anthropology as well, *inter alia*, in connection to the development of the symbolic understanding of culture (e.g., Douglas 1970; V. Turner 1967). The new ways of theorizing culture were systematically penetrating the mainstream of sociological studies. Bauman indicated, however, in his introduction to the second edition of *Culture as Praxis*, written at the end of the previous century, that at the beginning of the 1970s the very concept of culture was only poorly represented in the social sciences in Great Britain (1999, viii–ix). His undertaking of analyses devoted to this issue, which served to some extent as a continuation of his work conducted in Poland, contributed to a change in this state of affairs.

In the time period covered by this chapter – from his emigration out of Poland to the beginning of the 1980s – Bauman formed his theory of culture in opposition to both positivist and anti-positivist approaches in sociology. He claimed that neither of them acknowledged the complexity of the relationship between structure and agency. He also asserted that they did not serve as a proper basis for the development of critical thought, which remained – as I clearly emphasized in the first chapter of this book – the *signum specificum* of his sociology. The key term for his reflections on culture conducted during the time discussed here was *praxis*. Bauman applied it to both the structuration and the transformation of culture, but with the passing of time, the emphasis that he placed on the former phenomenon was replaced by a focus on the latter. The caesura, falling more or less at the halfway point of the 1970s, divides my own analysis into two parts. In the first part I will focus on the way Bauman attempted to transcend the binary opposition of determinism and voluntarism. The fundamental premise of his theory of culture at the time was presented in these words: "Being structures and being capable of structuring seem to be twin-kernels of the human way of life, known as culture" (Bauman 1973, 51). In the later portion of this chapter I will concentrate on Bauman's views pertaining to the role of culture in transcending existing conditions and forming the alternatives to them. Let these words be an introduction to this analysis:

"The most dramatically distinctive feature of culture is the notorious (though hotly denied by many scientists in the name of the ultimate success of the scientific venture) human ability to decline to learn, to resist the conditioning pressure, to 'make responses' to 'stimuli' which are not present in any imaginable material sense" (Bauman 1976d, 11). An important element of the considerations in this chapter will also be the connection of Bauman's theory of "culture as praxis" with his later thoughts on the genesis and development of modernity.

THEORY OF CULTURE AND THE PROBLEM OF CONFLATION

I decided to use, as a compositional frame for the analyses presented in this part of the chapter, Margaret Archer's theory of conflation, which she has been developing since the end of the 1980s (e.g., Archer 2000, 1995, 1988). She distinguished three types of conflation: "downwards," "upwards," and "central." The first relates to the deterministic view of structure in relation to agency. The second, on the contrary, is associated with an overly voluntarist image of an individual. The third is based on a co-constitutive vision of structure and agency that does not allow for examining the interdependencies between them. The reference to Archer's typology emerges from the fact that in many publications from the period under consideration here, Bauman criticized both downwards and upwards conflation in social theory (at the time, he obviously did not use these terms). Meanwhile, his own vision of culture as praxis (1973b) – being an effort to go beyond the limitations of these two approaches – was considered by Archer as a model example of central conflation (Archer 1988, 72–96). In the course of analyzing Bauman's concept, I will consider the legitimacy of this assessment. As in the other chapters of the book, I will highlight the sources of inspiration for his theory of culture at that time, evaluate it, and compare it with concepts and analyses developed in other periods of his work.

Archer described the assumption of downwards conflation in *Realist Social Theory* (1995) in the following way: "Individuals are held to be 'indeterminate material' which is unilaterally moulded by society, whose holistic properties have complete monopoly over causation, and which therefore operate in a unilateral and downward manner" (3). In her opinion, within the theories of culture founded on this premise – she listed as examples the works of Pitirim Sorokin, Talcott Parsons, and Claude Lévi-Strauss (Archer 1988, 25–45)[1] – individuals are reduced to properties of the system. Both Archer and, a few years earlier, Bauman (Bauman 1976e, 1–42; 1972a, 189–92) strongly criticized this approach. In their view, the focus on the processes of internalization of norms and values that is characteristic of downwards conflation cannot do justice to both human nature and the complexity of the world. "The structure," wrote Bauman (1973b), "... by its very definition is something relatively stable and constant, resistant to entropic erosion. The crux of the problem is, however, that this endemic constancy of the structure does not necessarily manifest itself, on the empirical level, in monotonous repetitiousness of its phenomenal outcomes" (62). Although both Bauman and Archer considered the striving to structure existing reality to be a fundamental property of culture, they also stated that it did not consist of recreating existing patterns but remained a continuous, dynamically changing process. Bauman wrote in this context about "the structured-structuring nature of praxis" (1973b, 77), and Archer proposed a theory of morphogenesis (e.g., 1995). Both of these concepts assume the active participation of individuals in the choice between competing rules. Both visions were formed in opposition to theories that portrayed humans as "systematically programmed robots" (Archer 1988, 72).

The criticism of the positivist approach to culture had another dimension in Bauman's case, related to the engaged nature of his work. He argued that a focus on the analysis of existing conditions may de facto legitimize them. "The philosophy of positivism," wrote Bauman in *Culture as Praxis*, "faithfully reflects this reality of the alienated world of humans" (1973b, 164). In opposition to this approach, he aimed to enhance human agency. Without diminishing the importance of structures, Bauman strove to create a theory that would take into account both the importance of adaptation to existing conditions and the ability to transcend them. As I will indicate, structuration and transformation were for him at that time two complementary properties of culture. It must be admitted, however, that in the early 1970s Bauman did not undermine all the premises of "the philosophy of positivism." He asserted that it was necessary to supplement it with a "cultural stance." By that he meant extending the scope of analysis to include reflections on alternative possibilities for the development of the social world (176, 177).

In *Realist Social Theory*, Archer wrote the following about upwards conflation: "The solution to the problem of structure and agency is again epiphenomenal, but this time it is the social structure which is passive, a mere aggregate consequence of individual activities, which is incapable of acting back to influence individual people" (1995, 4). *Ergo*, this type of conflation is distinguished by bolstering the significance of human agency at the cost of structure. The latter is grasped as an aggregate result of actions undertaken by the individuals, having the form of a consensus developed in the course of interaction or manipulation. In *Culture and Agency*, Archer singled out two types of upwards conflation: instrumental and technocratic (1988, 46–71). The first of them – exemplified by the philosophy of Antonio Gramsci[2] – referred to the ideological domination inherent in capitalist societies, consisting in the exploitation of one class by another. The second – discussed, for example, in the context of the theory of Jürgen Habermas[3] – is characteristic of industrial societies and consists of subordinating the cultural system to instrumental rationality. In her later works (e.g., 2000, 1995), Archer expanded her understanding of upwards conflation to include such orientations as symbolic interactionism, phenomenological sociology, and ethnomethodology. Bauman took a similar position with regard to these orientations, acknowledging that they placed too much emphasis on the role of individuals in the construction of social life, while ignoring structural constraints (see, for example, Bauman 1976e, 43–70; 1973c; 1972a, 192–7). While downwards conflation, in his opinion, presented an "oversocialized conception of man" (Wrong 1961, 183–93), the upwards one was characterized by a completely opposite, but equally erroneous, vision of human beings.

Among the aspects of Bauman's critique of anti-positivist orientations, I would like to direct particular attention to the fact that he highlighted their paradoxical convergence with the positivist stance. In their attempts to discover the way in which cultural reality is shaped in the processes of social interactions, they fulfill the descriptive and explanatory function of a science, without bringing it into the realm of critical discourse, he thought (Bauman 1973b, 165–9; 1973c). In this context it is worth quoting Jonathan Turner on ethnomethodology: "The 'methodology' in the ethnomethodological perspective does not address questions about the 'proper,' 'unbiased,' or 'truly scientific' search for knowledge; rather, ethnomethodology is concerned with the common methods people employ – whether scientists, housewives, insurance salesmen, or laborers – to create a sense of order about the situations in which they interact" (1974, 323). Bauman, like Turner, drew attention to the fact that the method of discovering meanings was not accompanied by an assessment of whether they were true or false. He recognized this property as petrifying the process of alienation. He even stated that in this respect the anti-positivist orientations were more dangerous than the positivist ones.[4]

The last of the types of conflation specified by Archer was described by her as "central." Initially – in *Culture and Agency* (1988, 72–96) – she illustrated it by reference to Bauman's concept of culture as praxis (Bauman 1973b) and Anthony Giddens's theory of structuration (Giddens 1984).[5] In her later works (e.g., 2000) Archer also pointed to the structural constructivism of Pierre Bourdieu (e.g., Bourdieu [1980] 1990, [1979] 1984). In distinction to downwards and upwards conflation, its central type is not reductionistic, because it takes into account the role of both structure and agency. In this approach, however, these dimensions are presented as interdependent. On the consequences of such theorization Archer wrote in *Being Human*: "[W]e are confronted with amalgams of 'practices' which oscillate wildly between voluntarism and determinism, without our being able to specify the conditions under which agents have greater degrees of freedom or, conversely, work under a considerable stringency of constraints" (2000, 6). According to Archer, the greatest weakness of central conflation is the impossibility of studying the mutual relationship between structure and agency. A direct consequence of this way of theorizing is the difficulty of formulating theses concerning cultural stability and change. In this context Archer negatively assessed Bauman's claims that culture "is, simultaneously, the objective foundation of the subjectively meaningful experience and the subjective 'appropriation' of the otherwise inhumanly alien world" (Bauman 1973b, 117).[6] In opposition to this approach, that she described as a "duality of structure," Archer presented a concept of "analytical dualism" (1988). Structure and agency, she recognized, both possessed emergent properties. Structure, in her view, preceded action and conditioned it, although it did not determine it. The effect of social interaction was either the reproduction (morphostasis), or the transformation (morphogenesis) of the cultural system.

Analyzing Bauman's theory of culture, Archer did not pay attention to the fact that it was inspired primarily by the work of two theoreticians, one of whom was classified by her as representative of downwards conflation, and the other, upwards conflation. The first of these was Claude Lévi-Strauss, whose work – as I demonstrated in the previous chapter – had a fundamental significance for the evolution of Bauman's work during his time at the University of Warsaw (Bauman [1968c] 2018). Continuing these theorizations, Bauman argued at the beginning of the 1970s that structures did not constitute a restriction on human creativity. They were rather "a network of communication within a set of elements" (1973b, 64), or, as he argued in reference to Noam Chomsky (1965), within "the set of generative rules" (Bauman 1973b, 76). The derivative of this understanding of structures was that Bauman used this term in a verbal form: he wrote about "structuring" and added that this process inevitably accompanied all human activity.

The second of the theorists referred to was Antonio Gramsci ([1948–51] 1971). In the previous chapter I pointed out that it was from him that Bauman borrowed the category of praxis (e.g., Bauman 1963). Bauman applied this term both to structuring chaos into a reality endowed with meaning and to transforming one way of organizing social reality into another. He argued that creativity materialized through activities oriented toward establishing and modifying structures, patterns, and institutions.[7] The inspiration that Bauman drew from the works of Lévi-Strauss and Gramsci led him to understand structure and agency as complementary phenomena. Bauman captured their mutual interrelationship in the following words: "The methodology of praxis radically opposes preferential treatment of any analytically separable aspect of the social process: from its perspective, the 'social structure and the 'cultural' (in the ideational sense of the distinction) facets of the process are as inseparable and resistant to all 'hierarchization' as are *signifant* and *signifié* in a sign-event" (1973b, 145–6).

It should be noted that although this belief appears to be fully representative of the concept of "duality of structure," Archer also identified several elements in Bauman's theory that seemed to question such an unequivocal classification (Archer 1988, 80–3). She pointed, for example, to a certain degree of independence that he ascribed to culture, when he claimed in *Culture as Praxis* that "[c]ultural data enjoy existence in their own right, though of a different kind from the reality typical of the 'natural universe.' Culture is not only intersubjective; it is indeed objective in its own specific sense" (1973b, 116). Archer argued, however, that Bauman did not problematize the consequences of this alleged autonomy of cultural system, but, on the contrary, he focused on presenting the mutual dependencies between it and the socio-cultural level. She also referred to Bauman's belief in the creative role of praxis in the process of structuring social reality. She argued, however, that Bauman did not consider praxis in relation to the socio-cultural system, because he defined the latter as "an attribute of community, capable of transcending the natural or 'naturalized' order and creating new and different ones" (Bauman 1973b, 118). Taking all this into account, it should be emphasized that Archer's analysis of these aspects of Bauman's theory led her to the conclusion that they did not so much exclude – but they even confirmed – the thesis about the conflationary character of his theory of culture, in the "central" sense of this term.

My view on this issue is different. As far as I am concerned, there is a lack of coherence between some of Bauman's theorizations of culture from the period that is considered here, and it is largely a derivative of the liminal nature of his sociology at that time. Using metaphorical language, it can be said that his theory of culture at that time was of a palimpsestic nature, as his earlier theorizations overlapped with the newer ones. In his works from the beginning of 1970s, one can find numerous references to the analyses he conducted earlier in Poland, as well as anticipations of his later theorizations.

The first group includes, among others, the thesis about the "objective" (external to individuals) character of culture that was inspired by the functionalism of Talcott Parsons and the sociologism of Émile Durkheim. In the introduction to the second edition of *Culture as Praxis*, published in 1999, Bauman wrote: "In tune with the prevalent sociological vision of three decades ago, I viewed culture as a feature of social reality; one of many 'social facts' to be adequately grasped, described and represented … I assumed that there was an objective phenomenon called 'culture.'" (1999, ix). However, Bauman also devoted much attention at that time to the issue of the autonomy of culture, which was a derivative of his earlier reflections that were inspired by revisionist Marxism and humanistic psychology.

"Culture is … the natural enemy of alienation. It constantly questions the self-appointed wisdom, serenity and authority of the Real," he argued (1973b, 176). Thus, although in the early 1970s Bauman strived to create a new theoretical model of the mutual dependencies between structure and agency, his previously developed ways of perceiving culture – as a mechanism of either the reduction or the proliferation of ambivalence – greatly influenced this research. These theorizations also had a significant impact on his subsequent analyses of the genesis and transformation of modernity. I will demonstrate this relationship with two examples.

In *Culture as Praxis* Bauman returned to his earlier – discussed in the previous chapter – analyses of phenomena that were filled with meanings of a varying, often contradictory, nature ([1968c] 2018, 94–118; 1973b, 120–57). Both in the late 1960s and in the early 1970s he argued that this kind of ambivalence might raise anxiety and uncertainty and even trigger the taboo mechanism. In the period discussed here he referred in this context to the works of Jean-Paul Sartre ([1943] 2001) and Mary Douglas (1966). Bauman quoted Sartre's analyses of the term *le visqueux*, meaning "viscous" or "glutinous," but also "vile, offensive and vulgar."[8] Referring to these thoughts, Bauman argued that the intrusion of that which was accorded the status of *le visqueux* – in the form of material objects, individual beings, or even entire social groups – was perceived in terms of a threat to identity. It therefore mobilized defensive actions, which could take the form of either physical separation of such phenomena or their expulsion. All these activities were oriented toward restoring a lost sense of order or a subjective experience of freedom (1973b, 137–8). Continuing these reflections, Bauman referred to the anthropological analyses of the phenomenon of "dirt" that Mary Douglas described in *Purity and Danger* (1966). He agreed with her perspective that striving to structure the world, as well as taking actions aimed at restoring the disturbed order, was a constitutive feature of human society.[9] It should be stressed that Bauman referred to the analyses of Sartre and Douglas when he reflected, in later years, on the constitutive features of modernity. The terms *le visqueux* and *dirt* were used by him in his reflections on attitudes toward "strangers" within this condition (e.g., Bauman 1997b, 7, 8, 26, 27). Bauman also used this analytical framework in his work on poverty, exclusion, and attitudes toward migrants (2016b, 2011a, 2004c). This issue will be the subject of my reflections in the following chapters.

Bauman also pointed out in the early seventies – just as he did at the end of the Polish period of his writings ([1968c] 2018, 116–18) – that the second half of the 1970s would be a time of definite change in the attitude toward ambivalence. It had not only gained a significant level of acceptance in society but even started to be valued and cherished. He argued that if this process continued, "human culture will face a revolution unmatched by the most drastic upheavals of the past, since the one aspect of it which has so far never been seriously challenged, and which has invariably emerged victorious and intact from the deep waters of revolutionary tumults and agitation, is the structure of human praxis" (1973b, 157). Bauman was still not fully convinced at the time that this change would actually take place. He finally gained such certainty in the mid-1980s when he began his analyses of the postmodern condition (e.g., 1988a; 1987), which will be discussed in the next chapter. At this point I would like only to quote a section of a paper of Bauman's from the 1990s, in which he reflected on the then contemporary change in the attitude toward the phenomena that were previously understood as *le visqueux*: "The essential difference between the socially produced modality of modern and postmodern strangers … is that while modern strangers were earmarked for annihilation, and served as bordermarks for the advancing boundary of the order-under-construction, the postmodern ones are, joyfully or grudgingly, but by common consent or resignation, here to stay … In an important respect, and for important reasons, ours in a *heterophilic* age" (1997b, 30).

Concluding this analysis, I would like to emphasize that Bauman's theory of culture at the beginning of the 1970s was in many ways a pioneering achievement. At a time that the domination of functionalism in social theory was being broken up by anti-positivist approaches, he created a theoretical concept free from the limitations of both of these orientations. Applying Margaret Archer's terminology, I have indicated how he was able to manage the Scylla of downwards conflation and the Charybdis of upwards conflations. In later years a similar path was followed by Pierre Bourdieu ([1980] 1990, [1979] 1984) and Anthony Giddens (1984). Although Archer considered all of these theories as exemplifications of central conflation, one may have doubts as to such a classification of Bauman's approach. This doubt emerges from the different ways of conceptualizing the relation between structure and agency that he offered. Taking this into account, his theory of culture from that time cannot be considered to be a coherent one. It is rather liminal in its nature because it contains references to both the Polish period of his writings and the harbingers of his later interests focused on the metamorphoses of modernity.

Finally, it is worth adding that it was not only Archer referring to Bauman's theory of culture; he also cited her work. In a review of *Culture and Agency*, published in 1989, he wrote that the emphasis on the meaning of the logical relationships between elements in the cultural system that was characteristic of her approach not only failed to capture the essence of cultural dynamics but also did not contribute to its development in social life. He claimed: "Archer tells her reader quite a lot about one logically elegant and analytically sophisticated way in which one can think about doing of culture. She tells much less about what culture does do" (1989d, 265). This second issue became, with the passing of time, an increasingly essential subject of his interests.

TRANSCENDENCE AS A MODALITY OF CULTURE

In this portion of the chapter I concentrate on the change in emphasis that took place in Bauman's sociology in the second half of the 1970s, consisting in an enhancement of the category of agency in relation to structure. Drawing on the metaphor borrowed from George Santayana, Bauman asserted then that culture was "a knife with its sharp edge pressed continuously against the future" (1973b, 172). This meant that it possessed a capability to create and bring to life alternatives to existing reality. In a conversation with Keith Tester at the beginning of the twenty-first century Bauman referred to this comparison and asserted: "Culture is about making things different from what they are; the future different from the present … Structures emerge at the far end of culture's struggle. They stand for the 'inevitable,' only to be eroded and in the end folded up, cut into pieces and dissolved by the culture's indefatigable and intransigent rebelliousness, pugnacity and swagger" (Bauman and Tester 2001, 31–2). I will point out the sources of this understanding of culture, with particular emphasis on *utopian thought*, *critical theory*, and *hermeneutics*. I will demonstrate how Bauman began to perceive transcendence as a modality of culture, and I will also evaluate his view on this issue.

Utopian thought was an exceptionally important point of reference for Bauman's theory of culture in the period considered here (Bauman 1976d; see, for example, Jacobsen 2016, 2008, 2007). From the outset, however, it must be noted that Bauman questioned the identification of "utopia" with unrestrained dreams or projects that had no chance of being implemented. He also rejected the critical way of relating to this concept, typical of the founders of historical materialism (Engels [1880] 1935),[10] that had been close to him at the beginning of his academic career (Bauman and Wiatr 1953, 75). Bauman understood the term *utopia* in a way that was innovative at the time but that is in fact consistent with most of the recent interpretations of the classic text by Thomas More ([1516] 2014; see, for example, Levitas 2013; Sargent 2010; Harvey 2000; Cousins and Grace 1994).[11] In *Socialism: The Active Utopia* Bauman wrote: "Whatever the nature of man as such, the capacity to think in a utopian way does involve the ability to break habitual associations, to emancipate oneself from the apparently overwhelming mental and physical dominance of the routine, the ordinary, the 'normal'" (1976d, 11). *Ergo*, Bauman identified utopia with a critical attitude toward norms, values, and practices characteristic of a given society, and an accompanying inclination to transcend them and create alternatives. He juxtaposed utopianism with "common-sense thinking," which he understood – both in the second part of the 1970s and in all later years (see, for example, 2000c, 202–16) – as the internalization of given premises that were reflected in routine practice.

Among the theorists who were most influential for Bauman's way of theorizing utopia, it is worth noting Karl Mannheim, Ernst Bloch, and Herbert Marcuse (see Aidnik and Jacobsen 2017; Jacobsen 2008; Levitas 1990, 168–72). All of them also significantly shaped the evolution of his theory of culture at that time. Bauman to a certain extent agreed with a view of Mannheim expressed in *Ideology and Utopia* that utopias "are not ideologies in the measure and in so far as they succeed through counteractivity in transforming the existing historical reality into one in accord with their own conceptions" ([1929] 1954, 176). He expanded, however, the understanding of this term to all concepts aimed at the change of the status quo, regardless of the final effect of actions initiated by them. He clearly tied the emergence of utopias to an ability, in his opinion constitutive of culture, to transcend existing conditions or to create alternative forms of organizing the social world.

Clarifying his position in the matter, and at the same time referring to another source of inspiration, he noted the following in conversation with Keith Tester: "To say 'culture' is to make another attempt to account for the fact that the human world (the world moulded by the humans and the world which moulds the humans) is perpetually, unavoidably and unremediably *noch nicht geworden* (not-yet-accomplished), as Ernst Bloch beautifully put it" (Bauman and Tester 2001, 32). The influence of the philosophy of the author of *Das Prinzip Hoffnung* was visible, *inter alia*, in Bauman's emphasis on the constructivist character of existing reality. Both Bauman's utopian thought and his theory of culture at the time were oriented toward the exploration of the potential that is manifested in every moment of history. Contrary to the assumption, commonly accepted as one of the fundamental premises of Marxism, he admitted – following Bloch – that the future was completely open and could lead to an infinity of various solutions (Bloch [1954–59] 1986).

Finally, the inspiration that Bauman drew from the work of Herbert Marcuse was founded on the identification of utopia with countercultural revolution, which had the goal of opposing "common sense" modes of thought and action (Marcuse 1972, 1964, 1955). Bauman fully agreed with the following statement of Marcuse's: "The revolution involves a radical transformation of the needs and aspirations themselves; cultural as well as material; of consciousness and sensibility; of the work process and leisure" (1972, 16–17). It should be noted, however, that Bauman was not an adherent of the majority of the political solutions proposed by Herbert Marcuse, and his attitude towards the New Left was deeply ambivalent (Bauman 1976d, 107–13). What made Bauman's work similar to Marcuse's, however, was a smooth combination of the denotative and conative functions of his language.

Bauman specified several functions that utopias – understood as "aspects of culture" (Bauman 1976d, 14) – fulfilled in the historical process. Firstly, they relativize the present; that is, they contribute to revealing its constructivist nature. In this regard they are reminiscent of political programs. However, in distinction from them, they are not limited by reflection on the difficulties in their implementation. Secondly, Bauman emphasized that utopian premises were generally formed in reference to actually existing reality. They reflect the specificity of historical conditions and evolve together with them. What allows them to transcend the status quo is – in Bauman's opinion, founded on Ernst Bloch's thought – "the principle of hope" (Bloch [1954–59] 1986). Bauman argued: "Hope supplies the missing link between practical and theoretical interests because it is intrinsically critical of the reality in which it is rooted. Again, it extends the meaning of realism to encompass the full range of possible options" (1976d, 15). Thirdly, utopian concepts are conditioned not only historically but also structurally. They arise within the frameworks of different social groups. The position in social structure determines the way of assessing reality and shapes the nature of alternatives to it. Fourthly, Bauman pointed to the significant role that utopias played in the process of historical change. They can be immediately implemented by political authorities, systematically penetrate social life, or serve as a reference point for the assessment of current processes. "In this triple role," wrote Bauman, "utopias enter reality not as the aberrations of deranged intellects, but as powerful factors acting from within what is the only substance of reality, motivated human action" (1976d, 14). It should be also noted that a particularly important element of Bauman's vision of the utopia was its "active" dimension. Far ahead of the reflections in this matter that would be made by Ruth Levitas (2013), Fredric Jameson (2005), or Russel Jacoby (2005), Bauman pointed out that utopian thinking took a continuous, processual, afinalistic form. Its goal was not to achieve a detailed plan of social or political order but to constantly relativize the status quo and to think of social reality as an open project.

All these premises of Bauman's concept of active utopia significantly influenced his theory of culture. As a result, the attempt to maintain a balance of emphasis between structure and agency, ongoing in Bauman's sociology since the end of the 1960s, was replaced a decade later by a clear shift toward the latter of these properties. In *Socialism: The Active Utopia* Bauman wrote about the need for "radical opposition to the conservative view of culture, as reduced to learning, to the detriment of creativity" (1976d, 11). In this context it can be said that his concept of culture as active utopia exemplified his view of utopian thinking.

In many ways Bauman's theory of culture at the time was in line with his vision of socialism as "the active utopia."[12] It assumed the need for a relativization of norms, institutions, and structures in contemporary societies from the point of view of socialist values. What is important – and will be developed further in the book – is that in creating this concept, Bauman referred critically to the societies on both sides of the Berlin Wall, which he considered to be "modern" formations (1976d, 130–2).[13] When Bauman was asked in 2005 about the parallels between his concepts of culture and socialism formulated in the 1970s, he replied: "The substance of both socialism and culture consists in demanding, pulling, nagging, prodding; they are archenemies of stillness and quietism and, above and most important of all, also of self-satisfaction and conceit. They are both inveterate and irreverent critics of reality, including the reality brought about in their names, that residual sediment of their past critique and demands" (cited in Tester and Jacobsen 2005, 93). I would like to pay particular attention to the issue of a continuous, unending transgression that was to characterize both culture and socialism. Just as Bauman's theory of culture at that time was formed in opposition to the vision of stable structures, his understanding of socialism contrasted with modern political ideologies. In the context of Bauman's vision of engaged sociology, it should also be noted that both concepts were characterized by a departure from representation in favour of critical revision of contemporary condition.

Turning to the analysis of the relationship between Bauman's understanding of culture and his view on critical theory, I refer to his book *Towards a Critical Sociology* (1976e). In it, he delineated an opposition between nature and culture. He identified nature with an area that was not subject to human volition and that determined a given order of events. He associated culture with the sphere of human creativity and its capability to actively transform the world. This opposition formed a foundation for his critique of the positivist paradigm, focused on the sphere of so-called second nature. This concept refers to the norms, customs, and traditions that are intended to model human action. In Bauman's opinion, this way of theorizing society and culture – related to the appreciation of regularity and predictability – was a manifestation of alienation from human praxis. He singled out as the most influential representatives of this approach Émile Durkheim and Talcott Parsons.

However, similar to his analyses in *Culture as Praxis* (1973b, 165–8), Bauman in *Towards a Critical Sociology* also criticized the anti-positivist orientation in social theory. He concentrated mainly on existentialism, of which he wrote: "With the same vehemence that Durksonians fight the 'mysterious notion of free will,' existentialist sociologists are bound to fight the 'mysterious notion of social necessity.' The change of direction does not detract from the intensity of the barrage" (1976e, 56). In Bauman's opinion, the anti-positivist approaches not only did not allow for drawing an adequate image of human society but also did not create a foundation for social transformations.

The way to overcome the limitations of the two opposite orientations was through critical sociology, argued Bauman. His view on this matter corresponded perfectly with and complemented his vision of active utopia that was formed at the same time. On the one hand, Bauman argued that critical sociology should concentrate on the role of existing structures. On the other hand, he emphasized their constructivist and changeable character.[14] It should also be noted that in line with the premises of the concept of active utopia and the related vision of culture, Bauman did not outline a vision of structures and institutions that would replace current ones. Instead, he pointed to the need to engage in a dialogue about their future shape. His view on this issue was related to his vision of hermeneutics, which I will present later in this chapter.

At this point, however, I would like to emphasize that Bauman's concept of critical sociology significantly influenced his view of modernity. His reflections on this condition appeared for the first time in his paper "Between State and Society," published in the first half of the 1970s (1973a). At that time they were closely related to analyses undertaken by Max Weber ([1922] 1968) and Reinhard Bendix (1960). A few years later, Bauman's attitude toward modernity began to be more and more critical, inspired in no small part by the works of the representatives of the Frankfurt School (e.g., Horkheimer and Adorno [1947] 1972). Following them, he claimed that the constitutive features of modernity derived from the philosophy of the Enlightenment. They included the imperative of continuous progress, the appreciation of science and technology, and the imposition of rational visions of organized order. Bauman pointed out that these assumptions were applicable to both the natural and the social world. This meant that human individuals were subjected to the processes of "cultivation." "The human environment, in its 'natural' and 'social' aspects alike, seemed passively to await the human modelling activity," wrote Bauman in *Socialism: The Active Utopia*, adding: "It would gladly reveal its secrets to an inquiring mind, and then it would obediently lend itself to an operation aimed at bringing it closer to human need. Hence the attitude of *techne*, of manipulation, inducing deliberate and planned change, first forged in the course of wrestling with Nature, could be, without much further reflection, stretched to embrace human relations" (1976d, 20). Bauman developed his view on the process of "cultural engineering" in the following years. It will be analyzed in detail in the next chapter.

The last perspective from which Bauman theorized culture in the period considered in this chapter was hermeneutics (Bauman 1978; see M. Davis 2020; Dawson 2017; Blackshaw 2005, 52–81; Tester 2004, 16–23).[15] In the book *Hermeneutics and Social Science: Approaches to Understanding* Bauman reflected on how the phenomenon of understanding was analyzed in the works of intellectuals such as Karl Marx, Max Weber, Karl Mannheim, Edmund Husserl, Talcott Parsons, Martin Heidegger, Alfred Schütz, and Jürgen Habermas. This choice can be considered at very least debatable, both because of the presence of certain names and because of the lack of broader references to the works of intellectuals such as Paul Ricoeur ([1969] 1974) and Hans-George Gadamer ([1960] 1975). However, this analytical perspective reflected the direction of Bauman's interest in hermeneutics. Peter Beilharz wrote in this context that Bauman "socializes, or sociologizes hermeneutics, viewing it as a practical and social rather than cerebral or merely intellectual challenge. The focus, in other words, is on intellectualizing life and concretizing the life of mind, rather than on cultivating a specific theory of reading" (Beilharz 2000, 69). Bauman was especially interested in the role that hermeneutics would play in both exposing the erroneous assumptions adopted within the framework of common-sense knowledge and replacing them with others, based on the right "understanding." His views on hermeneutics were thus fully in line with his theory of culture as active utopia and with his vision of critical sociology.

Consistent with the assumptions of both these concepts, Bauman argued that the process of understanding – both in social science and in social life – should not be aimed at achieving the indisputable truth.

In line with the idea of the "hermeneutic cycle," he indicated that the advancement of knowledge does not take the form of linear progression but "consists of an endless recapitulation and reassessment of collective memories – ever more voluminous, but always selective" (1978, 17). Mark Davis notes in this regard: "Everything is open to reinterpretation and nothing is ever finally decided upon now and forever" (2020, 34). What is more, Bauman was also inspired by Anthony Giddens's concept of "double hermeneutics" (Giddens 1976). In its context, Bauman reflected on the mutual relationships between the subject and the object of social research. "[T]he truth of sociology," Bauman wrote in *Hermeneutics and Social Science*, "is the derivative of an agreement reached (if at all) in the debate between sociologists and the objects of their study regarding phenomena whose control is shared between sociologists and their objects to the clear disadvantage of sociologists. The *truth of sociology has to be negotiated in the same way the ordinary agreement is*" (1978, 234; italics in the original). Taking all this into account, Bauman stated in the late 1970s that the role of intellectuals was not to discover, and then to impose onto individuals, particular ways of understanding the world. They should rather be engaged in a never-ending dialogue with the actors of social life. He developed these analyses in the next decade, in his book *Legislators and Interpreters* (1987).

These findings led Bauman to the conviction that a particularly important aspect of the process of understanding was the appropriate form of communication. No wonder then that of all the approaches to hermeneutics listed previously, he found Jürgen Habermas's theory of communication to be particularly important (Bauman 1978, 239–46; 1976e, 102–12; Habermas [1968] 1972).[16] Bauman wrote: "Habermas's model dashes hope. The model demonstrates that the rationality of discourse in cultural sciences, comparable to that of empirical-analytical science, cannot be codified without reference to the social dimensions of the debate; that, in other words, *the epistemology of hermeneutics cannot be detached from the sociology of communication*" (1978, 244; italics in the original). Bauman referred in *Hermeneutics and Social Science* to the rules of "undistorted communication" listed by Habermas and emphasized in particular the importance of an open dialogue and the equal rights between all those who participate in it. He was fully aware of the difficulties involved in implementing these assumptions and interpreted them through the prism of his concept of active utopia. In his opinion, they were like an "idealized horizon" that was to indicate the direction of efforts to be undertaken and to serve as a point of departure for assessing them.[17] Considering Bauman's later works, and especially his postmodern turn, it should be stated that many of the inspirations that he drew from the works of Jürgen Habermas did not last long. However, the assumptions about hermeneutics that he developed at that time (see M. Davis 2020; Blackshaw 2005, 52–81), as well as the vision of the culture of dialogue, remained constitutive features of his work (see Brzeziński 2020).

To conclude the analyses undertaken in this portion of the chapter, I would like to refer to the metaphor of the mountain pass that Bauman presented in *Socialism: The Active Utopia*.[18] At the end of that book he wrote: "Men climb, as it were, successive hills only to discover from their tops virgin territories which their never-appeased spirit of transcendence urges them to explore. Beyond each successive hill they hope to find peacefulness of the end. What they do find is the excitement of the beginning. Today as two thousand years ago, 'hope that is seen is not hope. For who hopes for what he sees?' (Paul to the Romans, 8.24)" (1976d, 141). This statement captures the essence of both Bauman's theory of culture at that time and his concepts of critical sociology and hermeneutics. Firstly, the metaphor of a mountain pass illustrates the importance of constantly transcending the status quo and reflecting on alternatives to it. Secondly, it emphasizes that the aforementioned process is to be carried out in relation to existing reality and not to the finalist idea of a perfectly designed order. Thirdly, Bauman's statement indicates the importance of the "principle of hope" as a mediator between theoretical research and practical activities.

Bauman's vision of culture as active utopia, based on these assumptions, can be the subject of various assessments. To some extent, it can be criticized as reductionist due to its strong appreciation of agency in relation to structures. However, this imbalance was most likely intentional and resulted from the utopian – in the sense in which Bauman used the term – attempt to change both cultural reality and the way of theorizing it. On the other hand, the novelty of this concept is evidenced, for example, by the fact that the assumptions concerning the theory of culture as the active utopia were present in all Bauman's later works. A statement from *Europe: An Unfinished Adventure*, published in 2004, can serve as one of many examples of the concept's impact: "Like our ancestors three centuries ago, we are on a rising slope of a mountain pass we have never climbed before and so have no inkling of what sort of a view will open up once we reach the top. We are not sure where the twisting gorge will lead us; one thing we are sure of is that we cannot settle and rest here, on a steeply rising path" (Bauman 2004a, 140).

CONCLUSION

Structuration and transformation are the two poles between which Bauman's theory of culture developed from the time of his emigration from Poland until the early 1980s. At the beginning of this period he devoted much attention to combining both poles into one theory of culture as "praxis" (Bauman 1973b). He applied this Gramscian term (Gramsci [1948–51] 1971) to transforming chaos into a reality endowed with meaning and to relativizing the latter. In this way he managed to overcome the limitations of the theories characterized by either downwards or upwards conflation (Archer 1988). In the second half of the 1970s, Bauman mainly focused, in his theory of culture, on the issue of transformation (Bauman 1976d). Inspired by, *inter alia*, Ernst Bloch's ([1954–59] 1986) concept of utopia, he began to understand culture as a potentiality remaining in a state of eternal unfulfilling, yet stimulating to constant activity. He argued that a constitutive feature of culture was to raise hope for transformations of the current way of structurization.

Both concepts – culture as praxis and culture as the active utopia – were very innovative in many respects. To a large extent they heralded the metamorphoses that took place in the following years in the theory of culture. However, both visions were not free from weaknesses. In the case of the first concept, it is worth emphasizing the lack of coherence between some of its aspects, and in the case of the second, attention should be paid to the strong appreciation of agency in relation to structures. It should be underlined as well that many of the aspects of the theory of culture, developed by Bauman at the time discussed here, significantly influenced his work in the following years. One such example is his concept of culture as a mechanism of repression, which presages his later work on the condition of modernity (1989c).

Another is his view on the growing role of ambivalence, which anticipates his analyses on postmodernity (1991a). Both issues will be discussed in the next portion of the book.

Closing this chapter, I would like to refer to the issue of the relationship between Bauman's theory of culture and his political thought, and in particular to draw attention to his interpretation of the social protests that erupted at the beginning of the 1980s in Poland (Bauman 1981) and Great Britain (Bauman 1982). In his analysis of the Polish Solidarity movement,[19] Bauman referred to the category of praxis as the factor responsible for breaking through existing structures and making attempts to replace them with new ones. He asserted that the liberation of the social forces of the time – which he considered to be the rare materialization of the Blochian concept of *novum* (Bloch [1954–59] 1986) – had the chance to break cultural hegemony and to create a new form of social organization. In accordance with his concept of active utopia (1976d), Bauman did not strive to describe the future scenario of events; he claimed that Poland found itself "at the crossroads" in which all eventualities seemed possible (1981, 54). In turn, what raised his hope for transformation on the Western side of the Berlin Wall was the growing social dissatisfaction with the reforms introduced by the conservative, Margaret Thatcher government. A breakdown in the labour market, rising prices of public services, and growing social problems led to the riots that erupted in 1981 in parts of large cities of Great Britain affected by exclusion. Bauman perceived this state of tension as a crisis of the social and political system that would most likely lead to the introduction of significant transformations (1982, 192–8). The events that took place not long afterwards proved the inaccuracy of his predictions in both of these cases. The introduction of martial law in Poland in 1981 and the strengthening of economic liberalism in Great Britain proved that if in essence culture is "a knife with its sharp edge pressed continuously against the future" (Bauman 1973b, 172), then it is a double-edged knife. It can serve for the transformation of existing reality, but also for the petrification of structures present in it.

4

FROM SYSTEMIC TO REPERTOIRE MODEL OF CULTURE: THE THEORY OF CULTURE BETWEEN MODERNITY AND POSTMODERNITY

INTRODUCTION

For most of the 1980s and all of the 1990s, Bauman's work was concentrated mainly on the question of the relationship between modernity and postmodernity (e.g., 1997b, 1995, 1992b, 1991a, 1989c, 1987). His analyses were considered some of the most significant in the debate on this issue (Rattansi 2017; Beilharz 2000; Smith 1999). They were an important point of reference for many intellectuals and also gained recognition among a wider audience. Bauman was very critical of the transformations taking place within modernity. He argued that this period was characterized by the development of disciplinary mechanisms and the deprivation of human freedom, as well as a striving to implement utopian blueprints. He discussed all these issues most fully in his book *Modernity and the Holocaust* (1989c). Bauman argued there that the Holocaust should not be interpreted as a denial of modernity but, on the contrary, as a materialization of its potential. At the same time, however, he pointed to the revolutionary changes that had taken place more or less since the middle of the twentieth century and had initiated the postmodern condition (e.g., Bauman 1991a, 1988a, 1987). They included the development of pluralism, the appreciation of human agency, and the breakdown of ethical codes. Although he was a keen supporter of these transformations, he also stressed many difficulties related to the postmodern condition. He wrote: "The discontents of modernity arose from a kind of security which tolerated too little freedom in the pursuit of individual happiness. The discontents of postmodernity arise from a kind of freedom of pleasure-seeking which tolerates too little individual security" (1997b, 3). As time passed, Bauman devoted more and more attention to the troubles of the postmodern condition, which was also reflected in his theory of culture.

The span of time described here was a period of particularly significant transformations with regard to the theorizations of culture (Bachmann-Medick [2006] 2016; Friedland and Mohr 2004; Bonnell and Hunt 1999). First of all, the importance of studies of culture increased in the social sciences and humanities. William H. Sewell Jr wrote on this issue: "[D]uring the 1980s and 1990s the intellectual ecology of the study of culture was transformed by a vast expansion of work on culture in a wide range of academic disciplines. The history of this advance differs in timing and content in each field, but the cumulative effects are undeniable" ([1999] 2005, 153). The aforementioned change was accompanied by significant transformations in the way culture was understood. The vision of culture as a coherent set of patterns, norms, and meanings was confronted with models that emphasized its heterogeneous nature. The belief in the isomorphism between geographic and cultural boundaries was replaced by an emphasis on the inherently heterogeneous character of culture. The attention previously directed to the transmission between generations was now turned to the issue of opposing the established order. Many theorists of culture have portrayed these changes with diametrically opposed models. Ann Swidler (1986) created the concept of culture as a "repertoire" or "tool kit," in contrast to the traditional approach, according to which culture provides the ultimate values for human action. Referring to her concept, Paul Di Maggio (1997) juxtaposed models of culture as a "seamless web" and "toolkit-repertoire," and Wendy Griswold (2013) contrasted the understandings of culture as "meaning systems" and "a tool kit."

Similar models of culture – which I refer to in this book as "systemic" and "repertoire" – determined Bauman's theorizations of this concept at that time (Bauman 1997b, 1991a, 1987). His analyses had a diachronic dimension and were related to his aforementioned vision of the transition from the modern to the postmodern condition. Bauman claimed that within modernity "the notion of culture was coined after the pattern of the *factory of order*" (1997b, 129). However, culture in the postmodern condition was presented by Bauman – as Polish sociologist Marian

Kempny interestingly noticed – as "a flexible repertoire of interpretative resources" (Kempny 1995, 188). In the two following parts of this chapter I will analyze Bauman's visions of culture within both the modern and the postmodern condition, pointing out the theoretical inspirations from which he drew. I will also make some critical comments with regard to his theorizations of culture and their applications to analyses of social phenomena.

CULTURE AS A DISCIPLINARY MECHANISM

William Turner's painting *Rain, Steam, and Speed* is one of the greatest studies in painting, presenting the relations between the agrarian era and the dynamically developing industrial civilization. It was painted in 1844, at a time that Great Britain was densely covered by a web of railway connections. These constituted a revolution in the field of transportation as well as a testimony to the developing process of humankind conquering nature. The train, which Turner captures in the painting, bursts onto the landscape, bathed in rain and country fog. In this way, the steam engine, and the formidable brick bridge stretching across the river that it traverses, dynamize the space and divide it into two. The opposition between nature and technology captured in this way was enacted by Turner on many other dimensions as well. On the right side of the painting he placed a cultivated field, and on it – barely visible and represented by a hazy mark – the figure of a farmer with a plow pulled by two horses. On the left side, he painted a small boat with passengers, travelling the river in the vicinity of another stone bridge. These details symbolize the traditional models of life receding. Turner contrasted them with the dynamism of the transformations that modernity brought with it. In front of the locomotive itself he placed the sketch of a rabbit fleeing, providing in this way a vision of the force and inexorable progress of technological civilization.

I have referenced Turner's painting because it resonates perfectly with the process of transition from "wild" to "garden" cultures that Bauman analyzed in relation to Ernest Gellner's *Nations and Nationalism* (Bauman 1987; Gellner 1983). Both intellectuals identified the "wild" cultures with communities in which norms, values, and practices were transmitted from generation to generation in a form that did not undergo significant changes. All these aspects of culture were perceived as a stable foundation of social life, possessing a religious provenance or derived from the laws of nature. The inviolability of tradition was also guarded by the elites of that society, whom Bauman gave the metaphorical name of "gamekeepers." According to him, "They lack … the sort of self-confidence needed to interfere with the trustees' timeless habits; it does not occur to them, therefore, that a state of affairs different from the one sustained by such habits could be contemplated as a realistic alternative" (Bauman 1987, 52). This does not mean that Bauman considered "wild cultures" to be coherent systems of values and meanings, as was the case with the anthropological concept of culture.[1] In *Modernity and Ambivalence* he wrote as follows about their characteristic attitude to otherness: "The pre-modern eye viewed difference with equanimity; as if it were in the pre-ordained order of things that they are and should remain different. Being unemotional, difference was also safely out of the cognitive focus" (1991a, 255). It can thus be said that, according to Bauman, it was not homogeneity but constant reproduction that was the distinctive feature of "wild" cultures.[2]

The way in which Bauman theorized premodern cultures was in significant contrast to many of the analyses that emerged in history and anthropology in the last decades of the twentieth century (e.g., Carrithers 1992; Peel 1987; Clifford and Marcus 1986; Fox 1985; Hobsbawm and Ranger 1983; Wolf 1982). For example, Eric Wolf, in his book *Europe and the People without History*, published in 1982, presented non-European cultures as perpetually changing and enmeshed in networks of mutual dependence. He clearly argued that this was true both before the colonial era and during active colonization, when these societies became part of the global transformation.[3] Referring, *inter alia*, to the work of Eric Wolf, Michael Carrithers claimed in the 1992 book *Why Humans Have Cultures: Explaining Anthropology and Social Diversity* that constant changeability was a constitutive feature of every culture. Following Roy D'Andrade (see Agar 1980, 11), Carrithers compared studying culture to studying snow in the middle of an avalanche (1992). Taking into account Bauman's constant dialogue with contemporary theories of culture, it might be surprising that the aforementioned arguments – developed, among others, by postmodern anthropologists (e.g., Clifford and Marcus 1986) – did not affect his work. However, it should be stated that Bauman, like many other intellectuals of the time (e.g., Beck, Giddens, and Lash 1994; Baudrillard [1981] 1983), believed that there was a threshold between premodern and modern cultures. He did not conduct detailed studies of the former but presented them as the negative of the latter. As I will point out, this was one of many examples of Bauman's use of the binary opposition in the period under discussion (M. Davis 2008b, 103–8).

The evolution of cultures from wild to garden took place, as Bauman argued, as a result of two major factors (Bauman 1987). The first concerned the progressive crisis of the feudal system, which made its further reproduction impossible. This appeared as a result of precipitous demographic growth, changes in structures of land ownership, the strengthening of capitalist markets, the development of manufacturing, the systematic migration of people from the countryside into the cities, and so forth. Taking into account the consequences of all these transformations – perfectly illustrated in the aforementioned painting by William Turner – Bauman wrote about a transformation from a culture in which life was reproduced from one generation to another to a reality shaped to an ever greater degree by human agency. "The forms of human life and conduct assumed did not seem any more part of the 'nature of things' or part of a divine order which would neither need nor stand human intervention," he claimed (1987, 94), and added: "Instead, human life and conduct appeared now as something which needed to be formed, less it should take shapes unacceptable and damaging to social order, much like an unattended field is swamped with weeds and has little to offer its owner." The activities mentioned here required intense legislative activity, modification of social control, and changes in the exercise of power.

In this context Bauman wrote about the second aspect of the genesis of modernity, which is a retreat of the elite from efforts to preserve social reality in an unchanging form, towards a reflection on the possibility of introducing fundamental social and cultural transformations. In accordance with the terminology that he introduced, this meant that the "gamekeepers" were replaced by "gardeners," who set themselves the goals of delineating new structures and institutions and removing all "weeds" that did not fit into the assumptions of the planned order (1987, 51–68). Tracing the genesis of this change, Bauman concentrated on the group that he called *les philosophes*. He indicated that this was not a coherent school of thought, nor a collective joined by experience or education. The factor that gave them a collective identity was, however, a belief in the need to found a new – permanent and harmonious – order based on the rule of Reason. Bauman described their stance as follows: "Truth is man-made, human reason is the highest authority, man is self-sufficient as the ordering force of human reality, reality itself is pliable, ready to be made, unmade and remade according to human – good or ill – will" (1987, 36). According to this view, tradition, religion, and folk culture severed people from comprehending their potential. Thus, liberating them from a state of "wilderness" and lifting them to the sphere of "civilization" required both disavowing their current way of life and conducting a remarkably ambitious program of education. *Ergo*, the "project of civilization" that *les philosophes* initialized assumed the intensification of activities related to education, control, and discipline.

As an introduction to the criticism of Bauman's theory of modern culture, presented later in this chapter, I would like to point out that his view on this issue is often accused of being simplistic. This also applies to his vision of *les philosophes*. For example, Ali Rattansi (2017, 21–34) argued that Bauman created the latter on the basis of a small selection of non-representative works of French intellectuals. This mode of analysis not only did not allow him to reflect on the complexity of the philosophy of the Enlightenment but also distorted its image. "Too many of the supposed 'legislators' were not simply rationalist and universalist," wrote Rattansi. "Nor did they believe in the inevitability of continuing progress or the unlimited applicability of the scientific method to any and all matters. In fact, they doubted that society could be ordered simply on rational principles and unbending discipline, revealed by indubitable truths valid for all time" (28). Although I agree with this argument in principle, I would also like to point out that Bauman's vision of *les philosophes* should be analyzed in the context of the methodological premises of his sociology at that time. One of its most characteristic features was the use of ideal types (Weber [1922] 1968).[4] Tony Blackshaw astutely observed: "In his use of ideal-types Bauman … recognized Weber's argument that they are merely abstract idealizations constructed from a *particular point of view*" (2005, 47, italics in original; see also Bauman 2007a, 26–8). And the "particular point of view" from which Bauman analyzed modern culture was of its disciplinary nature.

The seeds of this way of theorizing modern culture had appeared in the previous stages of Bauman's work. In the second chapter of this book I demonstrated that in the 1960s he devoted attention to the issue of reducing ambivalence by homogeneously oriented cultural systems. In *Sketches in the Theory of Culture* Bauman pointed out that they use different defence mechanisms to achieve this aim, including "the utilization of the institution of taboo, [and] efforts aiming towards cultural repression or psychical annihilation" ([1968c] 2018, 116). He was developing these analyses in the 1970s, inspired by the works of Jean-Paul Sartre ([1943] 2001) and Mary Douglas (1966). Referring to the analyses of the term *le viscaux* by the former, as well as to anthropological reflections by the latter on the issue of "purity," he analyzed the phenomenon of "thoroughness and consistency in imposing on the surrounding world whatever passes for the human order" (1973b, 139).[5] What is more, under the influence of Max Horkheimer and Theodor Adorno ([1947] 1972),[6] Bauman started to develop a critical attitude toward the Enlightenment in the 1970s. He pointed to the subordination of individuals to rationally organized projects, as well as to the brutal repression of those who advocated for alternative ways of life. Although Bauman focused these analyses mainly on the issue of communism, he – following Adorno and Horkheimer – was already referring to Nazism as well. "[T]he fascist tumours are natural outgrowths of the Enlightenment rather than its denial" (1976d, 125), Bauman wrote in 1976, anticipating his analyses contained in *Modernity and the Holocaust* (1989c).

All these inspirations not only formed the basis of Bauman's analyses of modernity – including the related theory of culture – but also were constantly referenced by him during the period discussed here. For example, the works of Sartre and Douglas were cited by Bauman in his then contemporary reflections on the "dream of purity." "Purity is an idea," he wrote in *Postmodernity and Its Discontents* (1997b, 5, 6), "a vision of the condition which needs to be created, or such as needs to be diligently protected against the genuine or imagined odds … Purity is a vision of things put in places different from those they would occupy if not prompted to move elsewhere, pushed, pulled or goaded;

and it is a vision of *order* – that is, of a situation in which each thing is in its rightful place and nowhere else." At the same time, the analyses of the Frankfurt School theorists played an extremely important role in Bauman's reflections on the disciplinary nature of modernity. In the introduction to *Modernity and Ambivalence* Bauman wrote: "Any reader of the book will certainly note that its central problem is firmly rooted in the propositions first articulated by Adorno and Horkheimer in their critique of Enlightenment (and, through it, modern civilization)" (1991a, 17). However, Bauman was by no means an uncritical reader of the aforementioned works. The "universal, extratemporal, and species-wide" (Bauman 1997b, 8) analyses of Sartre and Douglas were specified by him as being applicable in the context of the modern condition. As to the totalitarian character of the Enlightenment, outlined by Horkheimer and Adorno, Bauman argued that it had finally failed at the end of the last century (1991a, 17).

Bauman developed his theory of modern culture under the influence of many other intellectuals. Among them, I decided to concentrate on Sigmund Freud, Max Weber, and Michel Foucault. This choice stems from the importance Bauman ascribed to these authors in problematizing modernity (e.g., Bauman 1997b, 1991a, 1987). As far as Freud and Weber are concerned, Bauman claimed that thanks to them "the self-understanding of our (western, industrial, capitalist etc.) society has been given shape" (1983, 32). He stressed as well that they took opposing positions on many issues in theorizing modernity. Freud's emphasis on the tragedy of an individual entangled in a growing network of repression and compulsion contrasted with Weber's portrayal of the triumphant victory of human reason over the bonds of tradition.[7] Bauman undertook a dialogue with both perspectives and combined them into his own theory of modern culture. The work of Foucault played the role of a liaison in this respect. "When confronted with Foucault's re-writing of the history of industrial civilisation," wrote Bauman (1983, 33), "the otherwise radical controversies between competing interpretative traditions seem considerably less significant than their common assumptions and jointly accepted limits of the cognitively relevant." In the following analyses, however, I will stress that Bauman was also by no means an uncritical reader of the theories of Freud, Weber, and Foucault. He re-evaluated them and often pointed to their weaknesses.

In Freud's psychology, Bauman was especially interested in the issue of the relationship between two values: freedom and security (Bauman 1997b, 1987). As is well known, Freud claimed that the genesis of culture was related to the mechanisms of repression. On the one hand, culture suppress the drives of the individual, and on the other hand, it enables the creation of an ordered, predictable world (Freud [1930] 1962). Bauman adopted this belief via his reading of Norbert Elias's *Civilizing Process* (Elias [1939] 1997). He wrote: "Elias demonstrated that the 'suppression of instincts' which Freud deduced from the nature of mature modernity, was in fact a historical process which could be pinned down to the specific time, place and socio-cultural figurations" (Bauman 1987, 114). This historicizing interpretation of Freud's theory of culture enabled Bauman to combine it with Gellner's view of the transition from "wild" to "garden" cultures. Both theories emphasized the restriction of freedom in exchange for the promise of security.

As a harbinger of the subsequent analyses in this book, it is worth pointing out that, according to Bauman – and in opposition to Freud – the relationship between the two aforementioned values resembles the movement of the pendulum. Just as, in modern culture, freedom was taken from individuals for the sake of security, so in postmodern culture this relationship was reversed (Bauman 1997b). In turn, in the twenty-first century Bauman analyzed the movement of the pendulum in the other direction as well. As far as he was concerned, as part of the policy being developed by many countries in the name of security, individual freedom was limited in the time of "retrotopia" (2017c).

It should be stressed as well that Freud and Bauman problematized the relationship between culture and human nature to a large extent differently. Freud claimed that the human being was endowed with certain innate desires and instincts, and a predisposition to aggressive behaviour was one of them (e.g., Freud [1923] 1949). An important function of culture – and indeed the source of its genesis – is to suppress these drives. In *Civilization and Its Discontents* Freud argued: "Civilization, therefore, obtains mastery over the individual's dangerous desire for aggression by weakening and disarming it and by setting up an agency within him to watch over it, like a garrison in a conquered city" ([1930] 1962, 71). Bauman claimed that the human was inherently a moral being (1995, 1993). In an interview with Keith Tester, he explained his position on the matter: "'Being moral' does not, necessarily, mean 'being good.' But it does mean having eaten from the tree of knowledge of good and evil and knowing that things and acts may be good or evil" (Bauman and Tester 2001, 44). The innate human ability to make moral choices was the basis of Bauman's concept of postmodern ethics, which he began to develop in the late 1980s (Bauman 1990, 988b). Although this idea will be discussed in the next part of the chapter, it is worth pointing out here that, according to it, human society could exist not because it imposed moral obligations on individuals but because it consisted of moral beings. Freud's and Bauman's theories came together at the point where they both argued that the nature of the obligations imposed on an individual by culture could contribute greatly to a person's suffering.

The inspiration that Bauman drew from Weber also had a selective character (see du Gay 1999). Bauman wrote in *Legislators and Interpreters* that the conceptualizations of reason within modernity "reached its culminating point and fullest elaboration in Weber's vision of history as progressive rationalization, and of modern society as a radical break which disclosed its own past as, above all, the long domination of irrational conduct" (1987, 112). The fundamental role that Weber ascribed to instrumental rationality for the development of modern civilization was largely reflected in Bauman's analyses in the period discussed here (Bauman 1989c, 1987; Weber [1922] 1968). It must be admitted, however, that both sociologists focused on other aspects of this phenomenon and also assessed it differently. Weber concentrated primarily – though by no means exclusively – on the benefits of the increased effectiveness of organizational structures in modernity, previously bound either by traditional ties or by individual dependencies. He pointed out that the dominance of instrumental rationality made it possible for Western civilization to reach a level of development not available in any other part of the world ([1922] 1968, [1905] 1930). Bauman took a different perspective on this issue; he wrote about the "imprisonment" of individuals in "the iron cage of rationality." The consequence of this phenomenon was, in his opinion, the process of dehumanization. Paul du Gay commented on these differences as follows: "[W]hile Bauman's critical discourse on the bureau draws upon a theoretical lexicon that is self-consciously Weberian, its conclusions concerning the ethical and moral emptiness of bureaucratic conduct are the very antithesis of Weber's own. Indeed, both sociologically and historically, Bauman's analysis of the bureau diverges from Weber's in crucial respects, despite Bauman's claim to be following in Weber's footsteps" (1999, 578).

An excellent example of this approach to Weber by Bauman is the analyses of the latter devoted to the process of modern "adiaphorization" (Bauman 1995, 1993). Bauman derived this term from the Greek word *adiaphoron*, that is, things that are morally indifferent. He related it to the phenomenon of "the stripping of human relations of their moral significance, exempting them from moral evaluation, rendering them 'morally irrelevant'" (Bauman 1995, 133). In Bauman's opinion, the "iron cage" of rationality that characterized modernity was an excellent environment for the development of adiaphorization. In reference to Weber he wrote: "Through honour, discipline is substituted for moral responsibility. The delegitimization of all but inner-organizational rules as the source and guarantee of propriety, and thus denial of the authority of private conscience, become[s] now the highest moral virtue" (1989c, 22). The relationship of subordination within bureaucratic structures was, however, assessed differently by Weber and Bauman. Weber described the moral obligations related to performing official duties. It was well illustrated by his metaphorization of a profession as a "vocation" ([1917–19] 2004). Bauman emphasized that the subordination to internal regulations weakened or even completely suppressed the sense of morality (1993). As far as he was concerned, the process of excluding human actions from moral judgement, and their assessment from the perspective of other criteria, such as efficiency or compliance with a previously designed order, had led to tragic consequences in modernity. In *Modernity and the Holocaust* he wrote: "As the promotion of rationality to the exclusion of alternative criteria of action, and in particular the tendency to subordinate the use of violence to rational calculus, has been long ago acknowledged as a constitutive feature of modern civilization – the Holocaust-style phenomena must be recognized as legitimate outcomes of civilizing tendency, and its constant potential" (1989c, 28). Bauman's approach to the Holocaust as a product of modern culture will be analyzed in more detail later in this chapter.

The analysis of the relation between Bauman's and Foucault's theories of modern culture should begin by noting that the first reference to the work of the latter appeared in the book of the former entitled

Hermeneutics and Social Science: Approaches to Understanding (1978). Bauman pointed out there that the work of the French philosopher called into question the possibility of implementing in practice Habermas's concept of "undistorted communication" (Habermas 1972, 1970). He wrote: "The paramount obstacle standing in the way of true consensus is the structure of dominance, which defies both conditions of rational agreement" (Bauman 1978, 244). This reflection – though marginal at the time – was a harbinger of Bauman's theory of modern culture, influenced to a large degree by Foucault's philosophy. It is worth emphasizing above all that both intellectuals paid much attention to the issue of the asymmetry of power relations within modernity, symbolized, in their opinion, by Jeremy Bentham's panopticon (Bentham [1791] 2017). They argued that this institution, which allowed control to be exercised continuously, with full physical separation between supervisors and observers, became the guiding principle of the whole modern condition (Bauman 1988a; Foucault ([1975] 1977).[8] Bauman – following Foucault – wrote on this issue: "Prisons, workhouses, poorhouses, hospitals, mental asylums, were all by-products of the same powerful thrust to render the obscure transparent, to design conditions for redeploying the method of control-through-surveillance once the conditions of its traditional deployment proved increasingly ineffective" (1987, 45). Bauman developed these analyses in a number of publications.

For example, in *Memories of Class* (1982), Bauman analyzed the factory system from the perspective of imposing power over the bodies of workers. He emphasized that this practice exemplified not only the industrial sector but also the entire modern civilization. In an interview with Ian Varcoe and Richard Kilminster conducted about a decade after the publication of *Memories of Class*, Bauman stated that this book was "a farewell, not to the working class, but to the identity between the working class and the problem of injustice, and inequality" (Bauman 1992a, 206). Another example of how Bauman viewed the development of disciplinary power is his analyses of folk culture within modernity. In *Legislators and Interpreters* he wrote: "[A]ncient popular habits came under criticism and had been selected as objects of prosecution and legal prohibitions because of the false, or morally wrong, ideas they promoted, ideas contrary to scientific or moral truths as proclaimed and testified by the men of knowledge" (1987, 61). *Eo ipso*, folk culture was considered by modern intellectuals – or *les philosophes* – as the "weed" that needed to be eradicated. To do so, it was necessary, however, to cooperate with the authorities. Bauman, influenced by both Foucault ([1975] 1977) and Gellner (1983), argued that this alliance was made possible because both sides benefited from it. *Les philosophes* gained the opportunity to implement their visions of garden culture, while the authorities acquired the possibility of meaningfully increasing their influence on the people. This "cultural crusade" was accompanied by efforts to "educate people," which strengthened the congruence of state and culture.

It should be stressed, however, that Bauman did not accept uncritically Foucault's approach to modern culture. In an article entitled "Industrialism, Consumerism and Power" (Bauman 1983), he asserted – in opposition to the French intellectual – that disciplinary mechanisms were, to some extent, a characteristic feature of premodern societies as well. He claimed that the novelty of the seventeenth century was not the emergence but the "problematization" of discipline, both in social practices and in intellectual reflection. What is more, Foucault and Bauman had a completely different view of the question of the possibility of liberation from the panopticon-like modern condition. While the former did not have great hopes for its transformation, directing attention to acts of individual subversion, the latter continued to develop his utopian critical thought, the assumptions of which were presented in the previous chapter of this book (Bauman 1976d). Dennis Smith rightly noticed: "For Bauman, the self is not a prison in which we are trapped, but an inner generator waiting to be re-ignited. Foucault wants to escape the self. Bauman wishes to invigorate it" (1999, 181). An excellent example of the aforementioned strategy is Bauman's book *Modernity and the Holocaust*, in which, on the one hand, he analyzed the Holocaust as a consequence of the processes that took place within modernity, and on the other, he aimed to make a fundamental transformation in the approach to the issue of morality and responsibility.

Modernity and the Holocaust won the Amalfi Prize in 1989 and contributed to Bauman's receiving the Theodor W. Adorno Prize in 1998. It is one of the most widely discussed books in the social sciences and humanities of the last decades (see Palmer and Brzeziński 2022b). It begins with the juxtaposition of two metaphorical images of the Holocaust as "a picture on the wall" and as "a window" (Bauman 1989c, vii–xiv). The former highlights the fundamental differences between the Holocaust and modernity, just as a framed picture is separated from the wall. This view is related to the theory of culture – represented, among others, by Émile Durkheim ([1895] 1982) – according to which the norms and values of a given society are fundamental to the morality of individuals, and therefore their weakening led to the liberation of bestial instincts in humans. "In that world," wrote Bauman (1989c, vii), "murderers murdered because they were mad and wicked and obsessed with a mad and wicked idea. Victims went to the slaughter because they were no match to the powerful and heavily armed enemy. The rest of the world could only watch, bewildered and agonized, knowing that only the final victory of the allied armies of the anti-Nazi coalition could bring an end to human suffering." Bauman claimed that he cultivated this approach until he read the memoirs of first wife, Janina Bauman (J. Bauman 1986; see Pollock 2022; Wagner 2022), and then the books written by Raul Hilberg (1961) and Richard L. Rubenstein (1978). All these papers led him to change his attitude and recognize that "[t]he Holocaust was born and executed in our modern rational society, at the high stage of our civilization and at the peak of human cultural achievement, and for this reason it is a problem of that society, civilization and culture" (1989c, x). As a result, Bauman suggested that the Holocaust should be understood as "a window," because looking through it makes it possible to glimpse the genocidal potential of the modern condition.

The arguments presented by Bauman in *Modernity and the Holocaust* fully reflect the assumptions of his theory of modern culture. One of the most important perspectives through which he analyzed the genesis of the Holocaust was the concept of the "garden culture." He claimed: "Racism comes into its own only in the context of a design of the perfect society and intention to implement the design through planned and consistent effort. In the case of the Holocaust, the design was the thousand-year Reich – the kingdom of the liberated German Spirit ... It had no room for the Jews, as the Jews could not be spiritually converted and embrace the *Geist* of the German *Volk*" (1989c, 66). In terms of the metaphor of the garden culture, it can be said that the Jews were perceived by Nazi leaders as the "weeds" that were to be eradicated in order to make the vision of the perfect society a reality. In this context Bauman's arguments were very much the same as the arguments that were apparent in the works of the critics of utopian blueprints, such as Karl Popper ([1945] 2011), Hannah Arendt (1951), and Isaiah Berlin (1990). All of these demonstrated the direct relationship between the idea of a perfect society and the implementation of terror. It should be stressed, however, that Bauman's anti-utopian thought was limited to the visions that reflected the idea of the garden culture. In fact, he was a utopian intellectual in the sense in which he himself used this category in the book *Socialism: The Active Utopia*, discussed in the previous chapter (see Jacobsen 2008; Bauman 1976d).

The issue of modern bureaucratic civilization was very important in Bauman's analyses of the Holocaust. He argued that the norms, values, and procedures characteristic of modern organizations – with an emphasis on discipline, rationality, and hierarchical structure – were central to the realization of the Holocaust. "The murderous compound was made of a typically modern ambition of social design and engineering, mixed with the typically modern concentration of power, resources and managerial skills," wrote Bauman (1989c, 77). The relationship between modern bureaucracy and the Holocaust was analyzed by him on many different levels, ranging from the general principles of the ethics of obedience to the way in which ghettos and concentration camps operated. In all these cases, however, Bauman emphasized the particularly important role of the phenomenon of adiaphorization, that is, abandoning the moral evaluation of human actions. He stressed that the architecture of the Holocaust was discussed by the Nazi authorities and their collaborating scientists in terms of organizational and technical problems only. He also argued that the process of dehumanization of the victims of the Holocaust – recognizing them as *homo sacer* (Agamben [1995] 1998) – made their deaths no longer morally sanctioned. What is more, most of the perpetrators of the Holocaust, claimed Bauman, did not have murderous inclinations, but followed the orders of their superiors. "Bureaucracy's double feat is the moralization of technology, coupled with the denial of the moral significance of non-technical issues. It is the technology of action, not its substance, which is subject to assessment as good or bad, proper or improper, right or wrong. The conscience of the actor tells him to perform well and prompts him to measure his own righteousness by the precision with which he obeys the organizational rules and his dedication to the task as defined by the superiors," wrote Bauman (1989c, 160).

Bauman's concentration on the "gardening" and bureaucratic characteristics of modern civilization in his analyses of the Holocaust was accompanied by the marginalization of other factors of its genesis. For this reason, *Modernity and the Holocaust* has been criticized by many scholars (e.g., Ray 2022; Tokarska-Bakir 2022; Marshman 2008; Vetlesen 2005; Bauer 2001, 68–91). For example, it was emphasized that he did not pay attention to the issue of the brutality of the perpetrators. Arne Johan Vetlesen wrote in his book *Evil in Human Agency*: "The Holocaust, despite overwhelming efforts in that direction, never became a fully factory-like, cargo-eliminating undertaking along the lines suggested in Bauman's functionalist account" (2005, 35). Both in this book and in the article published several years later (Vetlesen 2022), he emphasized the exceptional importance of brutal instincts, hatred, and sadism in the course of the Holocaust. Another issue, the importance of which Bauman marginalized in his analysis of the Holocaust, was anti-Semitism. In line with his theory of culture at the time, according to which modernity was characterized by an obsessive attempt to both create order and eliminate ambivalence (Bauman 1991a), Bauman argued that it was not anti-Semitism but "allosemitism" (from Greek *allos*, "other") that played a crucial role in the course of the Holocaust. "While Bauman goes into great detail about the Jews' fundamental 'ambivalence' and estrangement, ultimately his landmark book argues that any group could have been the killers and any group could have been the victims," wrote Sophia Marshman (2008, 82–3; see also, for example, Tokarska-Bakir 2022; Goldhagen 1996).

Although it is beyond the scope of this book to address such critical remarks in detail,[9] I would like to emphasize that they do not, in my opinion, undermine either the strength of Bauman's argument or the essential purpose of his investigations. Bauman's analyses, although focused only on selected aspects of the genesis of the Holocaust, are an excellent study of the genocidal potential of modernity, as well as the processes of the social "normalization" of cruelty. By reinterpreting the aforementioned metaphor, it can be said that *Modernity and the Holocaust* is a window that provides insight into the structural and cultural determinants of violence (see Cheyette 2022; Palmer and

Brzeziński 2022a). Moreover, the dystopian image of the modern condition was for Bauman a starting point for outlining the utopian assumptions of a vision of social relations based on the concept of postmodern ethics (Bauman 1993), analyzed in the next part of the chapter. It appreciated both ambivalence and individual responsibility.

To conclude this part of the chapter, I would like to return to the painting by William Turner, *Rain, Steam, and Speed*. The work has received many different interpretations. It was read as a vision of the loss of the traditional world, a warning against the dangers of industrialization, a celebration of the opportunities offered by technological progress, and so forth. Ian Carter combined all these approaches, pointing to the ambivalence inherent in this work. He wrote: "*Rain, Steam and Speed* is about loss, but also about progress. To be more precise, it is about the casualties of progress and the impossibility of not changing. The radical instability of Turner's image is its most enduring feature" (1997, 4). In this respect, there is an important difference between Turner's and Bauman's visions of modernity, because the latter is unequivocally critical of this condition.

Inspired by the works of Freud – read through the prism of Elias's historical sociology – Bauman argued that within modernity the human being was caught in a perpetual web of regulations and commands. Under the influence of Weber's theory of rationalization, interpreted in the perspective of the Frankfurt School, he emphasized the totalitarian dimension of this period. What is more, following Foucault, Bauman compared the modern condition to Jeremy's Bentham vision of the panopticon. In fact, he brilliantly captured one of the faces of modernity but ignored its other dimensions. Stefan Morawski wrote on this issue: "Modernity is also … a constant anarchizing tendency that breaks up the established order; the constantly recurring anxiety and doubt in the ultimate meaning of existence, against the certainty that one wants to establish once and for all" (1999, 55, see Habermas [1985] 1987). It is precisely this ambiguity of modernity that is missing in Bauman's analyses.

However, it is also worth looking at this issue from a different angle. Bauman's theory of modern culture was one of the many examples of his usage of Weberian "ideal types" (Weber [1922] 1968). In the methodological section of his *Consuming Life*, published in 2007, Bauman wrote on this method: "'[I]deal types' (if properly constructed) are useful, and also indispensable, cognitive tools even if (or perhaps *because*) they deliberately throw light on certain aspects of described reality while leaving in the shade some other aspects considered to be of lesser or only random relevance to the essential, necessary traits of particular form of life. 'Ideal types' are not descriptions of reality: they are the tools used to analyze it" (2007a, 27). In the case of his theory of modern culture, Bauman "throws light" on its disciplinary nature, which he considered its most important feature, and, at the same time, intentionally left its other aspects "in the shade." This way of theorizing not only resulted from methodological premises but also was related to the assumptions of Bauman's critical sociology. His aim was both to highlight the dangers associated with the modern processes of rationalization, bureaucratization, and the resulting adiaphorization, and to indicate the need to shape contemporary society and culture on entirely opposed assumptions. This issue will be discussed in the next part of the chapter.

CULTURE AS A "FLEXIBLE REPERTOIRE OF INTERPRETIVE RESOURCES"

In order to illustrate the evolution of culture in the era of the development of European nationalism, Ernest Gellner juxtaposed the techniques of painting used by Oscar Kokoschka and by Amadeo Modigliani (Gellner 1983, 139, 140). The former built his compositions by layering various splotches of colour on top of each other, creating shapes that lacked clear outlines. The latter used a reduction of colour and strong lines to clearly distinguish the forms being represented. A discussion of Kokoschka's paintings has been used to describe the various and complicated relationships among social groups in Europe before the rise of nationalism, and a reference to Modigliani's work was intended to illustrate the ethnographic map that emerged as a result of the creation of nation states. These inspiring reflections were referred to a decade later by Ulf Hannerz. He claimed, however, that at that time cultural transformations had largely moved in the opposite direction to the one analyzed by Gellner. Describing this process as "the return of Kokoschka," he wrote: "If the painting cannot be quite the same as before, at least there seems to be again, in Gellner's terms, 'diversity and plurality and complexity,' 'ambiguous and multiple relations'" (Hannerz 1996, 66). This claim was an introduction to Hannerz's outline of the concept of creolization, which was intended to depict the process of the mutual interpenetration of cultures within the contemporary, globalized world. I believe that the term "the return of Kokoschka" is also a useful metaphor to describe the direction in which Bauman's theory of culture was evolving at the end of the previous century. This is because the issues of cultural pluralism and the proliferation of ambivalence form together an analytical framework for most of the analyses he conducted at the time.

An excellent illustration of the initial stages of Bauman's view of the cultural aspects of postmodernity are two of his articles from the first half of the 1980s: "Industrialism, Consumerism and Power" (1983) and "On the Origins of Civilisation: A Historical Note" (1985). One of the most important issues he discussed in the first of these was an interpretation of the development of consumer culture in the light of the mechanisms of the disciplinary society. Bauman argued that the practices of control characteristic of the modern condition did not by any means disappear at the end of the previous century. Rather, they fundamentally changed their form. At that time they had consisted in eliciting desires in people whose sense of self-worth was to an ever greater degree tied to the realization of those wishes. In Bauman's words, "consumerism does not mark any significant departure from the kind of society which emerged in Western Europe with the advent of industrialism. On the contrary, it seems to signify a fullest deployment to-date of the techniques of power which brought industrialism into existence" (1983, 41).

Similar thoughts are found in the second article mentioned above. Although most of it is devoted to the analysis of the origins of modernity, Bauman also referred to its contemporary transformations. On the one hand, he positively assessed the increasingly "polycentric" character of the culture at that time. On the other hand, he criticized the parallel development of the individualization process. Bauman asserted that the individual autonomy achieved in the framework of consumer culture was an evolved form of disciplinary power. It is worth stressing as well that this article contained a clear critique of the attitude of "many hermeneutically inspired versions of cultural study" (1985, 14). Most likely Bauman referred then to the postmodernist intellectuals, who in his view withdrew from the struggle to regain the true measure of human agency. Keith Tester and Michael Hviid Jacobsen wrote on this issue: "This, it seems, is an early version of Bauman's later attack on the 'postmodern sociologies'" (Tester and Jacobsen 2005, 164).

Regarding both articles, I assert that they have a liminal character. In them Bauman undertook to interpret new cultural phenomena in the context of conceptualizations that he had formerly applied to the analysis of the modern condition. These attempts were not fully successful because the theory of modernity as the disciplinary mechanism no longer corresponded to the reality of the time. This resembled the biblical parable about "pouring new wine into old wineskins" (Matthew 9:17). In the second half of the 1980s Bauman recognized that it was necessary to take on a new research perspective. In *Legislators and Interpreters* he wrote on the topic: "What has happened in recent years could be articulated as the appearance of a vantage point which allows the view of modernity itself as an enclosed object, an essentially complete product, an episode of history, with an end as much as a beginning" (1987, 117). Bauman's acceptance of this standpoint at the time – which initiated his identification with postmodern thought (Clifford and Marcus 1986; Lyotard [1979] 1984) – was the basis of significant transformations in his theory of culture.

Firstly, Bauman realized that attributes ascribed to modernity could no longer be used for an analysis of the contemporary condition. In the context of the theory of culture, this meant that its "systemic" model had to be replaced by a completely new one. *Eo ipso*, the characteristics of coherence and constancy ceased to accurately describe reality at the end of the twentieth century. Secondly, the postmodern perspective implicated the intensification of critical reflection on processes characteristic of modernity. In Bauman's view, looking at this period from a distance – as if at a finished epoch[10] – allowed for a complete assessment of the tragic consequences of phenomena such as the development of instrumental rationality, the widespread use of disciplinary practices, and thinking about the future in terms of a blueprint utopia. This approach was related to the belief that it was necessary to bolster attitudes with the opposite vector. Thirdly, the new theoretical framework determined a different approach to cultural transformations. These began to be interpreted as derivative of practices of deregulation, decomposition, and privatization. It was in this context that Bauman continued his reflections on the *development of consumer culture*, the *proliferation of ambivalence*, the *change in the role of intellectuals*, and the chances for the development of *postmodern ethics*. Next, I will focus on the critical analysis of his thoughts on these issues, juxtaposing them with the work of other theorists of the contemporary condition.

I have already emphasized that from the very beginning of his work Bauman pointed to the fundamental meaning of consumerism for the changes taking place in Western culture in the second half of the twentieth century. For example, in the second chapter I described in detail his model of the socially and culturally heterogeneous community ("Hths"), in which the market and the attitudes shaped by it constituted a fundamental mechanism of social integration (Bauman 1966a, 374–450). The convergence of these analyses with Bauman's diagnoses from the period under consideration here is well illustrated by the following statement from *Legislators and Interpreters*: "Features of the consumer culture explicable solely in terms of the logic of the market, where they originate, spill over all other aspects of contemporary life – if there are any other aspects, unaffected by market mechanism, left. Thus every item of culture becomes a commodity and becomes subordinated to the logic of the market either through a direct, economic mechanism or an indirect, psychological one" (1987, 166). *Ergo*, Bauman claimed that the constitutive feature of contemporary Western society was the commodification of social reality. He argued that consumerism was reflected in all levels of social life and that its importance continued to grow.

In the context of the analyses presented in the previous part of this chapter, it should be noted that, in Bauman's view, the disciplinary mechanisms characteristic of modernity were replaced in postmodernity by the phenomenon of seduction.[11] Tony Blackshaw commented on this issue: "The comfortable majority no longer lives in the shadow of tyranny of the state; instead they create their own turmoil, their own paroxysm, driven by market forces that they have no authority over, but which at the same time have no final authority over them. The turmoil is barely noticeable – publicly at least – it is simply how people live" (2008, 125). The change in the nature of external pressure from repression to seduction was manifested in the proliferation of ambivalence, claimed Bauman. He also argued that consumer culture was characterized by a specific *coincidentia oppositorum*: its continuity is a function of its constant transformations.

The way in which Bauman analyzed consumer culture at the end of the last century was to some extent similar to the work of Jean Baudrillard (see, for example, Baudrillard 1988, [1981] 1983; Bauman 1992a, 142–55).[12] Both intellectuals agreed on the matter of the increasing limitation of individual freedom that they believed was in part a result of the domination of the market. They also claimed that within the postmodern condition there was a process of continuous creation in the successive needs and desires of individuals that was impossible to ever completely satisfy. It was one of the contexts in which Baudrillard used the term *simulation*, which was also important in Bauman's theorizations (e.g., Bauman 1992a, 142–55). However, what differed between their perspectives was that Bauman directed particular attention to the relationship between the development of consumerist culture and the expansion of areas of poverty and misery (1987, 170–87).

Criticizing Baudrillard's work from this perspective, Bauman wrote: "To many people, much in their life is anything but simulation. To many, reality remains what it always used to be: tough, solid, resistant and harsh" (1992a, 155). Utilizing binary oppositions, Bauman argued that in contemporary society there was a clear division taking place, forming groups of people that he called the "seduced" and "repressed" or "free" and "flawed consumers" (1987, 149–87). Although both groups were subjected to pressure from the market, the distinction between them was in the extent to which they could fulfill the needs generated by consumer culture.[13] Elżbieta Tarkowska (2010, 259) wrote on this issue: "The drama of the 'new poor' in the world of consumption consists primarily in the fact that they are concerned with the principles and values of a consumer society which they cannot cope with: 'flawed consumers' or 'defective consumers,' as Bauman calls them, have no role in the world in which they live, they are completely useless, unnecessary, and what's more, they themselves constitute a problem to be solved."

Bauman's analysis of binary social divisions in consumer culture was accompanied not only by their criticism but also by an attempt to influence change in this regard. One of the ways in which he attempted to achieve this goal was to combine the conative and denotative functions of language (Jakobson 1960). In this context, Bauman often used terms, phrases, and metaphors that were meant to influence the sensitivity of the readers of his texts. Some of them – for example, his description of the group of the "repressed" as "human waste" or "outcasts" (Bauman 2004c, 1998d) – can be regarded as quite controversial. However, they were most likely a rhetorical provocation by means of which Bauman wanted to awaken the ethical impulse of his readers. In an interview with some Polish friends he claimed: "If I used to lecture, today I want to provoke ... to throw others from sleep, pierce the cobweb of routine, encourage to look again at matters so obvious that they are no longer noticeable" (Bauman, Kubicki, and Zeidler-Janiszewska 2009, 26).

Bauman was also strongly appealing to the need for revolutionary political and social changes in line with his aforementioned concept of active utopia (Bauman 1976d). He not only strongly supported the idea of the welfare state but also argued that this form of government should be an introduction to further changes. For example, in the book *Work, Consumerism and the New Poor* Bauman argued – following Claus Offe (1996) – for the separation of income entitlement from earning capacity, and the separation of work from the labour market (1998d). These ideas were supposed to be just one of the aspects of an entirely new social policy. Its assumptions also included changes on a global scale, which will be considered in the last chapter of this book.

Similarly to the studies of consumerism, the second aspect of Bauman's analyses of postmodern culture discussed here, the proliferation of ambivalence, was an extension of his reflections contained in works from the end of the 1960s and into the 1970s. In the second and third chapters of this book I referenced excerpts from *Sketches in the Theory of Culture* and *Culture as Praxis*, in which Bauman analyzed the then contemporary development of ambivalence. He stated that this phenomenon could have a revolutionary significance for the future of culture, and, from the perspective of the end of the last century, his predictions turned out to be prophetic. He also asked in 1968: "What is this innate tendency of the citizen of the twentieth century to a multiplicity of meanings? A sickness or a maturity? The illness of a sensile age? Or maybe an opportunity never before seen in history?" ([1968c] 2018, 118). His answers to these questions at the end of the twentieth century were ambivalent. Although he clearly pointed to the value of pluralism and heterogeneity, he also focused on the challenges that this new situation brought for both individuals and social institutions (1998d, 1997b).

In his analyses of the proliferation of ambivalence Bauman very often used metaphors (see M. Davis 2013; Jacobsen and Marshman 2008). In one of them he compared postmodern culture to the historical model of the consumer co-operative as it was created in 1844 in the form of the Society of Equitable Pioneers (Bauman 1997b, 127–40). He pointed out that this association became in fact a self-governed realm, whose members performed the dual function of "authors" and "actors." "Things which happen inside the ideal consumer cooperative are neither managed, nor random," wrote Bauman. "[U]ncoordinated moves meet each other and become tied up in various parts of the overall setting, only to cut themselves free again from all previously bound knots" (1997b, 134). Similarly, postmodern culture, Bauman argued, was becoming a more and more self-governing area. Its characteristic processes and phenomena were not directed or controlled. They arose as the results of autonomous practices undertaken by individuals. Hence, cultural development was almost entirely unpredictable.

By using the metaphor of a consumer co-operative, Bauman also highlighted another feature that was characteristic of postmodern culture. In the case of this association, it was not production but consumption that defined the share in the common wealth. A similar phenomenon took place in culture, claimed Bauman. "The orthodox models of culture were all creator-centered. The metaphor of the consumer co-operative suggests … a decisive shift in emphasis: it is precisely in the acts of consumption, in everyday authorship/actorship of 'ordinary consumers' … that everything cultural acquires its sense. It is here that the empty shells of signs fill with meaning; here the signs (already made meaningful) gain or lose value, which reverberates in the vacillations of the demand" (Bauman 1997b, 136, 137). Bauman therefore emphasized that the metaphor of a consumer co-operative should be complemented by the metaphor of the market.[14]

Many of the metaphors that Bauman applied in his analyses of the proliferation of ambivalence came from the realm of the visual arts (Bauman 1998b; 1997b, 95–102; [1995a] 2021). In one of his texts – which was found posthumously among the Papers of Janina and Zygmunt Bauman at the University of Leeds[15] – he interpreted the works of René Magritte as a visualization of the processes that characterized postmodern culture several decades later ([1995a] 2021). Bauman believed that the surreal worlds created on canvases by this artist anticipated the process of the development of ambivalence in the late twentieth century. He wrote: "Each object suggests the possibility of being something else than it is, or finding itself in a different place – and by the same token it reveals the uncertainty, 'merely possible' status of all others, even the most familiar and comfortingly 'natural' shape or location" ([1995a] 2021, 115).

In another paper, published in 1998 (1998b), Bauman referred to the meeting of Piet Mondrian and Alexander Calder that took place in 1930. He noted that Calder's admiration for Mondrian's suprematist compositions was accompanied by a suggestion to put his works of art in motion. Mondrian, however, did not agree with this idea. For Bauman, the reference to this meeting was a starting point for an analysis of the differences between modern and postmodern art. He emphasized that while the former was closely related to the idea of extratemporality, and therefore also immortality, the latter revealed the contingency of the world. Bauman extrapolated this conclusion to modern and postmodern culture.

In yet another text – the book *Legislators and Interpreters* – he noted: "Post-modern art is conspicuous for its absence of style as a category of artwork; for its deliberately eclectic character, a strategy which can best be described as one of 'collage' or 'pastiche,' both strategies aimed at defying the very idea of style, school, rule, purity of genre – all those things which underpinned critical judgements in the age of modernist art" (1987, 130). *Per analogiam*, Bauman pointed to the fundamental importance of the processes of pluralization, decomposition, and deregulation for culture at the end of the twentieth century. He argued that as a result of these processes, culture had ceased to be a coherent, homogeneous whole and had become a loosely connected repertoire of heterogeneous norms and practices, from which individuals were – to some extent – free to choose.

According to Bauman, these cultural metamorphoses were accompanied by convergent identity transformations (1992b). The evolution from modern to postmodern patterns of identity was presented by him via the juxtaposition of the metaphors of, on the one hand, a "pilgrim" and, on the other hand, a "tourist" and a "vagabond" (1997b, 83–94; 1996). While the pilgrim's whole life was subordinated to previously set goals, the tourist's and the vagabond's were characterized by a constant reorientation of identity. *Eo ipso*, contrary to the prospective temporal orientation characteristic of modernity, in postmodernity the continuous flow of time has been broken down into a multitude of loosely related moments.[16] It is also worth emphasizing that the difference between the tourist and the vagabond was the result of their diametrically opposed positions in the social structure. "[I]f the tourists move because they find the world irresistibly *attractive*," wrote Bauman (1997b, 93), "the vagabonds move because they find the world unbearably *inhospitable* ... The tourists travel because they want to; the vagabonds – because they have *no other choice*." The comparison of both strategies is largely consistent with the previously mentioned difference between the seduced and the repressed. Both illustrations clearly show the importance of structural conditions to Bauman's theory of culture.

Bauman reflected on the validity of using terms such as "system" or "boundaries" with regard to society and culture. Of the first, he wrote in *Intimations of Postmodernity*: "[T]he theory of postmodernity would do well if it disposed of concepts like *system* in its orthodox, organismic sense (or for that matter, *society*), suggestive of sovereign totality logically prior to its parts, a totality bestowing meanings on its parts, a totality whose welfare or perpetuation all smaller (and, by definition, subordinate) units serve; in short a totality assumed to define, and be practically capable of defining, the meanings of individual actions and agencies that compose it" (1992a, 190). Bauman suggested that the term *society* should be replaced with *sociality*, which would reflect "the processual modality of social reality, the dialectical play of randomness and pattern" (190).[17] In the 1999 introduction to the second edition of *Culture as Praxis*, he pointed out that the term *cultural boundaries* was less and less suited to the analysis of the reality of the then contemporary world. In his opinion, the polyphonic and heterogeneous cultural reality could not be identified with an area separated by borders. He compared it to a "borderland" where various influences constantly intertwined (1999, l–lii). Together with the metaphors of "collage," "pastiche," and "consumer co-operative," the vision of a permanent borderland illustrated Bauman's belief in the pluralistic, variabilistic, and rhizomatic nature of postmodern culture.

Bauman's theorization of the issue of the proliferation of ambivalence was consistent with the analyses of many other intellectuals in the late twentieth century (e.g., Featherstone 1991; Jameson 1991; Clifford and

Marcus 1986; Baudrillard [1981] 1983; Deleuze and Guattari [1980] 1987; Deleuze and Guattari [1972] 1977; Derrida [1969] 1981). At that time, there was a widespread belief that the vision of cultural cohesion should be replaced by an analysis of cultural heterogeneity, and that the assumption of an isomorphism between culture and a specific territory should be rejected in favour of theorizing intercultural relations (Connor 1989).

William Sewell Jr, whose analyses I referred to at the beginning of this chapter, addressed this issue critically in the following words: "This could lead to the conclusion that the notion of coherent cultures is purely illusory: that cultural practice in a given society is diffuse and decentered; that the local systems of meaning in a given population do not themselves form a higher-level, society-wide system of meanings. But such a conclusion would, in my opinion, be hasty. Although I think it is an error simply to assume that cultures possess an overall coherence or interrogation, neither can such coherence be ruled out a priori" ([1999] 2005, 171–2). I fully agree with this statement. As far as I am concerned, the very significant emphasis on the issue of the proliferation of ambivalence in Bauman's theory of culture at the end of the twentieth century, on the one hand, allowed him to excellently analyze the revolutionary cultural changes of that time, but, on the other hand, prevented him from reflecting on the factors of cultural stability.[18] Consequently, he did not paint a complete picture of the cultural reality of the late twentieth century. However, it is also worth noting that, as in the case of Bauman's vision of modern culture, his theory of postmodern culture should, in my opinion, be interpreted as an example of Weber's ideal type (Weber [1922] 1968). Therefore, it was meant more as a "cognitive tool to analyze reality" (Bauman 2007a, 27), than as a detailed description of reality. And in Bauman's theory of both modern and postmodern culture, the use of the concept of the ideal type was – as will be shown – closely related to the critical nature of his theory of culture.

This observation is an appropriate introduction to the third of the previously mentioned planes of analysis, that is, the change in the role of intellectuals. One of the functions that Bauman assigned to this group in postmodern culture was a direct consequence of the process of the proliferation of ambivalence (Bauman 1989b, 1987). He argued then that it was no longer possible for intellectuals to fulfill the role of "legislators," who had set the principles on which the social and cultural order was supposed to be based. Instead, they should assume the role of "interpreters," to translate between different traditions and promote a better understanding between them.[19] They should be both hermeneutically oriented researchers, interpreting practices and meanings, as well as mediators, assisting in the harmonious functioning of the contemporary world. In this respect, his thoughts were an extension of his analyses contained in *Hermeneutics and Social Science* (1978), which I considered in the previous chapter.[20]

Bauman's criticism of the legislative inclinations of modern intellectuals did not mean that he believed they were to abandon their efforts to transform social reality. As I have demonstrated, a constitutive element of his postmodern thought – including the theory of culture – was to emphasize the necessity of making social, political, and cultural changes. He pointed out that these transformations should concern, for example, reducing social inequalities, breaking the domination of consumer culture, and contributing to political changes (see, for example, Jacobsen and Hansen 2017; Carleheden 2008). In *Modernity and Ambivalence* Bauman wrote on this issue: "Postmodernity is not the end of politics, as it is not an end of history. On the contrary, whatever may be attractive in the postmodern promise calls for more politics, more political engagement, more political effectivity of individual and communal action (however much the call is stifled by the hubbub of consumer bustle, and however inaudible it becomes in a world made up of shopping malls and Disneylands, where all that matters is an enjoyable piece of theatre, and thus nothing matters really much)" (1991a, 276). This excerpt also effectively illustrates Bauman's belief that intellectuals must make efforts to break through the hustle and bustle of the postmodern world with their message. This was precisely the purpose for using the method of rhetorical provocation in his analysis of social exclusion. His use of binary oppositions, and his frequent theorization via metaphors, was also supposed to clearly emphasize social problems and the need to solve them (see, for example, M. Davis 2013).

Bauman's reflections on the role of intellectuals in postmodern culture were related to his concept of active utopia (1976d). In line with its assumptions, he argued that intellectuals should relativize postmodern reality, as well as present alternative paths of its development.[21] They are, however, not meant to form detailed institutional or structural solutions, as was the case with "blueprint" or "totalizing" utopias (Jacoby 2005; Alexander 2001). Their role is to indicate general assumptions and goals that these solutions should meet.[22] It is important to notice that active utopian thinking fully harmonizes with the nature of the postmodern condition. Firstly, this concept assumes the openness of the future; secondly, it stresses the need for the permanent critique of the status quo; and thirdly, it pays attention to the rich diversity and plurality of the world (Bauman 1976d, 9–17). As far as I am concerned, Bauman's aforementioned ideas regarding significant changes in social policy (1998d) and the "defamiliarization" of consumer culture (1987) should be interpreted from the perspective of this concept. The same concerns his vision of postmodern ethics, created by Bauman on the basis of the philosophy of Emanuel Levinas (Hirst 2014; Crone 2008; Junge 2001; Bauman 1995b, 1993; Levinas [1982] 1985; Levinas 1969 [1961]).

In the context of the analyses undertaken in the previous section of this chapter, it should be stressed that, according to Bauman, the proliferation of ambivalence (1991a) and "the fall of the legislators" (1987) were a chance for morality. Similarly to other representatives of the "ethical turn" taking place at the end of the last century (see T. Davis and Womack 2001; Garber, Hanssen and Walkowitz 2000; Fekete 1988), he claimed that in the then contemporary condition individuals became fully responsible for their moral choices. In modernity they were obliged to act according to clearly defined rules – which resulted in the phenomenon of adiaphorization – but the era of postmodernity had re-established their moral autonomy.[23] In *Life in Fragments* Bauman claimed: "The denizens of the postmodern era are, so to speak, forced to stand face-to-face with their moral autonomy, and so also with their moral responsibility. This is the cause of moral agony. This is also the chance the moral selves never confronted before" (1995b, 43). The concept of postmodern ethics that Bauman had been developing since the late 1980s (2000b, 1997a, 1995b, 1994, 1993, 1991b, 1990, 1988b) was based on a belief that the essence of morality was the infinite responsibility for the Other. In his opinion, "being for the Other" – as distinct from "being with the Other" – could not be codified, conventionalized, universalized, or rationalized in any way. The shape of this relationship was always *in statu nascendi*, entirely dependent on the needs of the

Other. *Ergo*, Bauman claimed that morality did not provide a sense of ontological security, as was the case with modern ethics, when the individual followed prescribed rules. "Moral life," he wrote, "the life of choice between good and evil, is … filled with the anxiety of self-reprobation and self-recrimination. To be moral means never to feel *good enough*" (Bauman and Tester 2001, 46). *Eo ipso*, morality was inherently aporetic.

On the one hand, the concept of morality without ethics perfectly corresponded to the previously described properties of postmodern culture, such as its pluralistic character or constant changeability. On the other hand, however, postmodern culture also created numerous barriers to morality, among which Bauman emphasized in particular the development of consumer culture and culture of individualism. Throughout his whole academic career Bauman argued that the first of these factors led to the commodification of human relations. This meant the instrumentalization of the self-Other relationship. Moreover, in his opinion, consumer culture was characterized by a reluctance to undertake long-term obligations, which was also contrary to "being for the Other" (see, for example, Bauman 1987, 170–87; 1983; 1966a, 374–450; see also Brzeziński 2018). The second of these factors was considered by Bauman in the context of the phenomenon of "*postmodern adiaphorization*" (2000a, 2000b). Unlike the modern version of adiaphorization, in which the individual was obliged to act in accordance with certain rules, its postmodern form "works through *dis*engagement and self-distantiation," claimed Bauman (2000b, 95). Taking responsibility for the Other does not fit the framework of the culture of individualism, in which the freedom to decide about oneself is the highest value. Taking all of this into account, Bauman claimed in 2001: "I am deeply worried that loving may well be on the way to becoming a forgotten, and seldom practiced, art. Without that art, there is little hope for morality; and less for just society" (Bauman and Tester 2001, 69). This doubt, however, did not lead Bauman to abandon the concept of postmodern ethics. On the contrary, until the very end of his life he pointed to the need to rely on it in terms of both interpersonal relations and social policy (see, for example, Bauman 2017c, 153–67; Bauman and Raud 2015; Bauman and Donskis 2013; Bauman 2008b). This will be one of the subjects of my analysis in the next chapter.

Bauman's concept of ethics evoked considerable controversy (e.g., Best 2017; Hookway and Ezzy 2017; Hirst 2014; Campbell and Till 2010; Crone 2008; Junge 2001). Some commentators argued that he "overemphasized the moral demand of the Other" (Hookway and Ezzy 2017, 39); others stressed "the un-sociological character of Bauman's project" (Hirst 2014, 190), that is, the inability to apply it in social life; others claimed that "there are no signs that Bauman's postmodern morality is part of a historical trend" (Crone 2008, 68), and so forth. Referring to these critical remarks, I would like to point to the following assumption of the concept of postmodern ethics: "The humankind-wide moral unity is thinkable, if at all … as the remote (and, so be it, utopian) prospect of the emancipation of the autonomous moral self and vindication of its moral responsibility; as a prospect of the self facing up, without being tempted to escape, to the inherent and incurable ambivalence in which that responsibility casts it and which is already its fate, still waiting to be recast into its destiny" (Bauman 1993, 15). These words clearly indicate that the concept of morality without ethics should be interpreted in the context of Bauman's idea of active utopia (Bauman 1976d). Postmodern ethics was in fact meant as a never attainable horizon, intended to evaluate the status quo and set the direction of changes. Similar observations were made by Bauman's Polish friend Stefan Morawski: "Can there be a more utopian blueprint of humankind than 'being-for' taking priority over 'being beside' or 'being with'? … These are not a sceptic's grimaces or ridiculing of Zygmunt's inconsequence. On the contrary, I would insist on the utmost greatness in his thinking just because it cannot limit itself to the frontiers of the contingent, heterogenous and fragmentary postmodernity, and outlines – beyond this territory – the chances of saving human dignity" (1998, 35, 36). The concept of postmodern ethics was therefore an excellent example of a critical aspect of Zygmunt Bauman's theory of culture.

Summarizing this part of the chapter, I would like to point out that for many other intellectuals Bauman's theory of postmodern culture was a reference point for analyzing the cultural reality at the end of the twentieth century. It was often referred to, *inter alia*, in researching such phenomena as the pluralization of social life, the proliferation of ambivalence, and the formation of culture of individualism. However, as

I have shown in this chapter, various criticisms have been directed toward this theory. It concerned such issues as its performative dimension and specifically the ways in which it was to serve as a tool for transforming the status quo; the inadequacy between the role that Bauman ascribed to consumer culture and the assumptions of postmodern ethics; and the hyperbolization of cultural deregulation and decomposition processes as the constitutive features of this theory. But regardless of various assessments of Bauman's vision of culture as "a flexible repertoire of interpretative resources" (Kempny 1995, 188), it should be concluded that it perfectly describes the most important changes that took place in the culture of the late twentieth century (Rattansi 2017, 101–79; Tester 2004, 131–56; Beilharz 2000, 122–69; Smith 1999, 136–66).

Referring once again to the analyses by Ernest Gellner and Ulf Hannerz, cited at the beginning of this part of the chapter, I would like to quote part of an article by the latter: "It could be, of course, that we really should have had Modigliani and Kokoschka get to work on canvas together, as there may be parts of the world where the neat surfaces really are even now clearly separated, and others which have a great deal more of the multiple relationships, the complexity, the ambiguity" (Hannerz 1996, 78). Thus, although Hannerz emphasized the dominant importance of the process of the heterogenization of cultural reality at the end of the twentieth century, he did not claim that systemic theories of culture would lose their explanatory power at that time. Stephen Vaisey expressed a similar conviction in a very interesting way about fifteen years later (2010). He claimed that instead of choosing between "seamless-web" and "toolkit-repertoire" models of culture, intellectuals should work out a perspective that would join them. Vaisey argued that similarly to the way in which reflections on the nature of light taking place in the sciences must take into account both its wave and its particle nature, so too a new theory of culture should address both aforementioned models. In this context it should be noted that, unlike Bauman's analyses from the end of the twentieth century, in the twenty-first century he increasingly included the issues of both the proliferation of ambivalence and the reduction of ambivalence in his theorizations (2017c, 2016b). I have called this process "Modigliani's return" and will describe it in the next chapter.

CONCLUSION

The end of the previous century was a time of far-reaching changes in the ways of conceiving culture in the social sciences and humanities. Many scholars critiqued the structuring function traditionally ascribed to this category and simultaneously indicated the need to bolster human agency. Bauman's thoughts were fully exemplary of this tendency. On the one hand, he decidedly strengthened his critique, which had lasted from the 1960s and the 1970s, of theories that brought out the "gardening" function of culture. On the other hand, he argued that theorization of culture required a focus above all on the problem of changeability, heterogeneity, and contingency. In both of these issues Bauman was inspired by the gamut of theories being developed at the time, and he frequently engaged in polemics with their authors. His analysis of the diminishing importance of the modelling functions of culture was largely consistent with the assumptions of postmodern thought.

It must, however, be emphasized that Bauman's attitude toward postmodern thought underwent various changes. In the first half of the 1980s he approached it with significant skepticism. This stemmed from, among other things, his belief that its representatives were characterized by a lack of engagement in efforts to transform existing reality. The change in his stance – which took place in the subsequent years – emerged partly from his belief that postmodernism offered a valuable perspective for both analyzing and criticizing the socio-cultural transformations of the end of the twentieth century. The focus on the issues of pluralism, ambivalence, and difference that were characteristic of postmodern thought fit perfectly into Bauman's critique of the disciplinary mechanism of the modern condition. Adopting the most important assumptions of postmodern thought, however, Bauman made many efforts to give it a critical and engaged character. With the passing of time he arrived, however, at the conclusion that these endeavours resembled the squaring of a circle.

Bauman's confirmation of this belief at the end of the last century should be considered in the broader context of the changes that took place in the humanities and in social thought at that time. Anthony Elliott wrote in connection with this issue: "By the late 1990s, the label 'postmodern' had everywhere – from academia to popular culture – become coterminous with a form of cultivated relativism in which 'everything goes.' It was, ironically, this very flattened and generalized view of the postmodern that Bauman wished to distance himself from with his new idea – outlined in the early 2000s – of 'liquidity'" (Elliott 2009, 295). Bauman's theory of culture, formulated in the framework of his new concept of liquid modernity, will be analyzed in the next chapter.

5

THE THEORY OF CULTURE IN LIQUID MODERNITY

INTRODUCTION

In the year 2000, Bauman published a book entitled *Liquid Modernity* (2000c), in which he presented a new analytic framework for the analysis of the contemporary condition. Its essence is the belief that the process of modernization has been the constitutive feature of Western civilization for several centuries. The differences that have emerged over time in the ways this process has been realized allow modernity to be divided into two periods, described as "solid" and "liquid." The first began during the eighteenth century and lasted through the first half of the twentieth century. It was characterized by the effort to create – in place of traditional society – an order based on fully rational premises. Using metaphorical language, Bauman argued that the "melting" of the elements of the previous formation was the path to the creation of new structures, institutions, and laws that were marked by an inviolable "solidity." In his view, however, the way in which modernizing efforts were realized in the second half of the twentieth century took an entirely different form. He pointed out that the metaphorical "crucible" into which previously existing solutions had been thrown had also melted the "smelting forms." Consequently, the definitive feature of the contemporary condition had become constant volatility, or "liquidity." "There are reasons to consider 'fluidity' or 'liquidity' as fitting metaphors when we wish to grasp the nature of the present, in many ways *novel*, phase in the history of modernity," wrote Bauman (2000c, 2). He analyzed this phase in numerous books, articles, and essays (Palmer, Brzeziński, and Campbell 2020).[1] As a result of his belief that the process of "liquification" was reflected in all dimensions of social life, he analyzed a wide variety of issues including, for example: transformations of identity, interpersonal relations, community patterns, local and global political strategies, economic processes, and labour market and consumer behaviour.[2] Near the end of his life, however, Bauman turned his attention to how, as a reaction to the uncertainty and unpredictability characteristic of today's condition, a new tendency emerged in the Western world based on a longing for the past, which was perceived as an oasis of safety and stability. He gave this type of nostalgia the name "retrotopia," presenting many examples of its significant influence on contemporary phenomena (2017c).

In the period under discussion here, the premises of postmodern thought became less and less popular (Rattansi 2017, 189–94). One of the causes of its decline lay in the fact that this intellectual current, shaped and developed in relation to the theory of modernity, had not acquired an autonomous status. Bauman, in an interview with Keith Tester at the beginning of this century, also admitted that the term *postmodernity* incorrectly pointed to the end of modernity, while "we are as modern as ever, obsessively 'modernizing' everything we can lay our hands on" (Bauman and Tester 2001, 97). In fact, in the twenty-first century many discourses of modernity have been revitalized and recontextualized. In addition to the theories of, *inter alia*, "late modernity" (Giddens 1991), "reflective modernity" (Beck, Giddens, and Lash 1994), and "another modernity" (Lash 1999) that emerged at the end of the twentieth century, many new ones have been created in the subsequent century. In this context, it is worth pointing to the concepts of "metamodernism" (Josephson-Storm 2021; Vermeulen and Van den Akker, 2010), "third modernity" (Zuboff 2019), and "digimodernism" (Kirby 2009).

It should also be stressed that many of the events that took place at the beginning of the twenty-first century did not support the thesis about the "decline of the grand narratives" (Lyotard [1979] 1984) that was characteristic of postmodern thought. Anthony Elliott wrote: "[S] ince the attack on the World Trade Center and the Pentagon of 9/11, and the follow-up war against Iraq in 2003, there is undeniably a growing societal sense that crises in contemporary culture are so deep and so pervasive that they demand new forms of political thinking, indeed a wholly fresh approach. It is in this sense that we might speak of the current generation as coming after postmodernism, most specifically as concerns the formulation of a new political agenda for tackling today's most pressing global problems" (2009, 265). In the context of the theory of culture, this meant that the further development of a "repertoire" understanding of this concept, emphasizing individualization, pluralism, and deterritorialization, was accompanied by the revitalization of "systemic" approaches, with a stress on collectivism, reduction of ambivalence, and cultural boundaries (Norris and Inglehart 2019). "Under the circumstances," wrote Wendy Griswold (2013, 40), "it once again seemed plausible to think of coherent cultural systems, generations of meaning for entire societies."

This chapter is divided into two parts, corresponding to the two primary thematic areas in Bauman's reflections on culture of the twenty-first century. An analysis of the first of these will emerge from an examination of the significance that he assigned to the process of individualization (e.g., Bauman and Leoncini 2018; Bauman and Raud 2015; Bauman 2004b, 2001d). Bauman even identified liquid modernity with "an individualized, privatized version of modernity, with the burden of pattern-weaving and the responsibility for failure falling primarily on the individual's shoulders" (2000c, 7–8). *Eo ipso*, within the contemporary condition identity takes the form of a continuous "task." Carrying it out requires, to a large extent, making a choice among a multitude of propositions, or "offers," that, in Bauman's opinion, contemporary culture comprises.[3] He also emphasized that the extent to which individuals could meet the requirements of the aforementioned "task" depended on the place that they occupied in the social structure. In this context, he pointed to the difference between de jure and de facto individualization (2000c, 38–41).

The second plane that was particularly important for the development of his theory of culture in the twenty-first century was the process of globalization (e.g., Bauman 2011a, 2008b, 2004a). In line with the assumptions of the "spatial turn" (Bachmann-Medick [2006] 2016, 211–44), he reflected on new ways of problematizing space, taking into account the intensification of global connections. Bauman aimed to reconceptualize concepts such as border, community, and cultural identity. He argued: "Motility, non-rootedness and global availability/

accessibility of cultural patters and products is now the 'primary reality' of culture, while distinct cultural identities can only emerge as outcomes of a long chain of 'secondary processes' of choice, selective retention and recombination (which, most importantly, do not grind to a halt once the identity in question does emerge" (1999, xlv). In his final publications, however, Bauman pointed out the symptoms of the revitalization of the systemic concept of culture. Reflections on this process were accompanied by the development of his concept of global responsibility (2017c).

THE CULTURE OF INDIVIDUALISM

The reflections in this part of the chapter begin with a brief discussion of the plot of Herman Hesse's novel *Steppenwolf* ([1927] 2001) which – though it was written during the 1920s – serves as an excellent illustration of contemporary changes in identity. It tells the story of Harry Haller, a fifty-year-old intellectual who experiences inner conflict caused by his identification with two opposing models of values. On the one hand, he is connected to the norms and practices proper to burghers; on the other hand, he feels a distaste for them, which materializes in his assuming the posture of an outsider. His awareness of the impossibility of reconciling this antinomy solidifies his emotional problems, which result in suicidal thoughts. Subsequent events – tied to becoming acquainted with Hermine, Pablo, and Maria – lead to a gradual change in his habits and ways of perceiving his own identity. The culmination of these changes is his visit to the Magic Theatre, where he can change into various incarnations and fluidly transcend any boundaries of space and time. After undergoing this ritual of initiation, Haller says: "I understood it all … I knew that all the hundred thousand pieces of life's game were in my pocket. A glimpse of its meaning had stirred my reason and I was determined to begin the game afresh. I would sample its tortures once more and shudder again at its senselessness. I would traverse not once more, but often, the hell of my inner being" (251).

The vision, emerging from these words, of the individual as a labile construct, subject to constant transformations, is relevant with regard to the contemporary discourses on the culture of individualism in the humanities and social sciences (e.g., Trueman 2020; Elliott and Lemert

2006; Beck and Beck-Grensheim 2002; Giddens 1991). This debate has been developing on the foundations of the belief that the social transformations taking place in the Western world since the second half of the twentieth century have led to a fundamental change in the relationship between the individual and society. In essence, the former became entirely responsible for shaping, but also constantly changing, his or her identity. On the development of the culture of individualism Bauman wrote in *Liquid Modernity*: "'[I]ndividualization' consists of transforming human 'identity' from a 'given' into a 'task' and charging the actors with the responsibility for performing that task and for the consequences (also the side-effects) of their performance ... As this happens, human beings are no more 'born into' their identities ... Modernity replaces the heteronomic determination of social standing with compulsive and obligatory self-determination" (2000c, 31, 32).

Małgorzata Jacyno (2007) listed four aspects of the sociogenesis of the culture of individualism. Firstly, she pointed out that during the counterculture movement the "puritan ethos," founded on the idea of "inner-worldly asceticism" (Weber [1905] 1930), had collapsed. In its place the individualism of the "new middle class" was formed with its own values such as mobility, creativity, and flexibility. Since the end of the last century Bauman had metaphorically portrayed this transformation as a change of the identity pattern of "pilgrim" to "tourist (1996). Secondly, in the course of the progressive rationalization, the individual had been assigned a double role: on the one hand, that of a subject endowed with agency and, on the other, that of an object of various, often opposing, external influences. This duality is reflected in the fusion of the freedom to decide for oneself and the tendency to follow the advice of experts. In these contexts, Bauman wrote in *Modernity and Ambivalence*: "Lay members of society must be rational, but they cannot be rational without being guided by the verdicts of science and without being offered algorithmic, or at least heuristic, prescriptions for action that carry approval of the experts" (1991a, 224). Thirdly, Jacyno drew attention to the change of the principle that integrated the social system. She argued that the aspirations of individuals to make sense of their experience were now limited mainly to the therapeutic discourse. This served as a reference point for shaping life goals and the visions of human happiness. Similar reflections were shared by

Bauman, who presented them in *Liquid Life* (2005) and *Identity* (2004b). Fourthly, the sources of the culture of individualism should be found, according to Jacyno, in the disintegration of traditional class structures and the culturalization of social differences. The life orientations and the lifestyles of individuals were of key importance in determining their social position in the current conjunction. Jacyno also referred to Bauman's vision of binary social divisions that was presented in the previous chapter of this book (Bauman 1998d). She claimed that they formed a new version of the division into the "saved" and the "damned" as described by Weber ([1905] 1930).

In the twenty-first century Bauman analyzed the process of individualization in all the dimensions listed above as part of his vision of the "liquification" of social reality (2001d). He associated the systematic increase of individualism with the weakening – or the "melting" – of structures, institutions, and community ties. Bauman argued that these adapted their temporary "shape" to the transformations taking place in the social reality. In this context he referred to the term, introduced by Ulrich Beck (2000), of "zombie categories," pointing out that the rules previously governing the trajectories of the lives of individuals and their ways of experiencing the world today had a de facto superficial character, that is, they resembled zombies. In *Liquid Modernity* he wrote: "These days patterns and configurations are no longer 'given,' let alone 'self-evident'; there are just too many of them, clashing with one another and contradicting one another's commandments, so that each one has been stripped of a good deal of compelling, coercively constraining powers. And they have changed their nature and have been accordingly reclassified as items in the inventory of individual tasks" (2000c, 7).

The situation outlined creates entirely new opportunities, as well as challenges for the individual. In this context, Bauman continued his reflections – which had started at the end of the twentieth century, within the postmodern thought (1999, 1991a, 1987) – on the subject of the range of human volition and agency. On the one hand, he observed that the liquid modern condition offered a massive and steadily broadening range of possibilities within every aspect of life. Moreover, most of the choices made today did not have an irrevocable character or close off the possibility of making use of other options. On the other hand, however, Bauman emphasized the limits of the availability of this repertoire of choice. In fact, he claimed that for one part of contemporary society emancipation had a de jure character, and for another, de facto (2013, 2011a).

What is more, Bauman pointed out that today's emancipation was the fate of individuals and not their choice because liquid modernity forced them to continuously redefine their life trajectories. Individualization also meant transferring onto individuals the burden of responsibility for all the results of their decisions, which could rarely be fully predicted. In the metaphorical but also hyperbolic way that was characteristic of his work, Bauman observed in *Stranger at Our Door*: "Devoured by that diffuse, dissipated and scattered fear that infiltrates and penetrates the whole life setting and the totality of life-pursuits, as capillary vessels do the totality of the living body, humans are abandoned to their own resources – puny and miserably flimsy assets by comparison with the grandiosity of existential liabilities" (2016b, 56). It should be stressed that – in line with the assumptions of his engaged sociology (see Bauman, Tester, and Jacobsen 2013; Bauman 2000c 202–16) – the critical dimension decidedly prevailed in Bauman's analyses of the culture of individualism. It is especially visible in the case of his analyses of love relationships, professional career patterns, and consumer behaviour.

In his analysis of love relationship, presented in the most detail in the book *Liquid Love: On the Frailty of Human Bonds* (2003), Bauman referred to the term, introduced by Anthony Giddens, of the "pure relationship." Giddens defined it as "one in which external criteria have become dissolved: the relationship exists solely for whatever rewards that relationship can deliver" (Giddens 1991, 6). Although both sociologists agreed on the origins of this form of love relations, Bauman emphasized issues other than those Giddens did (Bauman 2003; Giddens 1991). Instead of the value of feeling fulfillment as the foundation, he focused on the matter of its frequently short-lived, liquid nature. Bauman compared the pure relationship to an investment that would bring a specific gain to the participant. Thus, whenever the level of pleasure that was felt by either part of this relationship fell, that person might end it at any moment. In the conversation with Keith Tester, Bauman asserted: "[R]elationships are brittle and friable precisely because of their purity …

There must be more ties, and of a different sort, than notoriously erratic satisfaction for the relationship to be of benefit when harsh life tests are individually faced" (Bauman and Tester 2001, 123). Bauman offered, as opposed to the pure relationship, a vision of love based on an inalienable responsibility and a lasting engagement for the sake of the good of the Other (Jasińska-Kania [2010] 2016). It reflected his concept of postmodern ethics.

Another example that effectively illustrates the critical character of his analyses of the culture of individualism is the labour market (see, for example, Bauman, Bauman, Kociatkiewicz, and Kostera 2015; Bauman 2000c, 130–67). Referring, *inter alia*, to Richard Sennett's *Corrosion of Character* (1998), Bauman pointed to the systematic liquification of work trajectories (Bauman 2000c, 130–67). In presenting the structural context of this phenomena, he referred to the changes rapidly taking place in the ownership structure of enterprises, and the popularization of flexible forms of employment. Similarly to Sennett, he pointed out that the changes in the labour market required individuals to work out entirely new dispositions that were opposed to the building of stable collective ties. He expressed his criticism of this situation in the following words: "The place of employment feels like a camping site which one visits for just a few days, and may leave at any moment if the comforts on offer are not delivered or found unsatisfactory when delivered – rather than like a shared domicile where one is inclined to take trouble and patiently work out the acceptable rules of cohabitation" (2000c, 149). Bauman also highlighted that for the constantly expanding circle of people, the aforementioned changes meant the necessity of dealing with a very high degree of ontological uncertainty. Following Guy Standing, as well as developing his analyses presented in *Work, Consumerism and the New Poor* (Bauman 1998d), he devoted considerable attention to the condition of precarious workers (Standing 2011; see, for example, Bauman 2017b, 46–51). In this context, Bauman also developed analyses devoted to the culture of fear (2006).

As for consumer behaviour, according to Bauman, it was fundamental to the development of the culture of individualism (e.g., 2011c, 2007a, 2001b; Bauman and Rojek 2004). In the twenty-first century he wrote in this context about "the consumerist syndrome" that "consists above all in the emphatic denial of the virtue of procrastination and of the propriety and desirability of the delay of satisfaction" (2007a, 85). Bauman argued that under the influence of this syndrome, individuals were inclined to perceive reality as filled with "goods" that they should be chasing in order to satisfy individual desires, and then – after a short amount of time – abandon them and replace them with new ones (see Blackshaw 2008; M. Davis 2008b). Referring to his earlier division into wild and garden cultures (Bauman 1997b; Gellner 1983), he described the condition of being under the dominating influence of the consumerist syndrome– as a "hunting" one (2007c, 94–110; see Jacobsen 2008). This term was intended to emphasize that the life of individuals resembled hunting today, the rhythm of which was determined each time by a new prey. Hunting, Bauman claimed, comprised an entirely new form of utopian thinking. "For the gardeners," he wrote in *Liquid Times* (2007c, 109), "utopia was the end of the road; for the hunters it is the road itself. Gardeners visualized the end of the road as the vindication and the ultimate triumph of utopia. For the hunters, the end of the road can only be the lived utopia's final, ignominious *defeat*." In accordance with his critical theory of culture, Bauman perceived "hunting utopia" in dystopian terms.

These analyses – just like many other aspects of Bauman's vision of the culture of individualism – were criticized by some intellectuals. For example, commenting on Bauman's findings on love relationships, Janet Sayers (2007) negatively assessed their very starting point. In her opinion, a reliance on very general observations – often obtained from press materials – did not allow Bauman to reach a deeper understanding of this issue. While she appreciated the critical orientation of his analyses of love relationships, she also argued that he significantly overemphasized the role of "manic individualism" with regard to love relationships. In another text critical of Bauman's theory, Poul Poder (2007) focused on his analyses devoted to the work life. He asserted that by putting emphasis on the issue of the "liquid interpersonal relationships in flexible work life," Bauman did not analyze the factors that integrated team work in contemporary models of management. Poder decided to supplement these reflections with the latter factors. He wrote: "[E]mpowerment, engaged relationship between manager and employee, post-bureaucratic organization and team organization are also features of liquid work and they can be understood as integrative forces" (2007, 149–50). In yet another paper, Mateusz Marciniak (2011) decided to verify Bauman's theorizations on the dominant role of the consumerist syndrome in the current condition.[4] On the basis of quantitative research that he had conducted in the years 2005–10 among students at Adam Mickiewicz University in Poznań, Poland, he asserted that Bauman's writings on this issue (Bauman 2007a) were not reflected in reality. "The average student is 40% consumer-oriented towards reality in relation to Bauman's consumer fully mastered by this syndrome," Marciniak claimed (2011, 184–5). He observed, however, that if this study was repeated in the future, it would probably bring results that were closer to the vision presented by Bauman.

In all the critical commentaries referred to here, there is the repeated accusation that Bauman departed from a faithful account of the transformations connected to the emergence of the culture of individualism, in favour of presenting their deformed, one-dimensional image. It must be clearly noted, however, that his intention – emerging both from the methodological assumptions of his theorizations and from his focus on the conative function of the language (see M. Davis 2013; Blackshaw 2005, 52–81) – was not by any means to present the full complexity of the processes taking place in liquid modernity. In the context of the first of these issues I would like to refer to the fact – mentioned in the previous chapter of this book – that Bauman made use of the method of ideal types (2007a, 26–8). Therefore, empirical research conducted with the use of particular aspects of his theory of liquid modern culture should not have the goal of verifying it – as, for example, Mateusz Marciniak did – but rather of diagnosing to what degree a given collective reflects the premises of this theory. The second of the factors singled out is tied to the critical character of the reflections undertaken by Bauman (2000c, 202–16).[5] It was manifested in his efforts to expose – via hyperbolization – the negative aspects of the contemporary condition. It is from this perspective, I believe, that his analyses of the reification of interpersonal relations, systematic liquification of work trajectories, and the commodification of social reality should be interpreted. Bauman aimed both to elicit criticism of these phenomena – which required breaking through the barrier of common-sense thinking – and to search for alternatives to them. The fact that the publications he wrote in the last decades of his career were aimed at a broader audience (see Bauman and Tester 2001, 156–8) was particularly important for accomplishing these goals.

In the context of the properties of Bauman's sociology outlined here, it is also worthwhile to examine his findings that pertain to new kinds of collectivism within the culture of individualism (Bauman 2001d). As far as he was concerned, these forms – he called them "cloakroom" or "carnival" communities – were fully relevant to the properties of liquid modernity. The former metaphor was meant to express that, just as the audience members of a performance, after it is over, retrieve their coats and go to their respective homes, in the same way the feeling of "being together" has in the culture of individualism a very fleeting form. "Spectacles as the occasion for the brief existence of a cloakroom community do not fuse and blend individual concerns into 'group interest'; by being added up, the concerns in question do not acquire a new quality, and the illusion of sharing which the spectacle may generate would not last much longer than the excitement of the performance," wrote Bauman (2000c, 200). The reference to "carnival" served to indicate that the functioning of these formations was based above all on emotions and not on ethical engagement. This fact explained, in Bauman's opinion, both the speed of their creation and their ephemeral nature. "Explosive communities are events breaking the monotony of daily solitude, and like all carnival events they let off the pent-up steam and allow the revellers better to endure the routine to which they must return the moment the frolicking is over," claimed Bauman (2000c, 201).

Both of the statements cited here effectively illustrate Bauman's critical attitude toward these formations. This stemmed, above all, from the fact that these communities could not lead, in his view, to changes in the social world, and they actually detracted from undertaking any efforts that could have such effects. Demonstrating the futility of these efforts, he drew on examples of initiatives such as Occupy Wall Street or the Revolution of the Indignados (Bauman and Bordoni 2014). It should be noted, however, that Bauman did not concentrate on the examples of successful movements of cloakroom or carnival collectives.[6] He also did not examine the revolutionary possibilities that new media opened up for producing transformations by such formations (e.g., Brownlee 2020).

Bauman's reflections on cloakroom and carnival communities are part of the contemporary discourse on new forms of socialization (e.g., Click and Scott 2018; Krajewski 2014; Muggleton 2000; Mafessoli [1988] 1996). For example, in the late 1980s Michel Maffesoli created the concept of "neo-tribalism" ([1988] 1996). It postulates that contemporary communities are based not on economic or political factors but on shared passions or interests. Similarly to Bauman, Maffesoli ascribed a particular role in the formation of such collective groups to emotions. He pointed out that they allowed the creation of feelings of belonging, while their character was – in accordance with the characteristics of the contemporary condition – transitory and ephemeral. Maffesoli wrote that "in contrast to the stability induced by classical tribalism, neo-tribalism is characterized by fluidity, occasional gatherings and dispersal" ([1988] 1996, 76). It is also worth referring to Marek Krajewski's concept of "de-individuation." "[T]his term," wrote the Polish sociologist (2014, 14), "describes the process of occasional and relatively short-term alignment of a relatively large number of individuals who are different from each other on a daily basis." He emphasized that *de-individuation* does not mean "de-individualization," as the first term refers to the emotional bonds that arise between autonomous individuals. In a rich and highly diverse collection of examples of de-individuation, Krajewski included crowd behaviour, collective delusion, fashion, and consumer trends. He argued that all these phenomena allow for a temporary triumph over a feeling of uncertainty that is typical of the contemporary condition (Krajewski 2014). Bauman and Mafessoli – to whom Krajewski referred – had similar beliefs on the matter.

In all aspects of his reflections on the culture of individualism, Bauman devoted much attention to ethical issues (e.g., Bauman and Donskis 2013; Bauman 2008b; 2007b; 2000b, 83–9). In keeping with his analyses from the late twentieth century, he argued that the consequence of the rise of individualism was the spread of a liquid form of adiaphorization. It was because the vision of self-determining individuals promoted in contemporary culture remained at the other end of the continuum in relation to the imperative of taking responsibility for the Other. "Not that I am particularly selfish and would not be bothered by the well-being of the Other when my own interests are at stake; it is rather that I and the Other are similarly individuals … and so mutual dependency would be degrading and demanding for the Other as much as it is for me," claimed Bauman (2000b, 95). Developing these considerations in the twenty-first century, he reflected on the process of the mercantilization of morality (Bauman 2011a, 72–82; Bauman and Donskis 2013, 12–16). In this context, he analyzed such phenomena as buying products, a percentage of which was donated to charity, which he believed meant limiting the commitment to the Other to low-involvement financial assistance. According to Bauman, not only were such practices palliative, but they also gave the wrong sense of moral satisfaction. In *Collateral Damage* he wrote: "Emptying your wallet or debiting your credit card takes the place of the self-abandonment and self-sacrifice that moral responsibility for the Other requires. The side-effect, of course, is that by advertising and delivering commercialized moral painkillers, consumer markets only facilitate, instead of preventing, the fading, wilting, and crumbling of interhuman bonds" (2011a, 77).

Bauman's response to the processes of liquid modern adiaphorization and the commodification of morality was reflected in the further development of his critical thought (e.g., Bauman and Donskis 2013; Bauman 2008b). He painted a dystopian picture of the contemporary condition, thus wishing to indicate the need for its fundamental changes. Tony Blackshaw (2005, 79) aptly noted in this context: "[Bauman] uses the rage of storm to shout at his readers, as it were: 'look at the plight of these people and recognize your own conspiracy in their fates!' In this way, he alerts us to the sickness inherent in our own culture of excessive consumption, which we enjoy at the same time as we are busying ourselves erecting walls to keep out those who are fleeing poverty, war and persecution." What is more, in the twenty-first century, Bauman did not abandon the basic assumptions of his ethical thought, which he had developed since the late 1980s. On the contrary, he pointed out that the response to the crises related to the culture of individualism was the individual awakening of moral sensitivity. Until the end of his life he pointed to the need to develop an "ethical impulse" and at the same time outlined the threats related to the continuation of the status quo. And the more his expectations fell short of reality, the more he opposed it. In one of his essays published in the book entitled *44 Letters from the Liquid Modern World*, Bauman (2010a, 182–5) referred in this context to the *Myth of Sisyphus* by Albert Camus ([1942] 1955), the author who

– as I noticed in the second chapter – was of exceptional importance to his entire work. In this paper from 2010, as he had done half a century earlier, Bauman emphasized the importance of rebellion against existing reality, a rebellion that in itself made the human "stronger than his rock" (Camus [1942] 1955, 121).

Summing up these reflections, I will refer to the analyses of temporal transformations conducted by Bauman, which handily demonstrate the essence of his reflections devoted to the liquification of all structures, institutions, and communities (see, for example, Bauman 2007a, 100–6; 2000c, 91–129). Bauman argued that the model of "linear time" that had reflected the idea of progress in solid modernity was replaced in the liquid modernity by its entirely new form (see also Eriksen 2001; Bertman 1998; Virilio [1977] 1986). To describe it he used a term *pointillism*, borrowed from art where it describes a technique of painting in which hundreds of separate dots are applied to the canvas. Bauman's intention was to stress that the temporality of liquid modernity was reminiscent of a series of fleeting moments that are loosely connected and also subject to constant recombination. In a manner similar to the findings of Harry Haller mentioned at the beginning of this chapter, Bauman wrote: "Each new beginning may take you only so far, and no further; each new beginning augurs many new beginnings to come. Each moment has a vexing tendency to turn into the past – and in no time its own turn to be disabled will arrive" (2007a, 102). Among the most important perspectives through which Bauman analyzed the kind of temporality described here were the transformations in the ways of forming romantic relationships, paths of career development, consumerist culture, collective experiences, and moral actions. In each of these cases he pointed to the ephemeral nature of engagement and the lack of continuity between subsequent "episodes." He also emphasized, however, that these transformations had entirely different consequences for people for whom emancipation was a de facto form, and for those who experienced it de jure only. The latter not only did not have any control over time but had to independently grapple with the consequences of the process of "pointillization" (2013, 2011a). This way of describing social divisions in the culture of individualism may elicit justified criticism, in part for its simplified, binary character. However, it is important to observe that it has its source in critical theory.

At the conclusion of *Liquid Modernity* Bauman wrote: "The job of sociology is to see to it that the choices are genuinely free, and that they remain so, increasingly so, for the duration of humanity" (2000c, 216).

CULTURE IN AN AGE OF INTENSIFIED GLOBAL TIES

In his novel from the beginning of the twenty-first century, *Cosmopolis*, Don DeLillo (2003) presented one day in the life of New York multi-billionaire Eric Paker. He traverses Manhattan in his luxurious limousine filled with electronic devices. Together with his advisors, he tries to penetrate the essence of the connections in information about events taking place all over the world. On this basis he manages the financial assets of his clients, making multi-million-dollar transfers from one side of the globe to the other. Paker lives in pointillistic time and in deterritorialized space. However, over the course of the novel, his heretofore effective efforts to control reality – and influence it – turn out to be futile. What is more, the external world, which up to this point he had viewed from the window of his limousine, breaks into the automobile's interior with ever greater force. In New York there are protests against capitalism, and his life is increasingly in danger. In his novel, DeLillo describes a globalized world that falls into ever greater chaos. The structures and institutions existing within it lose their meaning in the face of a dramatic development of "space of flows" (Castells 1996). Social divisions are becoming more and more binary, and communication between those on opposite sides of the barricade is impossible.

The elements of the world presented in DeLillo's novel overlap perfectly with the way in which the process of globalization was described by Zygmunt Bauman over the years (e.g., Bauman and Mauro 2016; Bauman and Bordoni 2014; Bauman 2011a, 2008b, 2002, 1998a). At the end of the previous century, in *Globalization: The Human Consequences* he wrote about this phenomena as follows: "The deepest meaning conveyed by the idea of globalization is that of the indeterminate, unruly and self-propelled character of the world affairs; the absence of a centre, of a controlling desk, of a board of directors, of a managerial office. Globalization is Jowitt's 'new world disorder' under another name" (1998a, 59). In all of his work in later years, Bauman upheld the diagnosis presented in these words, focusing on the issue of the liquidity of the globalized condition. In this context, he used a term *interregnum* borrowed from Antonio Gramsci (Bauman 2010b, 200–5; Gramsci [1948–51] 1971). Bauman argued that the institutions called into existence in solid modernity de facto had ceased to function in its liquid form (they became "zombie" categories"). The consequences of this state of affairs included social disintegration, the petrification of social divisions, and a ubiquitous feeling of uncertainty (Bauman and Bordoni 2014; Bauman 2011a, 2006; see Tester 2004, 157–82).

It is worthwhile to situate Bauman's analyses of globalization on a map of positions represented by other intellectuals. To do so, I will make use of a very helpful typology presented by Andreas Busch at the turn of the century in a paper entitled "Unpacking the Globalization Debate: Approaches, Evidence and Data" (2000). Busch distinguished between three types of positions with regard to the process of globalization: liberal, skeptic, and moderately optimistic. The representatives of the first one refer mainly to the economic dimension of globalization, emphasizing that it makes it possible to increase the level of prosperity, achieve an ever more effective division of labour, intensify international trade, and so forth. The intellectuals included in the second group, on the contrary, believe that the development of global connections leads to negative consequences in the economic sphere – for example, they contribute to the increase in social inequalities – and also simultaneously weakens political structures, which are to an ever smaller degree capable of righting this situation.[7] The representatives of the third position, on the one hand, point to the threat posed by the contemporary condition but, on the other hand, remain moderately optimistic about the possibilities of limiting them and also opening up new opportunities.

Bauman's work belongs primarily to the second group of perspectives. This is well illustrated by a statement in *Liquid Fear*: "Thus far, ours is a wholly *negative* globalization: unchecked, unsupplemented and uncompensated for by a 'positive' counterpart which is still a distant prospect at best, though according to some prognoses already a forlorn chance" (Bauman 2006, 96). One of the sources of Bauman's singularly negative approach to globalization was the critical dimension of his work, including his theory of culture. As it will be shown, an expressive emphasis on the negative consequences of globalization was intended to stimulate alternative thinking in this area. *Ergo*, Bauman's analyses are also – to some extent – characteristic of the third position.

Bauman's theoretical analyses of culture in the era of the intensification of global ties are also worth considering in the context of the so-called *spatial turn* (Warf and Arias 2009; Bachmann-Medick [2006] 2016, 211–44). Within this orientation, space is grasped as a social construct, subject to a constant evolution as a result of human activity. The way in which it is problematized oscillates between two ends of a spectrum. On the one hand, attention is drawn to the increasing depreciation of the importance of space, thanks to the spread of modern means of communication. In this context Bachmann-Medick wrote: "In a situation characterized by free-flowing information, translocality, rootlessness and placelessness, space appears to be playing a subordinate role. Economics, politics and the mass media are increasingly following the lines of communication instead of remaining confined within ethnic, spatial, territorial or nation-state boundaries" ([2006] 2016, 213–14). On the other hand, it is assumed that the social, political, and economic transformations taking place during the last decades – related both to the opening of many formerly strictly guarded borders and to the emergence of new such borders, often based on different criteria – greatly enhance the importance of space. This leads to debates about the dynamics of the relationship between phenomena on a local and global scale, the emergence of "transnational spaces," and the consequences of migration movements. Both of the opposite theoretical perspectives described here were clearly present in Bauman's work in the twenty-first century.

An important source of inspiration for Bauman's cultural reflections on the "spatial turn" was Paul Virilio's concept of "the end of geography" (Virilio [1998] 2005). Its essence was the belief that the revolution that had taken place in the speed of movement and information transfer led de facto to the annihilation of space. Similarly to Virilio, though with a decidedly smaller dose of radicalism, Bauman asserted that the fundamental changes in socio-cultural reality that resulted from the end of geography demanded a redefinition of many concepts in social sciences and humanities. This pertains for example to the category of "border," which serves as a constitutive element of the systemic theories of culture. Bauman emphasized that although previously the life of the individual had taken place mainly in a strictly defined area, today every point on the map was an element of a web of relationships that encompassed the entire world. "Borders may be still in place, but they do not matter as much as they used to a mere half-century ago. Most certainly, they are not an obstacle for the drifting and gliding, skating and surfing, that fill the *Lebenswelt*," wrote Bauman in *Society under Siege* (2002, 21).

This observation was also related to a reflection on the meaning of the concept of "cultural identity" (Bauman and Mauro 2016). As far as Bauman was concerned, the norms and values characteristic of particular communities – previously separated by more or less tight borders – became a part of the "*global ecumene*." Ulf Hannerz, the author of this term, wrote that it "allude[s] to the interconnectedness of the world, by way of interactions, exchanges and related developments, affecting not least the organization of culture" (1996, 7). Similarly, in *Culture in a Liquid Modern World*, Bauman described the contemporary world as "an archipelago of diasporas": "Diasporas are dispersed and scattered over many formally sovereign territories; they ignore native pretensions to the primacy of local needs, demands and entitlements, and toss about in the snares of dual (or multi) citizenship – and, what is more, dual (or multiple) loyalty" (2011b, 35).

As far as Bauman was concerned, however, the phenomenon of the end of geography does not have a universal dimension. "[R]ather than homogenizing the human condition, the technological annulment of temporal/spatial distance tends to polarize it," he wrote in *Globalization: The Human Consequences* (1998a, 18). Drawing on his "will to dualism" (M. Davis 2008b, 103–8), Bauman argued that globalization had its own polar opposite, which was "localization" (2013, 2011a, 1998c). In his opinion, the benefits of the end of geography were actually available to only those who had the appropriate social, economic, and cultural capital. For the rest of society, the opportunities offered by globalization had a de jure dimension, not a de facto one. Bauman wrote: "Some can now move out of the locality – any locality – at will. Others watch helplessly the sole locality they inhabit moving away from under their feet" (1998a, 18). This observation was the basis of his concept of "glocalization" (1998c).

Through this concept, Bauman was developing his reflections on tourists and vagabonds, initiated in the 1990s (1997b, 83–94). He argued that while the liquid relationships to space characterized both of these groups, in the case of each they resulted from different premises. For tourists it was an expression of freedom, and for vagabonds it was an indispensable necessity. Among the liquid modern vagabonds Bauman paid special attention in the twenty-first century to refugees. He devoted to this issue, among others, the book *Strangers at Our Door* (2016b) – to which I will refer later in this book – as well as significant portions of the books *Liquid Times: Living in an Age of Uncertainty* (2007c) and *Wasted Lives: Modernity and Its Outcasts* (2004c).

One of the contexts in which Bauman analyzed the condition of refugees was Giorgio Agamben's concept of "biopower" (Agamben [1995] 1998). Following him, Bauman presented refugees as the contemporary *homo sacer*, thus emphasizing their suffering, the violence that affected them, and the fact that they were subjected to adiaphorization (Bauman 1989c). "What defines *homo sacer*," wrote Agamben ([1995] 1998, 82), "is … both the particular character of the double exclusion into which he is taken and the violence to which he finds himself. This violence – the unsanctionable killing that, in his case, anyone can commit – is classifiable neither as sacrifice nor as homicide, neither as execution of a condemnation to death nor as sacrilege."

In describing the strategies that are deployed in relation to refugees, Bauman also referred to the anthropology of Lévi-Strauss, and specifically to the two strategies of dealing with strangers that he discussed ([1955] 1961). The first, "antropoemic" one, takes the form of physical separation in camps. "Inside the fences of the camp," wrote Bauman in *Liquid Times* (2007c, 40), "they are pulped into a faceless mass, having been denied access to the elementary amenities from which identities are drawn and the visual yarns from which identities are woven." The second strategy, "anthropophagy," aims to eradicate the cultural differences of the refugees. "If the first strategy was aimed at the exile or annihilation of *the others*, the second was aimed at the suspension or annihilation of their *otherness*," wrote Bauman (2000c, 101).

His analyses devoted to the condition of both people subjected to "localization" and liquid modern "vagabonds" were part of his vision of "negative globalization." This approach, as I pointed out earlier, was an expression of the engaged nature of his work, including the theory of culture.[8] Bauman's intention, which he expressed explicitly in his publications on globalization, was to evoke sensitivity to the new dimensions of suffering in the current conjunction (2016b, 2011a, 2008b). In reference to his earlier works on postmodern ethics, he argued in the twenty-first century about the necessity of a significant – in fact, global – expansion of the scope of moral responsibility. He proved that the development of the global dependencies had led to the invalidation of the division into what Karl Jaspers termed "moral" and "metaphysical" guilt (Jaspers ([1947] 2001). *Eo ipso*, it is no longer possible to distinguish between the consequences of undertaking action or failing to act in contexts where one is a direct witness, and shared responsibility for the suffering that takes place all over the earth. In *Does Ethics Have a Chance in a World of Consumers?* (2008b, 72), Bauman wrote: "As never before, John Donne's words, 'Never send to know for whom the bell tolls; it tolls for thee,' represent the genuine solidarity of our fate; the point is, however, that the new solidarity of fate is as yet nowhere near being matched by the solidarity of our feelings, let alone our actions."

Bauman's teaching on the need to overcome the adiaphorizing properties of contemporary culture was accompanied by a highlighting of the need to introduce fundamental changes in politics. In this context, he wrote about the necessity of counteracting the separation between the rapidly developing "space of flows" (Castells 1996) and the structures of power remaining in the domain of nation states (Bauman and Bordoni, 2014). In Bauman's opinion, a fundamental transformation of the structures of power was needed in this regard. He argued that the new institutional order must convene with a worldwide network of economic ties. *Ergo*, it was necessary to give it a supranational character. "The logic of global responsibility," wrote Bauman (2004a, 137), "… prefers to pursue a new kind of global setting, in which the paths of economic initiatives anywhere on the planet will no longer be whimsical and guided by momentary gains alone, with no attention paid to side-effects and 'collateral causalities,' and no importance attached to the social dimensions of cost-and-effects balances."

Bauman considered the Kantian vision of the *allgemeine Vereinigung der Menschheit* to be a model of such a structure (Kant [1795] 1957).

It is worth recalling here that it assumed the founding of a systematically expanding federation of states that would commit to abstaining from the use of force for the sake of tangible economic benefits. What is particularly important from the point of view of the deliberations in this book is that Kant predicted that this process would be accompanied by the creation of a cosmopolitan consciousness among members of this federation. He wrote: "Since the narrower or wider community of the peoples of the earth has developed so far that a violation of rights in one place is felt throughout the world, the idea of a law of world citizenship is no high-flown or exaggerated notion" ([1795] 1957, 37). Both in the area of general premises of the institutional order and in the new ways of shaping intercultural relations, Bauman based his ideas on Kant's proposal, but it must also be emphasized that – in distinction from the author of the *Critique of Pure Reason* – he did not at all aim to describe the specific details of future laws, structures, and institutions. His thinking about the future remained in a framework of the concept of the active utopia (Bauman 1976d). His aim was to relativize the current state of the interregnum and to indicate general assumptions that should be made by future structures.

In 2004 Bauman pointed to the opportunities that, in terms of the possibility of creating the aforementioned political structure, as well as the accompanying new way of shaping intercultural relations, were provided by the progressive European integration (2004a). He emphasized that the European Union had developed a model of relations, assuming the peaceful coexistence of nations, despite different traditions and not infrequently violent and long-standing conflicts in the past. He argued in this context for the importance of the values on which the "European project" was based, such as freedom, solidarity, and self-criticism. Finally, he also highlighted the constitutive property for this part of the world of a tendency to constantly transcend the status quo. Bauman wrote: "Perhaps the sole steady element that made of European history a consistent and in the end cohesive story was the utopian spirit endemic to its identity, a forever not-yet-attained identity, vexingly elusive and always at odds with the realities of the day" (2004a, 36). Taking all of this into account, and also joining in the then contemporary discourse in social sciences and humanities (e.g., Giddens 2006; Beck and Grande [2004] 2007), Bauman asserted that the European project could be the avant-garde of a future cosmopolitan identity. On the one hand, he highlighted – in line with the assumptions of his utopian thought (Bauman 1976d) – the need of taking steps in this direction. On the other hand, however, he also pointed out the many, and ever increasing, difficulties that had to be conquered on the way. "The present momentum," he wrote in *Europe* (2004a, 135), "is shaped by two different (perhaps complementary, but then perhaps incompatible) logics – and it is impossible to decide, pre-empting history, which logic will ultimately prevail. One is the *logic of local retrenchment*; the other is the *logic of global responsibility and global aspiration*."

The analysis of the transformation taking place in the Old Continent over the course of the following years gave Bauman, however, less and less cause for optimism in both the possibility of building political structures capable of resisting negative globalization and the materialization of the accompanying vision of intercultural relations. In this context, he focused, first, on the effects of the financial crisis that broke out in 2008. In many of his publications of that time (e.g., Bauman 2011a; Bauman and Rovirosa-Madrazo 2009), Bauman pointed to the relationship between the increased sense of anxiety about the living condition and the changes in the attitudes toward cultural differences. For example, in *This Is Not a Diary*, he wrote: "'Culture' becomes a synonym for a fortress under siege, and the inhabitants of the fortress under siege are expected to manifest their loyalty daily, and give up, or at least radically curtail, any contacts with the outside world" (2012, 190). Secondly, Bauman assigned a significant role in the petrification of the aforementioned cultural change – which I called in the second chapter of this book "reduction of ambivalence" – to the threat of terrorist attacks in the twenty-first century. He argued that the fear they triggered – very often bolstered by some of the rulers who thereby seek to gain additional legitimization of their power– focused on cultural differences (2011a, 52–71; 2006, 129–59). In *Collateral Damage*, Bauman wrote that as a consequence "the mistrust of strangers, and the tendency to stereotype them all, or selected categories of them, as delayed action bombs bound to explode, grow more intense from their own logic and momentum, needing no further proof of their appropriateness and no additional stimuli from the inimical acts of the targeted adversary" (2011a, 70). Moreover, referring to the concept of the "state of exception" by Giorgio Agamben ([2003]

2005), Bauman claimed that the persistent terrorist threat was conducive to the development of the process of adiaphorization.

The reflections pertaining to the relationship between fear – on the grounds of both economic and security reasons – and the attitude toward "strangers" were continued by Bauman in connection with the outbreak of the European migration crisis in 2015 (Bauman 2016b). He interpreted this phenomenon, among others, through the prism of the previously discussed concepts of anthropoemy and anthropophagy, borrowed from Lévi-Strauss, and Giorgio Agamben's vision of state of exception. But then he, too, drew attention to the issue of rising populism and the increasing role that nationalist tendencies had begun to once again play in Western society (see Brzeziński 2020).

It should be noticed that the relationship between such phenomena and culture was to some extent present in his work – including his theory of culture – earlier. For example, in the first half of the seventies, in *Culture as Praxis*, he wrote that right-wing radicalism was characterized by "a widely diffused, unspecified and amorphic intolerance" (1973b, 152). On the genesis of this attitude, he wrote that "it selects the securely habitual reality, spreading all around, well founded, mirrored in scores of reciprocally reinforcing events, predictable and unobtrusively obvious, as the only tolerable (or, indeed, the only habitable) universe" (1973b, 151). Bauman made similar observations in his last publications in the second decade of the twenty-first century. Like many other intellectualists at the time (e.g., Applebaum 2020; Norris and Inglehart 2019; Hochschild 2016), he argued that a derivative of the development of populist and nationalist tendencies was appreciation of the aforementioned securely habitual reality. He described this process as a turn from proliferation to reduction of ambivalence, or – as I call it – from repertoire to systemic vision of culture.

In his book *Retrotopia* (2017c), Bauman also problematized these transformations in the context of the so-called nostalgic turn[9] (see Jacobsen 2020; Porter 2020; Salmose 2019). He claimed that longing for the past – or rather, for a mythologized vision of it – was increasingly influencing the contemporary social and cultural imaginary. In his analyses of this phenomenon he devoted most of his attention to the "restorative" form of longing for the past, specified by Svetlana Boym. She wrote that this type of nostalgia "attempts a transhistorical reconstruction of the lost home" (2001, xviii).[10] Bauman interpreted the restorative nostalgia as the opposite phenomenon to the process of the liquification of social reality. As far as he was concerned, in the face of an increasingly unstable present and an unpredictable future, the past appeared as an oasis of peace and comfort. "True to the utopian spirit, retrotopia derives its stimulus from the hope of reconciling, at long last, *security* with *freedom*," wrote Bauman (2017c, 8). A manifestation of this process is a more and more positive assessment of the structures, institutions, and norms characteristic of the past. *Per analogiam*, Bauman analyzed the growing criticism of both cosmopolitan thought and post-national politics in an increasing number of circles in this context (Bauman 2017b; 2017c; 2016b).

It is worthwhile to emphasize here that the transformations related to the nostalgic turn are in opposition to the assumptions of Bauman's utopian thought. The rise of nationalism is at the other end of the continuum in relation to his concept based on the Kantian vision of the *allgemeine Vereinigung der Menschheit*. The appreciation of cultural boundaries runs counter to his hopes for creating a cosmopolitan identity. And the rise to power of populist politicians stands in contradiction to the critical thinking that was constitutive of his works. The awareness of all these processes taking place did not, however, weaken the utopian potential of Bauman's work but, rather, solidified it. He argued all the more intensely in his final works that the only chance to oppose negative globalization lay in undertaking collective actions based on responsibility for the condition of the globalized world (Bauman 2017b, 144–9; 2017c, 153–67). What is more, continuing the reflections that he had been engaged in since halfway through the 1970s on the role of dialogue (1987, 127–48; 1978, 239–46; 1976e, 102–12), Bauman then pointed to its key role in the realization of the task.

In developing this perspective in the twenty-first century, Bauman drew support from Pope Francis's concept of "culture of dialogue." This was to be Bauman's point of departure for seeking solutions that responded to the needs of the contemporary world and simultaneously served as the foundation of peaceful coexistence and cooperation. In *Strangers at Our Door* (2016b, 18) Bauman wrote: "[I]nstead of refusing to face up to realities of the 'one planet, one humanity' challenges of our times, washing our hands and fencing ourselves off from the annoying differences, dissimilarities and self-imposed estrangements, we must seek occasions to come into a close and increasingly intimate contact with them – hopefully resulting in a *fusion* of horizons, instead of their induced and contrived, yet self-exacerbating, *fission*."

To finish this portion of the chapter, I will elaborate on elements of the critique of Bauman's theory of culture in the age of intensified global ties. Firstly, I would like to refer to his unambiguously critical position toward globalization. Although it was a derivative of the engaged nature of his work, I also believe that it is necessary to evaluate his position from the perspective of the descriptive and explanatory functions of sociology. In this matter I fully agree with George Ritzer, who – largely critical of the condition of the contemporary world – wrote: "There are certainly many negative aspects of the flows and processes related to globalization but I wouldn't risk the idea that globalization, as it is today, is completely negative. Awareness of the problems associated with globalization (such as environmental degradation; greater probability, speed and size of a pandemic) should not make us blind to its positive aspects (let us mention here at least the flow of life-saving drugs or medical personnel needed to contain the outbreak of a new pandemic)"[11] (2010, 240). Secondly, I would like to emphasize the dissonance in Bauman's work on globalization. He could have fully agreed with the following words of the chief of theory who was working for the main character of Donna DeLillo's novel *Cosmopolis*: "[Y]ou're dealing with a system that's out of control. Hysteria at high speeds, day to day, minute to minute" (2003, 85). Bauman's utopian thought was to overcome this chaos in both the political sphere (the *allgemeine Vereinigung der* Menschheit) and the cultural sphere ("the culture of dialogue"). However, he did not quite convincingly point to what might be the basis of this change. The question remains whether awareness of the growing crisis is capable of triggering a global transformation. Irrespective of this criticism, however, I fully share the following position of Mark Davis (2008a, 152): "[O]ne does not have to accept the full extent of the negative picture of the 'liquid world' that Bauman paints to agree that there remains much for the whole of humanity still to achieve, and to achieve together."

CONCLUSION

In the conversation with Keith Tester at the beginning of the twenty-first century, Zygmunt Bauman characterized the contemporary condition in the following way: "As to the shape [of the contemporary world], two parallel and closely connected processes make it what it is. First is seemingly unstoppable globalization, which takes power out of politics, and economics (the reproduction of livelihood) out of political control. Second is a complex process awkwardly dubbed 'individualization,' consisting in the 'phasing out,' one by one, of all societally woven and serviced safety nets at the time when individuals are called on to jump, each one on her or his own and to be bold and daring when they do" (Bauman and Tester 2001, 151). Reflection on the course and consequences of both these processes, which mutually condition each other, defined the framework of the work of Zygmunt Bauman in the twenty-first century. From the perspective of each one he analyzed the development of the mechanism of the liquification of social reality that is weakening the structures, institutions, and norms that had previously been its foundation. For culture, this meant that it took on an increasingly processual, heterogeneous, or repertoire character. Bauman wrote in this context about the "pointillization" of time, the "deterritorialization" of space, the emergence of "archipelago of diasporas," and so forth. In his final publications, however, he pointed to an opposite turn taking place in culture, consisting in the appreciation of clearly defined identities and neatly delineated borders. Further developing the way of describing cultural changes introduced by Ernest Gellner (1983), and then used by Ulf Hannerz (1996), it could be said that after "the return of Kokoschka" comes "the return of Modigliani."

Bauman's theoretical analyses of culture went hand in hand, not only with his reflections on the subject of the necessary changes taking place in the contemporary world, but also with an argument for the need of the individuals to take an active role in bringing them to fruition. In this context, it is worth recalling his statement, published in a Polish weekly several days after the attacks on the World Trade Center and the Pentagon on 11 September 2001: "The very fact of dependence is independent of us ... Also independent of us is the responsibility that emerges from this global interdependence. Only one thing is dependent on us: whether we acknowledge our responsibility and draw conclusions from it, or we take responsibility for this responsibility that fate has dealt to us, and act in accordance with this decision" (Bauman 2001c).[12] In all of his later years Bauman remained faithful to this conviction. He postulated the need to build up global responsibility in the context of, for example, successive terrorist attacks, the financial crisis in 2008, and the European financial crisis in the middle of the second decade of this century (Bauman 2016b, 2013, 2011a). Attempts to solve these problems, undertaken either within nation states or by supranational "carnival communities," he considered to be not only ineffective but even counterproductive. And although he himself largely emphasized the difficulties piling up on the way to counteract negative globalization, he all the more emphasized the need for fundamental political and cultural transformations. In this respect, the words from Franz Kafka's short story *Advocates*, with which Bauman ended *Europe: An Unfinished Adventure*, are significant: "So if you find nothing in the corridors open the doors, if you find nothing behind these doors there are more floors, and if you find nothing up there, don't worry, just leap up another flight of stairs. As long as you don't stop climbing, the stairs won't end, under your climbing feet they will go on growing upwards" (Kafka [1936] 1988, 451).

Conclusion

THE LEGACY OF ZYGMUNT BAUMAN'S THEORY OF CULTURE

Zygmunt Bauman's personal documents are collected at the University of Leeds, where he worked for his entire academic career in Great Britain. They can be found in the Special Collections of the university's library. Within this rich collection of materials there is, *inter alia*, the correspondence between Bauman and other pre-eminent intellectuals (such as Anthony Giddens, Agnes Heller, Shmuel Eisenstadt, Jürgen Habermas, and Claus Offe), illuminating the character of their intellectual ties. There are also various notes and jottings: handwritten notes on papers he was reading; initial sketches of ideas that were later developed in articles and books; and plans for further projects.[1] All these archival materials – which are written in several different languages – serve as an excellent source to examine how Bauman's thinking was shaped and evolved because they give particular insight into the inspirations behind his sociology. What is more, they also demonstrate the influence that his works had on other intellectuals and on the formation of particular methods and orientations in the humanities and social sciences of the last decades.

It is precisely the legacy of Bauman's work – with particular emphasis on his theory of culture – that will be the subject of my considerations here. My analysis will refer to the four different periods of his sociology outlined in this book. In each of them I will indicate the aspects of Bauman's theorization that played the biggest role in shaping the discourse on culture. At the same time, I will focus on the reasons that some of his analyses did not receive their due acknowledgment in the academic world. At the end I will consider some factors that could influence the reception of Bauman's theory of culture in the future.

In the second chapter of this book I pointed out that the approach to studying culture that was proper to Bauman's work in the 1960s contributed in an essential way to the creation of the turn in how this category was conceptualized in Polish sociology of the time. His work in 1967 with the Laboratory of Anthropology of the People's Poland, operating within the Department of General Sociology at the University of Warsaw, was an effort to institutionalize this approach (see Łuczeczko 2011, 65, 66). In the opening chapter of the book *Returns and Continuations: A Gift for Zygmunt Bauman* (Tarkowska 1995b) – a monograph containing articles by Polish researchers – Elżbieta Tarkowska assessed the legacy of this research group. She claimed: "The activity started on a grand scale was interrupted by March 1968 and the repressions that then affected Zygmunt Bauman and the environment of the department headed by him. The end of the Laboratory's activities was not, however, the final end of the work then initiated; thoughts, ideas, concepts have survived in various forms" (9). It must be acknowledged, however, that these inspirations, reflected in various studies and their resulting publications, did not lead to the creation of a separate school of the theory of culture. This situation was a direct consequence of Bauman's forced emigration, as well as the attitude of the Polish authorities toward him and his work (one of its manifestations was the decision to destroy the print run of *Sketches on the Theory of Culture*). And although – as the documents collected at the University of Leeds show – Bauman remained in correspondence with his close associates from the University of Warsaw, the influence of his theorization on Polish sociology over the years was very limited.[2]

A year after the publication of *Returns and Continuations*, a similar project was undertaken by Richard Kilminster and Ian Varcoe. The book they edited, entitled *Culture, Modernity, and Revolution* (1996), was meant to honour Bauman's work over two decades as the director of the Department of Sociology at the University of Leeds. Presenting his accomplishments in the introduction, they wrote: "He stimulated research on cultural themes as well as projects on the borderlines of sociology with social philosophy and the history of ideas and never recoiled from posing fundamental questions, even if they were uncomfortable" (2). This approach found an enduring reflection in the profile of the Department of Sociology that Bauman had headed until his retirement.

His personal documents collected at the University of Leeds can serve as a reference point for the analysis of his teaching and organization activities from that time. In recent years the legacy of Bauman's work at the University of Leeds is reflected in the activities of the Bauman Institute, established in 2010 by Mark Davis at the School of Sociology and Social Policy. This international centre is dedicated to developing the research and teaching in the areas that were especially important to Zygmunt Bauman, including his theory of culture (e.g., Bauman [1966–2015] 2021). Of Bauman's analyses during his time at the University of Leeds, his efforts to create a non-reductionist theory of culture are still of particular importance today (Bauman 1973b). As I pointed out in the third chapter, this issue was emphasized by, among others, Margaret Archer in *Culture and Agency* (Archer 1988). What is more, Bauman's then contemporary vision of utopia, understood as "aspect of culture" (Bauman 1976d, 14), is acknowledged as particularly valuable for contemporary utopian studies (see, for example, Jacobsen 2016, 72–4; 2008; Sargent 2010, 113–15; Levitas 1990, 168–78).

A decisive breakthrough in the reception of Bauman's work, both in academia and among a broader reading public, occurred at the end of the twentieth century. Although previously the importance of his work had been appreciated, especially among theorists of culture, philosophers of science, and researchers of socialist societies, at that time he gained worldwide recognition.[3] The work that played the most essential role in this regard was *Modernity and the Holocaust* (Bauman 1989c). The vision of modernity as the garden culture that this book offered has been the source of numerous commentaries and polemics (see Palmer and Brzeziński 2022b). Independently of some controversies that it evokes – though perhaps in part also because of them – it has permanently entered the annals of social sciences and humanities. Bauman's works in the postmodernist vein also met with a lively reception. Anthony Elliott wrote about this issue: "It is hard to imagine an analyst of the postmodern condition more theoretically sophisticated and consistently innovative than Bauman … Certainly the great strength of this research is his tenacity in pursuing the idea of the postmodern through its every shifting guise and mutation, from the economy to entertainment. He tracks cultural pressures, emotional torments and political dilemmas with a uniquely agile understanding, helping us to glimpse, if not the solutions, then at least the complexities of global postmodern transformations" (2009, 253,

254). The most essential aspect, from the point of view of theorizations of culture, was Bauman's analyses of the collapse of its systemic properties and the rise of the repertoire ones. His reflections, formulated on the basis of this conclusion, on the transformations of identity, on the role of intellectuals, or on consumer culture, have already become classics of social thought of the twentieth century (Bauman 1997b, 1991a, 1987). Of particular significance is also the critical dimension of the analyses conducted by Bauman in that period, which was accompanied by the development of his ethical thought (Bauman 1993). In the context of the legacy of Bauman's theory of modern and postmodern culture, it is also worth pointing out that his correspondence on these issues with very many eminent intellectuals is collected at the University of Leeds.

Bauman's reflections on the condition of culture in the twenty-first century, presented in the last chapter, remain one of the most read and discussed analyses of contemporary culture. Ulrich Beck wrote in this context: "In my opinion, and in the opinion of many others, Bauman's works are of greater importance to the current world than the works of any other contemporary thinker" (2010, 10). Bauman's analyses devoted to the process of individualization (2001d), the interpersonal relations (2003), and the consumption syndrome (2007a) gained exceptional recognition. They have been widely discussed in social sciences and humanities and have contributed to the development of the "sociological imagination" (Mills 1959) among a wider audience. What is more, the metaphor of liquidity has become an important analytical category in social sciences and humanities; in reference to it, the concepts of "liquid antiquity" (Holmes and Marta 2017), "liquid migrations" (Engbersen 2012), "liquid law" (Přibáň 2007), and so forth have been created. Bauman's vision of globalization has also been widely commented on. I emphasized in the fifth chapter that this concept had a clearly critical dimension and was related to his utopian thinking. Its development was accompanied by the outline of a vision of the future based on the Kantian concept of the *allgemeine Vereinigung der Menschheit* (Bauman 2004a; Kant [1795] 1957). This aspect of Bauman's work was especially important for the debate on cosmopolitan society characteristic of the beginning of the twenty-first century (see, for example, Alexander 2009; Beck and Grande [2004] 2007; Giddens 2006). Last but not least, his final publications – on retrotopia and the migration crisis (Bauman 2017c, 2016b) – have become a part of the contemporary discourse on populist and nationalist tendencies (see Norris and Inglehart 2019; Gingrich and Banks 2006).

I have shown in this book that the approach to Bauman's reflections on culture changed significantly throughout his life. At the end of his work at the University of Warsaw he was recognized as one of the most important Polish authorities in the field of theory of culture, and after March 1968, because of the interdiction of Polish authorities, his papers were not even cited by other scholars for two decades (Kraśko 1995, 33; Tarkowska 1995a, 18). However, while working in exile, he was initially known only to a small circle of intellectuals (Tester 2006) and then gained worldwide fame as an "interpreter" of the contemporary world.

The legacy of his work will also be subjected to changes in the future. The posthumous publication of his writings may be of some importance in this regard. For example, in 2018 an English translation of *Sketches in the Theory of Culture* was published, which gave insight into Bauman's very early works and allowed for an inquiry into the connections between it and his later theorizations (e.g., Brzeziński 2018). In 2021 a volume entitled *Culture and Art* (Bauman [1966–2015] 2021) was published, containing texts written by Bauman during each of the four periods of his work that I have described. Some of this material was found in the Special Collections of the University of Leeds Library; others had been published earlier only in Polish or were otherwise largely absent from intellectual discourse. In the coming years, further collections of previously unknown writings by Bauman will be published,[4] which will doubtless be accompanied by academic discussions. Other types of material held at the University of Leeds – Bauman's correspondence with other intellectuals, his personal notes, and initial plans for research projects – are still waiting to be published. Future, detailed analysis of them – a portion of which pertains to the theory of culture – will certainly contribute to the legacy of his work. Referring to Bauman's frequently repeated claim, after Santayana, that culture is "a knife with its sharp edge pressed continuously against the future" (Bauman 1973b, 172; Bauman and Tester 2001, 31), it can be said that the same will apply to the legacy of his theory of culture.

Notes

INTRODUCTION

1 These two ways of understanding culture should be perceived as ideal types; most of the definitions of culture belong somewhere on a continuum whose extremes are marked by these two.

CHAPTER ONE

1 The titles of the books published by Bauman in Polish have been translated by the author of this book into English.

2 This abbreviation was created by repeating the first two consonants of the word *heterogeneous*.

3 Bauman argued in *Culture and Society*: "Given the breadth and the versatility of the market, man in a Htht society has negative and positive relations with a number of people incomparably higher than that in any other society. However, these relations are, as a rule, of a market and competitive nature" (1966a, 425).

4 "Cultural norms," wrote Bauman (1966a, 444), "become part of the commodity market: one may purchase them or stop using them, relative to their pragmatic value."

5 Bauman applied this notion to a coherent, holistic set of characteristics shaped by market mechanisms in the members of modern society (Bauman 2007a; Bauman and Rojek 2004).

6 A continuity in Bauman's theoretical reflections on culture was also ensured by his constant reliance on the method of ideal types. Setting out to describe a socially and culturally heterogeneous community, he wrote: "Our construction will therefore be of an approximate nature. We will be talking about trends rather than facts, about probabilities rather than exception-free rules… We are trying to understand facts rather than describe them" (Bauman 1966a, 434). These methodological notes may, in fact, be applied to many of Bauman's reflections on culture in subsequent years. His analyses were frequently based on the creation of intellectual constructs, within which specific trends were brought into sharp focus, while counter-trends were ignored.

7 Bauman wrote in *Culture as Praxis*: "Positivism is … more than the philosophy of professional philosophers and the praxis of professional scientists. Its epistemological roots as well as axiological sprouts are intimately interwoven into the very texture of the human life-process in an alienated society" (1973b, 165).

8 This issue is a central theme of the book *Bauman and the West: Exile, Culture, Dialogue* by Jack Palmer (forthcoming).

9 One of the reasons behind this decision was Bauman's conviction that postmodernism did not provide a sound foundation for the development of critical thought (see Rattansi 2017, 189–94).

CHAPTER TWO

1 I will refer to this typology in more detail at the end of the first part of this chapter.

2 This did not mean any kind of definitive break in Bauman's analysis of political sociology. After his forced emigration from Poland he wrote several articles on the 1968 Polish political crisis (Bauman 1969a; 1969b, 7–23; 1968b), and in subsequent years he analyzed the political situation in Central-Eastern Europe (e.g., 1981, 1976a, 1974, 1973a, 1972c, 1971b).

3 The framework of Bauman's research in the Polish period of his work was limited by censorship (and the self-censorship related to it). In this respect, his focus on cultural issues in the second half of the 1960s gave him a much greater degree of freedom compared to that of his earlier studies in the field of political sociology. The issue of the social and political context of Bauman's work in Poland was described in detail by Izabela Wagner (2020).

4 Bauman was expected to take over a chair in the Sociology of Culture at the University of Warsaw, following Hochfeld's planned return to Poland in September 1966. After Hochfeld's death in July 1966, Bauman remained the head of the Department of General Sociology, and Józef Chałasiński was appointed as the chair in the Sociology of Culture. On the institutional and political aspect of this issue, see Wagner (2020, 249, 251).

5 Elżbieta Tarkowska (1944–2016) was a Polish sociologist specializing in the theory of culture; sociology and anthropology of time; and sociology of poverty. During her academic career she collaborated on various levels with Zygmunt Bauman. In 1995 she edited a collection of papers written by his associates of the period when he was in charge of the Department of General Sociology at the University of Warsaw (Tarkowska 1995b).

6 On the 1968 Polish political crisis, known also as March events, see Stola (2006) and Eisler (1998).

7 A significant portion of the editorial manuscript prepared for publication was discovered after years in the collections of the shared libraries of the departments of Philosophy and Sociology at the University of Warsaw, the Institute of Philosophy and Sociology of the Polish Academy of Sciences, and the Polish Philosophical Association, located at Krakowskie Przedmieście 3 in Warsaw. This text – along with the accompanying editorial materials that were preserved at the Ossolineum Publishing House in Wrocław (book folder no. B-196) – became the basis of the reconstruction of the work. It was published along with a new afterword written by Zygmunt Bauman (Bauman [1968c] 2018).

8 In line with the policy pursued in the countries of the Eastern bloc, Bauman highlighted in the 1950s the exceptional importance of "the culture of the masses." In an article written with Jerzy Wiatr, he pointed out that the culture of workers and peasants was a unique reservoir of values and beliefs (Bauman and Wiatr, 1953, 80–3).

9 It is worth recalling here Bauman's statement regarding his and Leszek Kołakowski's attitude to communist ideology after the Second World War: "[W]e had both believed that the programme of the Polish communists in 1944/45 was the only one that gave us some reason to hope that our country could escape from the backwardness of the pre-war era and the cataclysm of the war; that it was the only programme that could solve the nation's problems of moral degeneration, illiteracy, poverty and social injustice" (Bauman and Haffner [2017] 2020, 9).

10 Bauman divided the British labuor movement into four phases: embryonic (1750–1850), "comes of age" (1850–90), mass mobilization (1890–1924), and consolidation (1924–55). In each of them he studied the dependencies between the working class, the organized labour movement, and its elites.

11 Among the various methods of research carried out by Bauman during his work in Poland, there was also quantitative research. Later in his work he repeatedly criticized the quantitative methodology.

12 See Prazmowska (2016).

13 See Kemp-Welch (2006).

14 It should be noted, however, that Bauman remained a member of the Polish United Workers' Party until 1967.

15 It is also important in the context of intellectual relations that Bauman and Hochfeld were friends.

16 This paper will be published in English in Zygmunt Bauman's *History and Politics: Selected Writings, Vol.* 2, translated by Katarzyna Bartoszyńska (Cambridge: Polity Press).

17 From 1956 to 1960 Stanisław Ossowski was also director of the Department of Cultural Theory and Social Transformations of the Institute of Philosophy and Sociology of the Polish Academy of Sciences.

18 In 1957 Hochfeld transformed his chair from Historical Materialism to Sociology of Political Relations.

19 In the conversation with Keith Tester in 2001, Bauman regretted that Osowski's concepts – among them his reflections on culture – were almost completely unknown outside Poland (Bauman and Tester 2001, 22).

20 This text was written in 1955 and published in 1956, a few months before the Polish October.

21 Fragments of this paper were published in English in Ossowski (1998).

22 This probably happened after Albert Camus was awarded the Nobel Prize for Literature in 1957. Perhaps Bauman read a samizdat translation of Camus's *Rebel* into Polish, which was published by the Literary Institute in Paris in 1958.

23 In line with Camus's concept, Bauman's idea of the rebel was not only personal; it concerned the necessity to change the social and political condition. Camus wrote on that matter: "[F]rom the moment that a movement of rebellion begins, suffering is seen as a collective experience – as the experience of everyone. Therefore the first step for a mind overwhelmed by the strangeness of things is to realize that this feeling of strangeness is shared with all men and at the same time the human race suffers from the division between itself and the rest of the world. The unhappiness experienced by a single man becomes collective unhappiness. In our daily trials, rebellion plays the same role as does the '*cogito*' in the category of thought: it is the first clue. But this clue lures the individual from his solitude. Rebellion is the common ground on which every man bases his first values. I *rebel* – therefore we *exist*" ([1951] 1953, 28).

24 *The Prison Notebooks* (*Quaderni del carcere*) were written by Antonio Gramsci between 1929 and 1935, when he was imprisoned by the Italian fascist regime. They were first published in Italian in six volumes between 1948 and 1951. A selection of the texts contained in *The Prison Notebooks* was first published in Polish in 1950.

25 In the early 2000s, Bauman admitted that it was largely due to his inspiration by Gramsci's thoughts that he did not abandon Marxism, despite his growing disappointment with the situation in his home country. He said: "In a paradoxical way Gramsci saved me from turning into an anti-Marxist, as so many other disenchanted thinkers did, throwing out on their way everything that was, and remained, precious and topical in Marx's legacy. I read good tidings in Gramsci's *Prison Notebooks*: there was a way of saving the ethical core, and the analytical potential I saw no reason to discard from the stiff carapace in which it had been enclosed and stifled" (Bauman and Tester 2001, 26).

26 Kroeber and Kluckhohn also described an "incomplete" way of defining culture. Due to its analytic uselessness, this type is generally omitted in discussions of their classification. This will also be the case in this chapter.

27 Pierre Boulez (1925–2016) was a French composer, conductor, and animator of musical life. He was one of the leaders of the post-war musical avant-garde and an outstanding interpreter of the classics of twentieth-century music.

28 Bauman presented this distinction in the book *Culture and Society*, published in Polish in 1966, a fragment of which was published in English in 2021 ([1966] 2021). The attributive understanding of culture relates to the constitutive features of human beings as a species. The distributive approach "does not indicate what is common to all people and comprises their major attribute, differentiating humans from all that is not human – but what differentiates one group of people from another" ([1966] 2021, 2).

29 It is worth quoting in this context an excerpt from a sketch written by Grazia Deledda, an Italian writer and Nobel Prize winner, who described life in her hometown of Nuoro in Sardinia as follows: "Una leggera sfumatura di progresso, che è sempre il segno del tempo e che dice pochissimo, ha modificato qualche rito, e le vesti. Ma il lutto e la gioia, le credenze e la religione, i pregiudizi e le passioni, sono sempre le stesse" (1894, 5). [A slight nuance of progress, which is always the sign of time and which says very little, has changed some rituals and the clothes. But mourning and joy, beliefs and religion, prejudices and passions, are always the same" (trans. D. Brzeziński).]

30 Over the next decade, Bauman's attitude to Parsons's work changed entirely. In the 1970s, Bauman shaped his theory of culture in opposition to the works of the author of *The Social System* (see, for example, Bauman 1976e).

31 It should be stressed that the inspiration Bauman drew from structural semiotics was limited by the Marxist foundations of his sociology. In a paper entitled "Marx and the Contemporary Theory of Culture" (1968a), prepared for a Paris symposium in May 1968 to consider Marx's significance for social sciences and humanities (see Hobsbawm 2002, 246–62), Bauman wrote: "[W]ithout renouncing any of Lévi-Strauss's methodological discoveries, we must try to avoid the blind alley into which he was led by his philosophy. We must designate the reality in relation to which culture – that specifically human aspect of active existence – functions as a sign" (1968a, 28). *Ergo*, Bauman rejected Lévi-Strauss's belief that the primary concern for humanities and social sciences should be reflection on the structure of human thinking. From the general premises of Marxism he derived a conviction of the necessity to concentrate on the modes of organization – or "structurization" – of the human material world.

32 About the relationship between adopting cultural models and the stability of the social system, Bauman wrote: "The purely abstract theoretical model of culture, fulfilling this function in an excellent way, would assume the complete identity of the individual-assimilationist directive (patterns of behaviour) with the socio-accommodating directive (institutional requirements, or – as Parsons writes – structural-functioning ones" ([1968c] 2018, 157). Bauman simultaneously emphasized that this situation was never realized in social practice.

33 In a Polish book, *The Society We Live In*, Bauman wrote: "Conscience is not 'innate,' but has a social origin ... When we take a closer look at what our 'private' conscience demands of us, we will recognize in its demands precisely those requirements that our environment imposes on us" (1962b, 44).

34 In "Towards a Semiotic Theory of Culture," Bauman wrote in this context as follows: "A living organism is constructed according to the needs of a 'structuralized' world, and only in such a world can it prosper. It is naturally predisposed to acquaint itself with the structure of events around it" ([1968c] 2018, 56). In the case of the human, he added, the need discussed here refers not only to adaptation to the environment but also to the active role in organizing it and guaranteeing harmonious co-operation between individuals.

35 Kroeber and Kluckhohn (1952, 70–1) decided to also distinguish genetic definitions of a residual character. Within them culture is described through an opposition to properties that characterize the natural order. Both anthropologists thought, however, that such approach was "unsatisfactory for the purposes of formal definition."

36 It is worth quoting in this context a statement from the editorial review of *Sketches in Theory of Culture* from 1967, written by the Polish literary critic and historian Stefan Żółkiewski: "[T]his and the previous work [*Culture and Society*] of docent Bauman is of a pioneering nature. It effectively introduces the problems of current research in the field of cultural anthropology and its theory. The value of Bauman's book does not only lie in its initiating possibilities, in opening up intellectual and research perspectives in a field little known in Poland. It also lies in the original attempts to solve the fundamental theoretical questions of cultural anthropology" (1967, 14). This review has been preserved in the editorial folder of *Sketches in the Theory of Culture*, located in the archives of the Ossolineum Publishing House, Wrocław, Poland (card catalogue no. B-196).

37 In 1966 the conference "The Languages of Criticism and the Sciences of Man" took place at Johns Hopkins University in Baltimore, Maryland, where breakthrough concepts were presented by, *inter alia*, Jacques Derrida and Roland Barthes (Macksey and Donato 1970). This year is usually regarded as the symbolic beginning of post-structuralism.

38 See letters from Julia Kristeva to Zygmunt Bauman, 8 March 1967 and 22 January 1968, in Janina and Zygmunt Bauman Papers, MS2067/B/5/1.

39 Bauman's theory of heterogeneous culture from that time is similar to the image of culture as a "tool kit" presented two decades later by Ann Swidler (1986). They both critically revised the model of culture as a coherent set of patterns, values, and meanings and claimed that it was in fact an ever-expanding "repertoire … which people may use in varying configurations to solve different kinds of problems" (Swidler 1986, 273).

40 Bauman wrote the following on this topic: "The whole world presents itself to me as a collection of things, and since I am free to choose between its various kinds, I imagine myself to be an authentic personality by the very fact that this choice has been presented to me. When I choose things, I get the illusion that I choose myself; in a way it really is; I choose myself as a combination of goods" (1966a, 440).

CHAPTER THREE

1 Archer's and Bauman's interpretations of the anthropology of Claude Lévi-Strauss ([1958] 1963) were completely different. Bauman not only did not consider Lévi-Strauss's theory to be conflationary but was inspired by its description of a dynamic, processual vision of culture (Bauman [1968c] 2018). I began to discuss this issue in the previous chapter; it will also be the subject of my reflections in the following portion of the book.

2 It is appropriate to highlight the difference in Archer's and Bauman's evaluations of Antonio Gramsci's theory of culture. Archer interpreted his work as an example of the instrumental version of upwards conflation due to his emphasis on the role of cultural hegemony in the process of maintaining social order (1988, 56–62). As I pointed out in the previous chapter, in his analysis of Gramsci's works Bauman (1963) focused as much on the issue of cultural hegemony, understood by him as a reality external to individuals, as on the attempts to break it.

3 Bauman's perspective on Habermas's thought in the 1970s was significantly different from Archer's approach (see Bauman 1978). It will be one of the issues discussed in a later portion of this chapter.

4 Bauman wrote: "What has been revered as 'the social reality' by the positive social scientist is degraded to the status of a contingent, varying by-product of the 'typifying' work of the 'members' … When everything is equally valid, since 'experienced,' nothing can be relied upon as the sure way out of the predicament" (1973b, 168).

5 Bauman referred to Giddens's structuration theory in his article collected in the book *Social Theory of Modern Societies: Giddens and His Critics* (Bauman 1989a). He asserted that Giddens took on a task of the scale of Talcott Parsons, and in carrying out this task, he did not avoid the pitfalls of the latter. In his view, Giddens was unable to convincingly demonstrate that the rules and resources that were supposed to create a social structure possessed an entirely different status than the one that the representatives of functionalism ascribed to cultural norms.

6 Archer also critiqued the thesis, constitutive for Giddens's theory, according to which "the structural properties of social systems are both medium and outcome of the practices they recursively organize" (Giddens 1984, 25). Analogously, she criticized Bourdieu's attempt to resolve the dilemma between determinism and voluntarism in his theory of structural constructivism (Bourdieu [1979] 1984).

7 Bauman combined this approach with structuralist assumptions, as evidenced by these words: "Since all cultural praxis consists in imposing a new, artificial order on the natural one, one has to look for the essential culture-generating faculties in the domain of the seminal ordering rules built into the human mind" (Bauman 1973b, 119).

8 Sartre wrote in *Being and Nothingness*: "I am no longer the master in arresting the process of appropriation. It continues. In one sense it is like the supreme docility of the possessed … and in another sense there is underneath this docility a surreptitious appropriation of the possessor by the possessed" ([1943] 2001, 609).

9 Bauman wrote in *Culture as Praxis*: "It would … be hard to imagine how society, or indeed any kind of ordered network of human relationships, would be possible in the first place, were there not a propensity to ordering praxis built into the human animals" (1973b, 139).

10 Marx and Engels juxtaposed "scientific socialism" and "utopian socialism" and described Henri de Saint-Simon, Charles Fourier, and Robert Owen as representatives of the latter current. They argued that utopian socialism was based on erroneous premises (among others, it did not take into account the leading role of the proletariat) and also led to false ideas about social change (this concerned, for example, sketching detailed rules for the functioning of future social system) (e.g., Engels [1880] 1935).

11 For example, in this context, David Harvey wrote as follows: "I had always thought that the purpose of More's *Utopia* was not to provide a blueprint for some future but to hold up for inspection the ridiculous waste and foolishness of his times, to insist that things could and must be better" (2000, 281). Lyman Tower Sargent made a similar statement: "All utopias ask questions. They ask whether or not the way we live could be improved and answer that it could. Most utopias compare life in the present and life in the utopia and point out what is wrong with the way we now live, thus suggesting what needs to be done to improve things" (2010, 5).

12 Bauman used the metaphor of "a knife with its sharp edge pressed continuously against the future" for both of the aforementioned categories (1976d, 12; 1973b, 172).

13 Bauman emphasized at that time the similarities between socialism and capitalism. For example, he argued that in spite of the official narrative in the Eastern bloc countries about their axiological superiority, the norms and values characteristic of capitalist formations significantly contributed

to the shaping of their social life. Bauman also drew attention to the process of the progressing implementation of the politics characteristic of socialist ideology in Western countries, the derivative of which was the growing popularity of the welfare state. In connection with all these processes he wrote: "Increasingly, the drama is seen not as a struggle between socialism and capitalism (two consecutive systems of social organization), but between socialism and commonsense (two alternative ways of tackling the human condition). The conclusion that the fate of the battle, and the responsibility for it, falls on the shoulders of each and every individual, follows almost by itself" (1976d, 131, 132).

14 Peter Beilharz wrote on this issue: "Sociology, for Bauman, then, is political or more directly, radical … for it moves around concerns such as freedom, dependence, solidarity, contingency. In this regard sociology indeed is dangerous, if only it lives up even to the most modest of its dreams, for to be critical is precisely to be open to arguments for change, in whatever direction" (2000, 46).

15 Bauman's reflections pertaining to hermeneutics had appeared already in his earlier work. For example, in the text entitled "Towards a Semiotic Theory of Culture," published in *Sketches in the Theory of Culture*, he considered the role of the process of understanding in the Marxist humanities. He pointed, in this context, to the value of a research method "that would allow us to 'understand' cultural facts by reference to social structure, and consequently would also allow us to discern that social structure, emerging from the given empirical facts of culture" ([1968c] 2018, 33).

16 Habermas's most important work on the issue of communication, *The Theory of Communicative Action* (Habermas [1981] 1984–87), was published three years after *Hermeneutics and Social Science* was released. This concept, however, had been systematically developed by him during the previous years (e.g., Habermas [1968] 1972).

17 On the cultural dimension of these efforts Peter Beilharz stated as follows: "If sociology as a utopia were successful, then understanding and communal life would be more closely interconnected. Utopia would connect science and life, not suspend or submerge them" (2000, 69).

18 Bauman borrowed this metaphor from Reinhart Koselleck (see, for example, Koselleck [1979] 2004).

19 On the Polish Solidarity movement see, for example, Brier (2021), Bloom (2013), and Cirtautas (1997).

CHAPTER FOUR

1 The anthropological concept of culture was described in the second chapter of this book.

2 Bauman characterized traditional, "premodern" cultures similarly in his earlier works. In the second chapter of this book I analyzed his concept of the socially and culturally homogeneous community ("Hmhm") that he presented in *Culture and Society: Preliminaries* (1966a, 235–92). Culture in this model was characterized by syngenism, and social structure by synergy. Seven years later, in *Culture as Praxis*, Bauman argued that a coherence of norms dominating in premodern societies implicated a lack of vulnerability to cultural difference. In this context, he used the term *cultural blindness* (1973b: 134), which also effectively reflects his view of wild cultures.

3 Contrary to the vision of "people without history," Wolf redefined the semantic fields of "society" and "culture" in the following way: "'Societies' emerge as changing alignments of social groups, segments, and classes, without either fixed boundaries or stable internal constitution … 'A culture' is thus better seen as a series of processes that construct, reconstruct, and dismantle cultural materials, in response to identifiable determinants" (1982, 387).

4 On the methodological premises of Weber's concepts, Bauman wrote most extensively in a chapter of his book *Hermeneutics of Social Science* (1978, 69–88).

5 Referencing Douglas's *Purity and Danger*, Bauman made the following statement in 2001: "It took some time for that inspiration to sink in and even longer to take root and give fruit: to realize that most if not all of the forbidding nastiness of human degradation and socially produced indignity is the by-product of the search for order and fear of disturbance, brought to its radical, obsessive extreme by modernity, itself a desperate response to collapse of the self-reproducing order of the *ancient régime*. I suppose that when writing *Socialism: The Active Utopia* I came to the threshold of that realization: it shows in the premonition that what the socialist utopia needed was to redeploy itself a 'counterculture of *modernity*.' But it took a few more years to think the consequences" (Bauman and Tester 2001, 53).

6 On the relation between Bauman and the Frankfurt School see Jacobsen and Hansen (2017).

7 Bauman stressed that both Freud's and Weber's approaches to modernity were not unambiguous and also underwent evolutions. On the one hand, in his later writings Weber pointed out the difficulties emerging from the development of instrumental reason. On the other hand, Freud, alongside pointing out the difficulties emerging from the suppression of instincts and drives, also perceived certain positive aspects of this process for social life (Bauman 1983, 32).

8 From this perspective, Bauman also developed his critique of the positivist orientation in social sciences. For example, in *Freedom* he drew a relationship between panopticism and positivism in sociology. Referring to the work of Talcott Parsons – criticized by him since the early 1970s – he wrote: "*Panopticon* may be compared to Parsons' laboriously erected model of the social system. What both works seek is nothing less than a model of well-balanced, equilibrate, cohesive human cohabitation, adaptable to changing tasks, capable of reproducing the conditions of its own existence, producing maximum output (however measured) and minimum waste" (1988a, 20).

9 Together with Jack Palmer, I have published an edited volume that addresses this issue: Palmer and Brzeziński (2022).

10 Bauman's views on the relations between modernity and postmodernity were not unambiguous and evolved over time (see Bauman 2000c). This is one of the subjects of the following chapter.

11 "The new mode of domination," wrote Bauman in 1987, "distinguishes itself by the substitution of seduction for repression, public relations for policing, advertising for authority, needs-creation for norm-imposition. What ties individuals to society today is their activity as consumers, their life organized around consumption … Individuals willingly submit to the prestige of advertising, and thus need no 'legitimation' beliefs" (167, 168).

12 The issue of the relationship between Bauman's theory of consumer culture and the works of other authors is discussed in detail, *inter alia*, in Jacobsen and Hansen (2017), M. Davis (2008b), and Blackshaw (2005, 111–40).

13 "The distinction between the two," wrote Mark Davis, "is based upon relative levels of freedom and dependency, understood as the ability to follow one's own free will and the necessity to comply with the will of others. For the seduced and the repressed, it is the consumer market that mediates this relative level of freedom. In short, the market provides the

acid test of eligibility for inclusion in the consumer society" (2008b, 103).

14 Bauman also compared the development of culture to the phenomenon of Markov chains, in which the probability of each successive event depends only on the state immediately preceding it (1992b, 165).

15 This piece is an essay that was attached to a letter written by Zygmunt Bauman (see Brzeziński et al. 2021, xxvi).

16 In this respect, Bauman's theory of culture corresponded to the "schizophrenic" visions of the contemporary condition presented by both Fredric Jameson (1991) and Gilles Deleuze and Félix Guattari ([1980] 1987; [1972] 1977).

17 Among Bauman's inspirations for this way of theorizing postmodern culture, it is worth mentioning Georg Simmel (Frisby and Featherstone 1997). According to Bauman, the polysemic, fragmentary, and variabilistic cultural reality presented by the author of *The Philosophy of Money* was an accurate anticipation of the processes that were fully revealed at the end of the twentieth century. He wrote: "Simmel's sociology had no room for 'society': Simmel was after the mystery of *sociality* … [R]eality emerged from Simmel's writings as so many splinters of life and crumbs of information; a far cry from the complete, all-embracing, harmonious and systematic models of 'social order' or 'social structure' offered by other sociologists and considered de rigeur by the social sciences of the time" (1991a, 185).

18 The issue of cultural cohesion, however, was incorporated back into Bauman's theory of culture in the twenty-first century (see, for example, Bauman 2017c, 2016b), which I will analyze in the next chapter.

19 Bauman wrote on this issue: "To be effectively and consequentially present in a postmodern habitat, sociology must conceive of itself as a participant (perhaps better informed, more systematic, more rule-conscious, yet nevertheless a participant) of this never ending, self-reflexive process of reinterpretation and devise its strategy accordingly. In practice, this will mean in all probability, replacing the ambitions of the judge of 'common beliefs,' healer of prejudices and umpire of truth with those of clarifier of interpretative rules and facilitator of communication; this will amount to the replacement of the dream of the legislator with the practice of an interpreter" (1992a, 204).

20 It is also worth noticing that Bauman's reflections on the role of contemporary "interpreters" were exemplary of the "translational turn"

that emerged in the humanities and social sciences in the late 1980s (Venuti 2000; Bassnett and Lefevere 1990). Doris Bachmann-Medick presented its assumptions as follows: "It is no longer possible to ignore the need for processes of cultural translation and their analysis, whether it is in cross-cultural contact, interreligious relations and conflicts, the integration strategies of culturally and ethnically diverse societies or examinations of the interfaces between the natural sciences and the study of culture. The globalized condition of world society, in particular, calls for increased attention to the problem of cross-cultural contact and the obstacles and room for maneuver in our dealings with cultural differences" ([2006] 2016, 175).

21 What is more, according to Bauman – inspired in this regard by Ernst Bloch ([1954–59] 1986) – intellectuals should inspire hope that the necessary social, political, and cultural transformations will be made. On his own utopian thinking, Keith Tester and Michael Hviid Jacobsen wrote: "With his faith in humanity and his commitment to the pursuit of possibilities, Bauman can be identified as a 'utopian of hope'" (Tester and Jacobsen 2005, 33).

22 In 2001 Bauman stated: "I no longer believe (as I did, to my shame, once believe) that 'the ends justify the means,' and I do not believe it for the simple reason that ends cannot be humane if they require inhuman means to be promoted. And so the dialogue with the experience of free men and women is the only door which can be used. That does not by itself mean that it will be used; a lot of effort is needed to open it and keep it open" (Bauman and Tester 2001, 157).

23 It is worth noting again at this point that in the 1960s Bauman considered conscience to be a "social product" (1962b, 45).

CHAPTER FIVE

1 Some of these publications take the form of a dialogue with other intellectuals or journalists.

2 Describing the number of subjects analyzed by Bauman in the course of this century, Michael Hvid Jacobsen, Sophia Marshman, and Keith Tester (2007, 14) described this period of his work as "the mosaic phase."

3 Bauman compared culture to "one of the departments of a world which has been fashioned into a gigantic department store experienced by people who have been turned into consumers first and foremost" (2011b, 17).

4 On the various aspects of the critique of Bauman's vision of consumer culture see Blackshaw (2008, 126–30).

5 In a conversation with Gabriela Ziewiec and Paweł Kozłowski, Bauman said on the subject: "In our society of individuals *de jure*, the society, so to speak, of the individualization of problems of supra-individual provenance, there is growing ... an unstoppable social need ... for open and conscious participation of sociology in dialogue with human experience (I mean the common experience of hoi polloi ...); the need for sociology to participate in the interpretation and continual reinterpretation of the meaning of this experience; to revealing such connections and conditions of individual vicissitudes and actions that go beyond the scope of individual view and may remain invisible for other partners in the dialogue" (Bauman, Ziewiec, and Kozłowski 2009, 4).

6 Protests against the Anti-counterfeiting Trade Agreement in Europe can be cited here as one of the numerous examples of such successful movements.

7 In a typology of attitudes toward globalization that is similar to that of Andreas Busch, Anthony Elliott described this perspective in the following way: "Alongside the sceptics of globalization were to be found the antiglobalizers. The anti-globalization brigade, in all its manifestations from anti-capitalist protesters to policy think-tanks, put forward a list of powerful charges cataloguing the sins of globalization. Globalism was allegedly empowering multinational corporations and speculative finance, compounding inequality and eroding democracy, promoting Western imperialism and the Americanization of the world, destroying environmental standards, as well as brutalizing the public sphere and the state governmental structures through which it operates. The emergence of a planetary-scale global market with ever-decreasing tariffs, ever-greater international production, as well as more integrated financial markets with higher trade flows, had unleashed a turbo-charged capitalism of unprecedented forms of economic exploitation and political oppression. Or so argued the anti-globalizers" (2009, 313).

8 In this context, it is worth recalling the words of Henning Bech referring to Bauman's particular sociological genre: "It is that of a *call* – an attempt to make an appeal to a possible ethical impulse that may inhere in human beings, by opening passways through the soundscapes of modern roar and postmodern barking so that we may not remain deaf to the unconditional call from those who need us" (Bech 2007, 374).

9 Katharina Niemeyer wrote on this issue: "There has always been a fascination for the, as we often call them, 'good old times.' But who would have thought, given the 1990s' imaginings of a future filled with technology, that the beginning of the new century would in fact be marked by an increase in expressions of nostalgia, and in nostalgic objects, media contents and styles?" (2014, 1). Simon Reynolds claimed: "This kind of retromania has become a dominant force in our culture, to the point where it feels like we've reached some kind of tipping point" (2010, xiv).

10 Boym distinguished two types of nostalgia: "restorative" and "reflective." She wrote: "Restorative nostalgia does not think of itself as nostalgia, but rather as truth and tradition. Reflective nostalgia dwells on the ambivalences of human longing and belonging and does not shy away from the contradiction of modernity. Restorative nostalgia protects the absolute truth, while reflective nostalgia calls it into doubt" (2001, xviii).

11 It is worth noticing that Ritzer wrote these words about a decade before the outbreak of the Covid-19 pandemic.

12 This paper will be published in English translation in: Zygmunt Bauman, *History and Politics: Selected Writings, Vol. 2*, translated by Katarzyna Bartoszyńska (Cambridge: Polity Press; forthcoming).

CONCLUSION

1 Among the many other materials gathered in the Janina and Zygmunt Bauman Papers at the Leeds University Library are the publications he studied, texts that he reviewed for academic presses, and documents pertaining to his work at universities in Warsaw, Tel Aviv, and Leeds.

2 Some of Bauman's papers written before 1968, including those on the theory of culture, were translated into other languages than Polish, including English, Italian, French, Hungarian, Hebrew, Czech, Slovak, and Serbo-Croatian. However, due to the passage of time, their influence also diminished. In recent years, initiatives have been taken to renew interest in his early theory of culture on a global scale (Bauman [1968c] 2018).

3 A crucial role in spreading Bauman's work to a wider audience was played by the change in the style of Bauman's writings that took place at the end of the twentieth century. This systematically resembled the exoteric discourse, relevant to his vision of sociology as "an ongoing dialogue with human experience" (Bauman and Tester 2001, 40).

4 Currently in production are two volumes: *History and Politics* and *Theory and Society*. They will form a trilogy, along with *Culture and Art* (Bauman [1966–2015] 2021). Work is also underway on Zygmunt Bauman's autobiography, found among the papers gathered at the Leeds University Library. It will be published as *My Life in Fragments* in fall 2022.

References

ARCHIVE MATERIALS

"Cultural Focus and Semiotic Density." Unpublished research project proposal, pp. 1–3. In Janina and Zygmunt Bauman Papers, MS2067/3/1.

Janina and Zygmunt Bauman Papers, Special Collections, University of Leeds Library.

Letters from Julia Kristeva to Zygmunt Bauman. 8 March 1967 and 22 January 1968. In Janina and Zygmunt Bauman Papers, MS2067/B/5/1.

Żółkiewski, Stefan. 1967. *Review of a Manuscript of Zygmunt Bauman's Book "Sketches in the Theory of Culture."* The book folder of *Sketches on the Theory of Culture*, 1967–68, Archives of the Ossolineum Publishing House, Wrocław, Poland, no. B-196.

BOOKS AND ARTICLES

Aidnik, Martin, and Michale Hviid Jacobsen. 2017. "Not Yet: Probing the Potentials and Problems in the Utopian Understanding of Ernst Bloch and Zygmunt Bauman." In *Beyond Bauman: Critical Engagement and Creative Excursions*, edited by Michael Hviid Jacobsen, 136–62. London: Routledge.

Agamben, Giorgio. (1995) 1998. Homo sacer: *Sovereign Power and Bare Life*. Translated by Daniel Heller-Roazen. Stanford, CA: Stanford University Press.

– (2003) 2005. *State of Exception*. Translated by Kevin Attell. Chicago: University of Chicago Press.

Agar, Michael. 1980. *The Professional Stranger: An Informal Introduction to Ethnography*. New York: Academic Press.

Alexander, Jeffrey C. 2001. "Robust Utopias and Civil Repairs." *International Sociology* 16, no. 4: 579–92.

– 2009. "'Globalization' as Collective Representation: The New Dream of a Cosmopolitan Civil Sphere." In *Globalization and Utopia: Critical Essays*, edited by Patrick Hayden and Chamsy el-Ojeili, 28–39. Basingstoke, UK: Palgrave Macmillan.

Appadurai, Arjun. 1996. *Modernity at Large: Cultural Dimension of Globalization*. Minneapolis: University of Minnesota Press.

Applebaum, Anne. 2020. *Twilight of Democracy: The Seductive Lure of Authoritarianism*. New York: Anchor Books.

Archer, Margaret. 1988. *Culture and Agency. The Place of Culture in Social Theory*. Cambridge: Cambridge University Press.

– 1995. *Realist Social Theory: The Morphogenetic Approach*. Cambridge: Cambridge University Press.

– 2000. *Being Human: The Problem of Agency*. Cambridge: Cambridge University Press.

Arendt, Hannah. 1951. *The Origins of Totalitarianism*. New York: Schocken Books.

Bachmann-Medick, Doris. (2006) 2016. *Cultural Turns: New Orientations in the Study of Culture*. Translated by Adam Blahut. Berlin: De Gruyter.

Barthes, Roland. (1967) 1977. "The Death of the Author." In *Image, Music, Text*. Translated by Stephen Heath, 142–8. New York: Hill & Wang.

Bassnett, Susan, and André Lafevere, eds. 1990. *Translation, History and Culture*. London: Printer Publishers.

Bateson, Gregory. (1935) 1972. "Culture Contact and Schismogenesis." In *Steps to an Ecology of Mind: Collective Essays in Anthropology, Psychiatry, Evolution, and Epistemology*, 71–82. Northvale, NJ: Jason Aronson.

Baudrillard, Jean. (1981) 1983. *Simulation*. Translated by Paul Foss, Paul Batton, and Philip Beitchman. New York: Semiotext(e).

Bauer, Yehuda. 2001. *Rethinking the Holocaust*. New Haven, CT: Yale University Press.

Bauman, Janina. 1986. *Winter in the Morning: A Young Girl's Life in the Warsaw Ghetto and Beyond, 1939–1945*. New York: Free Press.

Bauman, Zygmunt. 1955. "Od mitu 'społeczeństwa managerów' do apologii dywersji i agresji." *Myśl filozoficzna* 1:168–96.

– 1957a. "O potrzebie socjologii partii." *Myśl Filozoficzna* 2:3–26.

– 1957b. "Traktat o biurokracji." *Twórczość* 9:103–18.

– 1957c. *Zagadnienia centralizmu demokratycznego w pracach Lenina*. Warsaw: Książka i Wiedza.

– 1959. *Socjalizm brytyjski: Źródła, filozofia, doktryna polityczna*. Warsaw: Państwowe Wydawnictwo Naukowe.

– (1960a) 1972a. *Between Class and Elite: The Evolution of the British Labour Movement; A Sociological Study*. Translated by Sheila Patterson. Manchester, UK: Manchester University Press.

– 1960b. *Kariera: Cztery szkice socjologiczne*. Warsaw: Iskry.
– 1962a. "Social Structure of the Party Organization in Industrial Works." *The Polish Sociological Bulletin* 3–4:50–64.
– 1962b. *Społeczeństwo, w którym żyjemy*. Warsaw: Książka i Wiedza.
– 1962c. "Struktura władzy społeczności lokalnej." *Studia Socjologiczno-Polityczne* 12:7–30.
– 1962d. "Values and Standards of Success of the Warsaw Youth." *The Polish Sociological Bulletin* 1–2:77–90.
– 1963. "Antonio Gramsci – czyli socjologia w działaniu." *Kultura i Społeczeństwo* 1:19–34.
– 1964a. "Bieguny analizy kulturowej." *Studia Socjologiczne* 3:51–91.
– 1964b. *Zarys marksistowskiej teorii społeczeństwa*. Warsaw: Państwowe Wydawnictwo Naukowe.
– 1965. "Osobowość – kultura – struktura społeczna." *Studia Socjologiczne* 2:203–33.
– 1966a. *Kultura i społeczeństwo: Preliminaria*. Warsaw: Państwowe Wydawnictwo Naukowe.
– (1966b) 2021. "Culture and Society: Semantic and Genetic Connections." Translated by Katarzyna Bartoszyńska. In *Culture and Art: Selected Writings, Vol. 1*, 1–32. Cambridge: Polity Press.
– (1966–2015) 2021. *Culture and Art: Selected Writings, Vol. 1*, translated by Katarzyna Bartoszyńska. Cambridge: Polity Press.
– 1967a. "Modern Times, Modern Marxism." *Social Research* 3:399–415.
– (1967b) 2021. "Notes beyond Time." Translated by Katarzyna Bartoszyńska. In *Culture and Art: Selected Writings, Vol. 1*, 33–49. Cambridge: Polity Press.
– 1968a. "Marx and the Contemporary Theory of Culture." *Social Science Information* 3:19–33.
– 1968b. "O frustracji i kuglarzach." *Kultura* 12:5–21.
– (1968c) 2018. *Sketches in the Theory of Culture*. Translated by Katarzyna Bartoszyńska. Cambridge: Polity Press.
– 1969a. "The End of Polish Jewry: A Sociological Review." *Bulletin on Soviet and East European Jewish Affairs* 3:3–8.
– 1969b. "Przedmowa." In Zygmunt Bauman et al., *Wydarzenia marcowe 1968*, 2–23. Paris: Instytut Literacki.
– 1971a. "20 Years After: Crisis of Soviet-Type Systems." *Problems of Communism* 6:45–53.
– 1971b. "Social Dissent in the East European Political System." *Archives Européennes de Sociologie* 1:25–51.

– 1971c. "Use of Information: When Social Information Becomes Desired." *Annals of the American Academy of Political and Social Science* 1:20–31.

– 1972a. "Culture, Values and Science of Society." *The University of Leeds Review* 2:185–203.

– 1972b. "Praxis: The Controversial Culture-Society Paradigm." In *Rules of the Game: Cross-Disciplinary Essays in Scholarly Thought*, edited by Teodor Shanin, 303–21. London: Tavistock.

– 1972c. "The Second Generation Socialism: A Review of Socio-cultural Trends in Contemporary Polish Society." In *Political Oppositions in One-Party States*, edited by Leonard Bertram Shapiro, 217–40. London: Macmillan.

– 1973a. "Between State and Society." *International Journal of Contemporary Sociology* 1:9–25.

– 1973b. *Culture as Praxis*. London: Routledge & Kegan Paul.

– 1973c. "On the Philosophical Status of Ethnomethodology." *Social Review* 1:5–23.

– 1973d. "The Structuralist Promise." *The British Journal of Sociology* 1:67–83.

– 1974. "Officialdom and Class: Bases of Inequality in Socialist Society." In *The Social Analysis of Class Structure*, edited by Frank Parkin, 129–48. London: Tavistock.

– 1976a. "East Europe and Soviet Social Science: A Case Study in Stimulus Diffusion." In *The Influence of East Europe and the Soviet West on the USSR*, edited by Roman Szporluk, 91–116. New York: Praeger.

– (1976b) 2021. "Jorge Luis Borges, Or Why Understanding Is Not What it Seems to Be." In *Culture and Art: Selected Writings, Vol. 1*, 84–102. Cambridge: Polity Press.

– 1976c. "The Party in the System Management Phase: Change and Continuity." In *Authoritarian Politics in Communist Europe: Uniformity and Diversity in One-Party States*, edited by Andrew C. Janos, 81–108. Berkeley: Institute of International Studies, University of California.

– 1976d. *Socialism: The Active Utopia*. London: George Allen & Unwin.

– 1976e. *Towards a Critical Sociology: An Essay on Common-Sense and Emancipation*. London: Routledge & Kegan Paul.

– 1978. *Hermeneutics and Social Science: Approaches to Understanding*. London: Hutchinson.

– 1981. "On the Maturation of Socialism." *Telos* 47:48–54.

– 1982. *Memories of Class: The Pre-history and After-Life of Class*. London: Routledge & Kegan Paul.

– 1983. "Industrialism, Consumerism and Power." *Theory, Culture & Society* 3:32–43.

– 1985. "On the Origins of Civilisation: A Historical Note." *Theory, Culture & Society* 3:7–14.

– 1987. *Legislators and Interpreters: On Modernity, Post-Modernity and Intellectuals*. Cambridge: Polity Press.

– 1988a. *Freedom*. Milton Keynes, UK: Open University Press.

– 1988b. "On Immoral Reason and Illogical Morality." *Polin* 3:294–301.

– 1989a. "Hermeneutics and Modern Social Theory." In *Social Theory of Modern Societies: Giddens and His Critics*, edited by David Held and John B. Thompson, 34–55. Cambridge: Cambridge University Press.

– 1989b. "Legislators and Interpreters: Culture as Ideology of Intellectuals." In *Social Structure and Culture*, edited by Hans Haferkamp, 313–32. Berlin: De Gruyter.

– 1989c. *Modernity and the Holocaust*. Cambridge: Polity Press.

– 1989d. Review of *Culture and Agency: The Place of Culture in Society*, by M.S. Archer. *History of the Human Sciences* 2:260–5.

– 1990. "Effacing the Face: On the Social Management of Moral Proximity." *Theory, Culture & Society* 1:5–38.

– 1991a. *Modernity and Ambivalence*. Ithaca, NY: Cornell University Press.

– 1991b. "The Social Manipulation of Morality, Moralizing Actors, Adiaphorizing Action." *Theory, Culture & Society* 1:139–53.

– 1992a. *Intimations of Postmodernity*. London: Routledge.

– 1992b. *Mortality, Immortality and Other Life Strategies*. Cambridge: Polity Press.

– 1993. *Postmodern Ethics*. Oxford: Wiley-Blackwell.

– 1994. *Alone Again: Ethics after Certainty*. London: Demos.

– (1995a) 2021. *Einstein Meets Magritte: Postmodernity Is Born*. In *Culture and Art: Selected Writings, Vol. 1*, 114–18. Cambridge: Polity Press.

– 1995b. *Life in Fragments: Essays in Postmodern Morality*. Oxford: Basil Blackwell.

– 1996. "From Pilgrim to Tourist – Or a Short Story of Identity." In *Questions of Cultural Identity*, edited by Stuart Hall and Paul du Gay, 18–36. London: Sage.

– 1997a. "Morality Begins at Home; Or, Can There be a Levinasian Macro-Ethics?" In *Closeness: An Ethics*, edited by Harald Jodalen and Arne Johan Vetlesen, 218–45. Oslo: Scandinavian University Press.

– 1997b. *Postmodernity and Its Discontents*. Cambridge: Polity Press.
– 1998a. *Globalization: The Human Consequences*. New York: Columbia University Press.
– 1998b. "On Art, Death and Postmodernity – And What They Do to Each Other." In *Stopping the Process: Contemporary View on Art and Exhibition*, edited by Mika Hannula, 21–34. Helsinki: Nordic Institute for Contemporary Art.
– 1998c. "On Glocalization: Or Globalization for Some, Localization for Some Others." *Thesis Eleven* 54:37–49
– 1998d. *Work, Consumerism and the New Poor*. Milton Keynes, UK: Open University Press.
– 1999. *Culture as Praxis*. New edition. Sage: London.
– 2000a. "Am I My Brother's Keeper?" *European Journal of Social Work* 1:5–11.
– 2000b. "Ethics of Individuals." *Canadian Journal of Sociology* 1:83–96.
– 2000c. *Liquid Modernity*. Cambridge: Polity Press.
– 2001a. *Community: Seeking Safety in an Insecure World*. Cambridge: Polity Press.
– 2001b. "Consuming Life." *Journal of Consumer Culture* 1:9–29.
– 2001c. "Imiona cierpienia, imiona wstydu." *Tygodnik Powszechny* 38:9.
– 2001d. *The Individualized Society*. Cambridge: Polity Press.
– 2002. *Society under Siege*. Cambridge: Polity Press.
– 2003. *Liquid Love: On the Frailty of Human Bonds*. Cambridge: Polity Press.
– 2004a. *Europe: An Unfinished Adventure*. Cambridge: Polity. Press.
– 2004b. *Identity: Conversations with Benedetto Vecchi*. Cambridge: Polity Press.
– 2004c. *Wasted Lives: Modernity and Its Outcasts*. Cambridge: Polity Press.
– 2005. *Liquid Life*. Cambridge: Polity Press.
– 2006. *Liquid Fear*. Cambridge: Polity Press.
– 2007a. *Consuming Life*. Cambridge: Polity Press.
– 2007b. "The Liquid Modern Adventures of the 'Sovereign Expression of Life.'" In *Concern for the Other: Perspectives on the Ethics of K. E. Løgstrup*, edited by Svend Andersen and Kees van Kooten Niekerk, 113–38. Notre Dame, IN: University of Notre Dame.
– 2007c. *Liquid Times: Living in an Age of Uncertainty*. Cambridge: Polity Press.
– 2008a. "Bauman on Bauman – Pro Domo Sua." In *The Sociology of Zygmunt Bauman: Challenges and Critique*, edited by Michael Hviid Jacobsen and Poul Poder, 231–40. Aldershot, UK: Ashgate.
– 2008b. *Does Ethics Have a Chance in a World of Consumers?* Cambridge, MA: Harvard University Press.

– 2010a. *44 Letters from the Liquid Modern World*. Cambridge: Polity Press.
– 2010b. "Conclusion: The Triple Challenge." In *Bauman's Challenge: Sociological Issues for the 21st Century*, edited by Mark Davis and Keith Tester, 200–5. Basingstoke, UK: Palgrave Macmillan.
– 2011a. *Collateral Damage: Social Inequalities in a Global Age*. Cambridge: Polity Press.
– 2011b. *Culture in a Liquid Modern World*. Cambridge: Polity Press.
– 2011c. "Selves as the Objects of Consumption." In *Beyond the Consumption Bubble*, edited by Karin M. Ekström and Kay Glans, 85–98. London: Routledge.
– 2012. *This Is Not a Diary*. Cambridge: Polity Press.
– 2013. *Does the Richness of a Few Benefit Us All* Hannerz*?* Cambridge: Polity Press.
– 2016a. "'Liquid modernity' Fifteen Years After (2015)." In *The New Bauman Reader: Thinking Sociologically in Liquid Modern Times*, edited by Tony Blackshaw, 391–402. Manchester, UK: Manchester University Press.
– 2016b. *Strangers at Our Door*. Cambridge: Polity Press.
– (2017a) 2018. Afterword to *Sketches in the Theory of Culture*. Translated by Katarzyna Bartoszyńska, 251–5. Cambridge: Polity Press.
– 2017b. *A Chronicle of Crisis, 2011–16*. London: Social Europe Edition.
– 2017c. *Retrotopia*. Cambridge: Polity Press.
– 2017d. "Some of the Foremost Challenges to the Status Quo." *Studia Socjologiczno-Polityczne: Seria Nowa* 2:31–46.
Bauman, Zygmunt, Irena Bauman, Jerzy Kociatkiewicz, and Monika Kostera. 2015. *Management in a Liquid Modern World*. Cambridge: Polity Press.
Bauman, Zygmunt, and Carlo Bordoni. 2014. *State of Crisis*. Cambridge: Polity Press.
Bauman, Zygmunt, and Leonidas Donskis. 2013. *Moral Blindness*. Cambridge: Polity Press.
Bauman, Zygmunt, and Peter Haffner. (2017) 2020. *Making the Familiar Unfamiliar: Conversation with Peter Haffner*. Translated by Daniel Steuer. Cambridge: Polity Press.
Bauman, Zygmunt, Roman Kubicki, and Anna Zeidler-Janiszewska. 2009. Życie w kontekstach. Rozmowy o tym, co za nami i o tym, co przed nami. Warsaw: Wydawnictwa Akademickie i Profesjonalne.
Bauman, Zygmunt, and Thomas Leoncini. 2018. *Born Liquid*. Cambridge: Polity Press.

Bauman, Zygmunt, and Ezio Mauro. 2016. *Babel*. Cambridge: Polity Press.
Bauman, Zygmunt, and Rein Raud. 2015. *Practices of Selfhood*. Cambridge: Polity Press.
Bauman, Zygmunt, and Chris Rojek. 2004. "The Consumerist Syndrome in Contemporary Society: An Interview with Zygmunt Bauman." *Journal of Consumer Culture* 3:291–312.
Bauman, Zygmunt, and Citlali Rovirosa-Madrazo. 2010. *Living on Borrowed Time*. Cambridge: Polity Press.
Bauman, Zygmunt, and Keith Tester. 2001. *Conversations with Zygmunt Bauman*. Cambridge: Polity Press.
Bauman, Zygmunt, Keith Tester, and Michael Hviid Jacobsen. 2013. *What Use Is Sociology?* Cambridge: Polity Press.
Bauman, Zygmunt, and Jerzy Wiatr. 1953. "O roli mas w historii." *Myśl Filozoficzna* 3:69–99.
– 1957. "Marksizm a socjologia współczesna." *Myśl Filozoficzna* 1:3–23.
Bauman, Zygmunt, Gabriela Ziewiec, and Paweł Kozłowski. 2009. "*Świat niedoskonały. Nowe Książki* 6:4–9.
Bech, Henning. 2007. "Bauman's Call." In *Bauman beyond Postmodernity: Critical Appraisals, Conversations and Annotated Bibliography, 1989–2005*, edited by Michael Hviid Jacobsen, Sophia Marshman, and Keith Tester, 369–74. Aalborg, Denmark: Aalborg University Press.
Beck, Ulrich. 2000. "*Zombie* Categories." In *The Art of Life: On Living, Love and Death*, edited by Jonathan Rutheford, 35–51. London: Lawrence.
– 2010. "Odmiany indywidualizacji – perspektywa kosmopolityczna." Translated by Michał Bogdan. In *Zrozumieć nowoczesność. Księga Jubileuszowa Zygmunta Baumana*, edited by Andrzej Chrzanowski, Wiesław Godzic, and Anna Zeidler-Janiszewska, 9–15. Warsaw: Wydawnictwo Officyna.
Beck, Ulrich, and Elisabeth Beck-Gernsheim. 2002. *Individualization: Institutionalized Individualism and Its Social and Political Consequences*. London: Sage.
Beck, Ulrich, Anthony Giddens, and Scott Lash. 1994. *Reflexive Modernization: Politics, Tradition and Aesthetics in the Modern Social Order*. Cambridge: Polity Press.
Beck, Ulrich, and Edgar Grande. (2004) 2007. *Cosmopolitan Europe*. Translated by Ciaran Cronin. Cambridge: Polity Press.
Beilharz, Peter. 2000. *Zygmunt Bauman: Dialectic of Modernity*. London: Sage.

Bendix, Reinhard. 1960. *Max Weber: An Intellectual Portrait*. Garden City, NY: Doubleday.

Benedict, Ruth. (1929) 1931. "The Science of Custom." In *The Making of Man: An Outline of Anthropology*, edited by Victor Francis Calverton, 805–17. New York: The Modern Library, Inc.

– 1934. *Patterns of Culture*. New York: Houghton Mifflin.

Benjamin. Walter. (1940) 1969. *Illuminations: Essays and Reflections*. Translated by Harry Zohn. New York: Schocken Books.

Bentham, Jeremy. (1791) 2017. *Panopticon: The Inspection House*. Whithorn, UK: Anodos Books.

Berlin, Isaiah. 1990. *The Crooked Timber of Humanity: Chapters in the History of Ideas*. Edited by Henry Hardy. London: Murray.

Bertman, Stephen. 1998. *Hyperculture: The Human Cost of Speed*. Westport, CT: Praeger.

Best, Shaun. 2017. "Voice and Generalized Other in the Ethical Writings of Zygmunt Bauman." In *Beyond Bauman: Critical Engagement and Creative Excursions*, edited by Michael Hviid Jacobsen, 46–64. London: Routledge.

Blackshaw, Tony. 2005. *Zygmunt Bauman*. London: Routledge.

– 2008. "Bauman on Consumerism – Living the Market-Mediated Life." In *The Sociology of Zygmunt Bauman: Challenges and Critique*, edited by Michale Hviid Jacobsen and Poul Poder, 117–35. Aldershot, UK: Ashgate.

Bloch, Ernst. (1954–59) 1986. *The Principle of Hope*. Vols. 1–3, translated by Neville Plaice, Stephen Plaice, and Paul Knight. Oxford: Basil Blackwell.

Bloom, Jack M. 2013. *Seeing through the Eyes of the Polish Revolution: Solidarity and the Struggle against Communism in Poland*. Leiden: Brill.

Bonnell, Victoria E., and Lynn Hunt, eds. 1999. *Beyond the Cultural Turn: New Directions in the Study of Society and Culture*. Berkeley: University of California Press.

Bordoni, Carlo. 2016. *Interregnum: Beyond Liquid Modernity*. Bielefeld, Germany: Transcript Verlag.

Bourdieu, Pierre. (1979) 1984. *Distinction: A Social Critique of the Judgment of Taste*. Translated by Richard Nice. Cambridge, MA: Harvard University Press.

– (1980) 1990. *The Logic of Practice*. Translated by Richard Nice. Cambridge: Polity Press.

Boym, Svetlana. 2001. *The Future of Nostalgia*, New York: Basic Books.

Brier, Robert. 2021. *Poland's Solidarity Movement and the Global Politics of Human Rights*. Cambridge: Cambridge University Press.

Brownlee, Billie Jeanne. 2020. *New Media and Revolution: Resistance and Dissent in Pre-uprising Syria*. Montreal: McGill-Queen's University Press.

Brzeziński, Dariusz. (2017) 2018. "A Message in a Bottle: On the Recovered Work of Zygmunt Bauman." In *Sketches in the Theory of Culture*, by Zygmunt Bauman, vii–xxv. Cambridge: Polity Press.

– 2018. "Consumerist Culture in Zygmunt Bauman's Critical Sociology: A Comparative Analysis of His Polish and English Writings." *Polish Sociological Review* 1:77–94.

– 2020. "Culture of Dialogue in the Context of the Rise of Nationalism: On the Engaged Nature of Zygmunt Bauman's Writings." *Culture & Society* 2:33–50.

Brzeziński, Dariusz, Mark Davis, Jack Palmer, and Tom Campbell. 2021. "Culture and Art in the Sociological Imagination of Zygmunt Bauman." In *Culture and Art: Selected Writings, Vol. 1*, by Zygmunt Bauman. xi–xxxix. Cambridge: Polity Press.

Busch, Andreas. 2000. "Unpacking the Globalization Debate: Approaches, Evidence and Data." In *Demystifying Globalization*, edited by Colin Hay and David Marsh, 21–48. Basingstoke, UK: Palgrave.

Campbell, Tom, Mark Davis, and Jack Palmer. 2018. "Hidden Paths in Zygmunt Bauman's Sociology: Editorial Introduction." Theory, Culture & Society 35, no. 7–8: 351–74.

Campbell, Tom, and Chris Till. 2010. "Resistance towards Ethics." In *Bauman's Challenge: Sociological Issues for the 21st Century*, edited by Mark Davis and Keith Tester, 172–88. Basingstoke, UK: Palgrave Macmillan.

Camus, Albert. (1942) 1955. *The Myth of Sisyphus, and Other Essays*. Translated by Justin O'Brien. New York: Knopf.

– 1953. *The Rebel*. Translated by Anthony Bower. London: Hamish Hamilton.

Carleheden, Mikael. 2008. "Bauman on Politics – Stillborn Democracy." In *The Sociology of Zygmunt Bauman: Challenges and Critique*, edited by Michael Hviid Jacobsen and Poul Poder, 175–92. Aldershot, UK: Ashgate.

Carrithers, Michael. 1992. *Why Humans Have Cultures: Explaining Anthropology and Social Diversity*. Oxford: Oxford University Press.

Carter, Ian. 1997. "Rain Steam & What?" *Oxford Art Journal* 20, no. 2: 3–4.

Castells, Manuel. 1996. *The Rise of the Network Society*. Vol. 1 of *The Information Age: Economy, Society and Culture*. Cambridge, MA: Blackwell.

Chałubiński, Mirosław. 2006. "The Sociological Ideas of Stanisław Ossowski:

His Life, Fundamental Ideas and Sociology in Polish and World Science." *Journal of Classical Sociology* 3:283–309.

Cheyette, Bryan. 2022. "Off-the-Scene: An Afterword." In *Revisiting Modernity and the Holocaust: Heritage, Dilemmas, Extensions*, edited by Jack Palmer and Dariusz Brzeziński, 232–45. Abingdon, UK: Routledge.

Chomsky, Noam. 1965. *Aspects of the Theory of Syntax*. Cambridge, MA: MIT Press.

Cirtautas, Arista Maria. 1997. *The Polish Solidarity Movement: Revolution, Democracy and Natural Rights*. London: Routledge.

Click, Melissa A., and Suzanne Scott, eds. 2018. *The Routledge Companion to Media Fandom*. London: Routledge.

Clifford, James, and George E. Marcus. 1986. *Writing Culture: The Poetics and Politics of Ethnography*. Berkeley: University of California Press.

Connor, Steven. 1989. *Postmodernist Culture: An Introduction to Theories of the Contemporary*. New York: Blackwell.

Cousins, A.D., and Damian Grace, eds. 1994. *More's Utopia and the Utopian Inheritance*. Lanham, MD: University Press of America.

Crone, Manni. 2008. "Bauman on Ethics – Intimate Ethics for a Global World?" In *The Sociology of Zygmunt Bauman: Challenges and Critique*, edited by Michael Hviid Jacobsen, and Poul Poder, 59–74. Aldershot, UK: Ashgate.

Czerwiński, Marcin. 1965. "Uwagi krytyczne o socjologii kultury." Kultura i Społeczeństwo 3:9–28.

Dawson, Matt. 2017. "Keeping Other Options Alive: Zygmunt Bauman, Hermeneutics and Sociological Alternatives." In *Beyond Bauman: Critical Engagement and Creative Excursions*, edited by Michael Hviid Jacobsen, 224–42. London: Routledge.

Davis, Mark. 2008a. "Bauman on Globalization – The Human Consequences of a Liquid World." In *The Sociology of Zygmunt Bauman: Challenges and Critique*, edited by Michael Hviid Jacobsen and Poul Poder, 137–53. Aldershot, UK: Ashgate.

– 2008b. *Freedom and Consumerism: A Critique of Zygmunt Bauman's Sociology*. Aldershot, UK: Ashgate.

– ed. 2013. *Liquid Sociology: Metaphor in Zygmunt Bauman's Analysis of Modernity*. Farnham, UK: Ashgate.

– 2020. "Hermeneutics *contra* Fundamentalism: Zygmunt Bauman's Method for Thinking in Dark Times." *Thesis Eleven* 156, no. 1: 27–44.

Davis, Todd F., and Kenneth Womack, eds. 2001. *Mapping the Ethical Turn: A Reader in Ethics, Culture and Literary Theory*. Charlottesville: University Press of Virginia.

Deledda, Grazia. 1894. *Tradizioni popolari di Nuoro in Sardegna*. Rome: Forzani e C. Tipografi Del Senato.

Deleuze, Gilles, and Félix Guattari. (1972) 1977. *Anti-Oedipus. Capitalism and Schizophrenia*. Vol. 1, translated by Robert Hurley, Mark Seem, and Helen R. Lane. Minneapolis: University of Minnesota Press.

– (1980) 1987. *A Thousand Plateaus: Capitalism and Schizophrenia*. Vol. 2, translated by Brian Massumi. Minneapolis: University of Minnesota Press.

DeLillo, Don. 2003. *Cosmopolis*. London: Picador.

Derrida, Jacques. (1967) 1976. *Of Gramatology*. Translated by Gayatri Chakravorty Spivak. Baltimore, MD: John Hopkins University Press.

– (1969) 1981. *Dissemination*. Translated by Barbara Johnson. Chicago: University of Chicago Press.

DiMaggio, Paul. 1997. "Culture and Cognition." *Annual Review of Sociology*, 263–87.

Dostoevsky, Fyodor. (1872) 2000. *Demons*. Translated by Richard Pevear and Larissa Volokhonsky, London: Everyman.

Du Gay, Paul. 1999. "Is Bauman's Bureau Weber's Bureau? A Comment." *British Journal of Sociology* 4:575–87.

Douglas, Mary. 1966. *Purity and Danger*. London: Routledge & Kegan Paul.

– 1970. *Natural Symbols: Explorations in Cosmology*. London: Barrie & Rockliff, Cresset Press.

Durkheim, Émile. (1895) 1982. *The Rules of Sociological Method*. Translated by W.D. Halls. New York: Free Press.

Eisler, Jerzy. 1998. "March 1968 in Poland." In *1968: The World Transformed*, edited by Carole Fink, Philipp Gassert, and Detlef Juner, 237–52. Cambridge: Cambridge University Press.

Elias, Norbert. (1939) 1997. *Civilizing Process: The History of Manners and State Formation and Civilization*. Translated by Edmund Jephcott. Oxford: Blackwell.

Elliott, Anthony, ed. 2007. *The Contemporary Bauman*. London: Routledge.

– 2009. *Contemporary Social Theory: An Introduction*. London: Routledge.

Elliott, Anthony, and Charles Lemert. 2006. *The New Individualism: The Emotional Costs of Globalization*. London: Routledge.

Engbersen, Gotfried. 2012. *Migration Transitions in an Era of Liquid Migrations: Reflections on Fassmann and Reeger*. In *European Immigrations: Trends,*

Structures and Policy Implications, edited by Marek Okólski, 91–105. Amsterdam: Amsterdam University Press.

Engels, Frederick. (1880) 1935. *Socialism: Utopian and Scientific*. Translated by Edward Aveling. New York: International Publishers.

Eriksen, Thomas Hylland. 2001. *Tyranny of the Moment: Fast and Slow Time in the Information Age*. London: Pluto Press.

Evens, T.M.S., and Don Handelman. 2006. *The Manchester School: Practice and Ethnographic Praxis in Anthropology*. New York: Berghahn.

Featherstone, Mike. 1991. *Consumer Culture and Postmodernism*. London: Sage.

Fekete, John, ed. 1988. *Life after Postmodernism: Essays on Value and Culture*. Basingstoke, UK: Macmillan Education.

Foucault, Michel. (1969) 1972. *The Archaeology of Knowledge and the Discourse on Language*. Translated by A.M. Sheridan Smith. New York: Pantheon Books.

– (1975) 1977. *Discipline and Punish: The Birth of the Prison*. Translated by Alan Sheridan. New York: Pantheon Books.

Fox, Richard G. 1985. *Lions of the Punjab: Culture in the Making*. Berkeley: University of California Press.

Freud, Sigmund. (1923) 1949. *The Ego and the Id*. Translated by Joan Riviere. London: Hogarth Press and the Institute of Psycho-Analysis; Toronto: Clarke, Irwin.

– (1930) 1962. *Civilization and Its Discontents*. Translated by James Strachey. New York: W.W. Norton.

Friedland, Roger, and John Mohr. 2004. *Matters of Culture: Cultural Sociology in Practice*. Cambridge: Cambridge University Press.

Frisby, Davis, and Mike Featherstone, eds. 1997. *Simmel on Culture: Selected Writings*. London: Sage.

Gadamer, George. (1960) 1975. *Truth and Method*. Edited by John Cumming and Garret Barden. Translated by William Glen-Doepel. London: Sheed & Ward.

Garber, Marjorie, Beatrice Hanssen, and Rebecca L. Walkowitz, eds. 2000. *The Turn to Ethics*. New York: Routledge.

Gellner, Ernest. 1983. *Nations and Nationalism*. Oxford: Basil Blackwell.

Giddens, Anthony. 1976. *New Rules of Sociological Method: A Positive Critique of Interpretative Sociologies*. New York: Basic Books.

– 1984. *The Constitution of Society: Outline of the Theory of Structuration*. Cambridge: Polity Press.

– 1991. *Modernity and Self-identity: Self and Society in the Late Modern Age*. Stanford, CA: Stanford University Press.

– 2006. *Europe in the Global Age*. Cambridge: Polity Press.

Gingrich, Andre, and Marcus Banks, eds. 2006. *Neo-nationalism in Europe and Beyond: Perspectives from Social Anthropology*. New York: Berghahn Books.

Goldhagen, Daniel J. 1996. *Hitler's Willing Executioners: Ordinary Germans and the Holocaust*. New York: Vintage Books.

Gramsci, Antonio. (1948–51) 1971. *Selections from the Prison Notebooks*. Edited and translated by Quentin Hoare and Geoffrey Nowell Smith. London: Lawrence & Wishart.

Griswold, Wendy. 2013. *Cultures and Societies in a Changing World*. Thousand Oaks, CA: Sage.

Gumplowicz, Ludwik. 1899. *The Outlines of Sociology*. Translated by Frederic W. Moore. Philadelphia: American Academy of Political and Social Science.

Habermas, Jürgen. (1968) 1972. *Knowledge and Human Interest*. Translated by Jeremy Shapiro. Boston: Beacon Press.

– 1970. "Towards a Theory of Communicative Competence." *Inquiry: An Interdisciplinary Journal of Philosophy* 13, nos. 1–4: 360–75.

– (1981) 1984–87. *The Theory of Communicative Action*. Vols. 1–2. Translated by Thomas A. McCarthy. Boston: Beacon Press.

– (1985) 1987. *The Philosophical Discourse of Modernity: Twelve Lectures*. Translated by Frederik Lawrence. Cambridge: Polity Press.

Hall, Stuart, and Tony Jefferson, eds. 1976. *Resistance through Rituals: Youth Subcultures in Post-War Britain*. London: HarperCollins Academic.

Hannerz, Ulf. 1996. *Transnational Connections: Culture, People, Places*. London: Routledge.

Harvey, David. 2000. *Spaces of Hope*, Berkeley: University of California Press.

Hesse, Herman. (1927) 2001. *Steppenwolf*. Translated by Basil Creighton. London: Penguin Books.

Hilberg, Raul. 1961. *The Destruction of the European Jews*. Chicago: Quadrangle Books.

Hirst, Benjamin Adam. 2014. "After Lévinas: Assessing Zygmunt Bauman's 'Ethical Turn.'" *European Journal of Social Theory* 17, no. 2: 184–98.

Hobsbawm, Eric. 2002. *Interesting Times: A Twentieth-Century Life*. New York: Pantheon Books.

Hobsbawm, Eric, and Terence Ranger. 1983. *The Invention of Tradition*. Cambridge: Cambridge University Press.

Hochfeld, Julian. (1957) 1982. "Kelles-Krauza marksizm otwarty." In *Marksizm, Socjologia, Socjalizm. Wybór Pism*, 190–202. Warsaw: Państwowe Wydawnictwo Naukowe.

– 1958. "Marksizm a socjologia stosunków politycznych." *Studia Socjologiczno-Polityczne* 1:3–24.

Hochschild, Arlie Russell. 2016. *Strangers in Their Own Land: Anger and Mourning on the American Right*. New York: New Press.

Hoggart, Richard. 1969. *Contemporary Cultural Studies: An Approach to the Study of Literature and Society*. Birmingham, UK: Centre for Contemporary Cultural Studies.

Holmes, Brooke, and Karen Marta. 2017. *Liquid Antiquity*. Athens, Greece: Deste Foundation for Contemporary Art.

Hookway, Nicholas, and Douglas Ezzy. 2017. "Aesthetic and Relational Ethics: Beyond Bauman's Postmodern Ethics." In *Beyond Bauman: Critical Engagement and Creative Excursions*, edited by Michael Hviid Jacobsen, 29–45. London: Routledge.

Horkheimer, Max, and Theodor Adorno. (1947) 1972. *Dialectic of Enlightenment*. Translated by John Cumming. Stanford, CA: Stanford University Press.

Jacobsen, Michael Hviid. 2007. "Solid Modernity, Liquid Utopia – Liquid Modernity, Solid Utopia: Ubiquitous Utopianism as a Trademark of the Work of Zygmunt Bauman." In *The Contemporary Bauman*, edited by Anthony Elliott, 217–40. London: Routledge.

– 2008. "Bauman on Utopia – Welcome to the Hunting Zone." In *The Sociology of Zygmunt Bauman: Challenges and Critique*, edited by Michael Hviid Jacobsen and Poul Poder, 209–30. Aldershot, UK: Ashgate.

– 2016. "Liquid Modern 'Utopia' – Zygmunt Bauman on the Transformation of Utopia." In *Utopia: Social Theory and the Future*, edited by Michael Hviid Jacibsen and Keith Tester, 69–96. London: Routledge.

– ed. 2017. *Beyond Bauman: Critical Engagement and Creative Excursions*. London: Routledge.

– ed. 2020. *Nostalgia Now: Cross-Disciplinary Perspectives on the Past in the Present*. Abingdon, UK: Routledge.

Jacobsen, Michael Hviid, and Claus D. Hansen. 2017. "Critical Theory Old and New: Theodor W. Adorno Meets Zygmunt Bauman in the Shopping Mall." In *Beyond Bauman: Critical Engagement and Creative Excursions*, edited by Michael Hviid Jacobsen, 107–35. London: Routledge.

Jacobsen, Michael Hviid, and Sophia Marshman. 2008. "Bauman on Metaphors – A Harbinger of Humanistic Hybrid Sociology." In *The Sociology of Zygmunt Bauman:. Challenges and Critique*, edited by Michael Hviid Jacobsen and Poul Poder, 19–39. Aldershot, UK: Ashgate.

Jacobsen, Michael Hviid, Sophia Marshman, and Keith Tester. 2007. *Bauman beyond Postmodernity: Critical Appraisals, Conversations and Annotated Bibliography, 1989–2005*. Aalborg, Denmark: Aalborg University Press.

Jacoby, Russel. 2005. *Picture Imperfect: Utopian Thought for an Anti-Utopian Age*. New York: Columbia University Press.

Jacyno, Małgorzata. 2007. *Kultura indywidualizmu*. Warsaw: Wydawnictwo Naukowe PWN.

Jakobson, Roman. 1960. "Closing Statement: Linguistics and Poetics." In *Style in Language*, edited by Thomas A. Sebeok, 350–77. Cambridge. MA: MIT Press.

Jameson, Fredric. 1991. *Postmodernism, Or, The Cultural Logic of Late Capitalism*. Durham, NC: Duke University Press.

– 2005. *Archaeologies of the Future: The Desire Called Utopia and Other Science Fictions*. London: Verso.

Jasińska-Kania, Aleksandra. (2010) 2016. "The Fluidity of Love and Hate: Zygmunt Bauman on Death, Love, and Hatred." Translated by Katarzyna Bartoszyńska. *Revue Interntionale de Philosophie* 3:327–46.

Jaspers, Karl. (1947) 2001. *The Question of German Guilt*. Translated by E.B. Ashton. New York: Fordham University Press.

Josephson-Storm, Jason Ānanda. 2021. *Metamodernism: The Future of Theory*. Chicago: University of Chicago Press.

Junge, Matthias. 2001. "Zygmunt Bauman's Poisoned Gift of Morality." *British Journal of Sociology* 1:105–19.

– 2008. *Bauman on Ambivalence – Fully Acknowledging the Ambiguity of Ambivalence*. In *The Sociology of Zygmunt Bauman: Challenges and Critique*, edited by Michael Hviid Jacobsen and Poul Poder, 41–56. Aldershot, UK: Ashgate.

Kafka, Franz. (1936) 1988. "Advocates." Translated by Tania Stern and James Stern. In *The Collected Short Stories of Franz Kafka*, 449–51. London: Penguin.

Kant, Immanuel. (1795) 1957. *Perpetual Peace*. Edited by Lewis White Beck. Indianapolis, IN: Bobbs-Merrill.

Kelles-Krauz, Kazimierz. 2018. *Marxism and Sociology: A Selection of Writings by Kazimierz Kelles-Krauz*. Edited by Helena Chmielewska-Szlajfer. Warsaw: Wydawnictwa Uniwersytetu Warszawskiego.

Kempny, Marian. 1995. "O roli kategorii kultury w myśleniu socjologicznym. Przypadek Zygmunta Baumana." In *Powroty i kontynuacje. Zygmuntowi Baumanowi w darze*, edited by Elżbieta Tarkowska, 177–93. Warsaw: Wydawnictwo IFiS PAN.

Kemp-Welch, Tony. 2006. "Dethroning Stalin: Poland 1956 and Its Legacy." *Europa-Asia Studies* 58, no. 8: 1261–84.

Kilminster, Richard, and Ian Varcoe. 1996. "Addendum: Culture and Power in the Writings of Zygmunt Bauman." In *Culture, Modernity, and Revolution: Essays in Honour of Zygmunt Bauman*, edited by Richard Kilminster and Ian Varcoe, 215–47. London: Routledge.

Kirby, Alan. 2009. *Digimodernism: How New Technologies Dismantle the Postmodern and Reconfigure Our Culture*. New York: Bloomsbury Academic & Professional.

Kłoskowska, Antonina. 1964. *Kultura masowa. Krytyka i obrona*. Warsaw: Państwowe Wydawnictwo Naukowe.

Koselleck, Reinhart. (1979) 2004. *Futures Past: On the Semantics of Historical Time*. Translated by Keith Tribe. New York: Columbia University Press.

Kossak, Jerzy. 1987. *Teoria kultury Karola Marksa i problemy współczesnego humanizmu*. Warsaw: Książka i Wiedza.

Krajewski, Marek, ed. 2014. *Deindywiduacja. Socjologia zachowań zbiorowych*. Warsaw: Fundacja Nowej Kultury Bęc Zmiana.

Kraśko, Nina. 1995. "O socjologii zaangażowanej Zygmunta Baumana." In *Powroty i kontynuacje. Zygmuntowi Baumanowi w darze*, edited by Elżbieta Tarkowska, 22–37. Warsaw: Wydawnictwo IFiS PAN.

Kristeva, Julia. (1969) 1980. *Desire in Language: A Semiotic Approach to Literature and Art*. Edited by Leon Roudiez. Translated by Thomas Gora and Alice Jardine. New York: Columbia University Press.

Kroeber, Alfred, and Clyde Kluckhohn. 1952. *Culture: A Critical Review of Concepts and Definitions*. Cambridge, MA: Museum.

Kurczewski, Jacek. 1988. "A Self-Commissioned Sociology for the People: Ossowski on Marxism and Marxist Societies." *Polish Sociological Review* 2:95–113.

Lash, Scott. 1999. *Another Modernity: A Different Rationality*. Oxford: Blackwell.

Leach, Edmund. 1964. "Anthropological Aspects of Language: Animal Categories and Verbal Abuse." In *New Directions in the Study of Language*, edited by Eric. H. Lenneberg, 22–63. Cambridge, MA: MIT Press.

Levinas, Emanuel. (1961) 1969. *Totality and Infinity: An Essay on Exteriority*. Translated by Alphonso Lingis. Pittsburgh, PA: Duquesne University Press.

– (1982) 1985. *Ethics and Infinity: Conversations with Philippe Nemo*. Translated by Richard A. Cohen. Pittsburgh, PA: Duquesne University Press.

Lévi-Strauss, Claude. (1955) 1961. *A World on the Wane*. Translated by John Russel. London: Hutchinson.

– (1958) 1963. *Structural Anthropology*. Translated by Claire Jacobson and Brooke Grundfest Schoepf. New York: Basic Books.

Levitas, Ruth. 1990. *The Concept of Utopia*. London: Philip Allan.

– 2013. *Utopia as Method: The Imaginary Reconstitution of Society*. Basingstoke, UK: Palgrave Macmillan.

Linton, Ralph. 1945. *The Cultural Background of Personality*. New York: D. Appleton-Century.

Łuczeczko, Paweł. 2011. "Socjologiczne badania nad kulturą a nauki etnologiczne. Historia romansów i rozstań oraz jej konsekwencje." *Roczniki Historii Socjologii* 1:57–86.

Lyotard, Jean-François. (1979) 1984. *The Postmodern Condition*. Translated by Geoff Bennington and Brian Massumi. Minneapolis: University of Minnesota.

Macksey, Richard, and Eugenio Donato, eds. 1970. *The Structuralist Controversy: The Languages of Criticism and the Sciences of Man*. Baltimore, MD: Johns Hopkins University Press.

Mafessoli, Michel. (1988) 1996. *The Time of Tribes: The Decline of Individualism in Mass Society*. Translated by Don Smith. London: Sage.

Malinowski, Bronisław. 1944. *A Scientific Theory of Culture and Other Essays*. Chapel Hill: University of North Carolina Press.

Mannheim, Karl. (1929) 1954. *Ideology and Utopia: An Introduction to the Sociology of Knowledge*. Translated by Louis Wirth and Edward Shils. London: Routledge & Kegan Paul.

Marciniak, Mateusz. 2011. *Orientacje konsumpcyjne młodzieży akademickiej. Perspektywa Baumanowska*. Kraków, Poland: Impuls.

Marcuse, Herbert. 1955. *Eros and Civilization: A Philosophical Inquiry into Freud*. Boston: Beacon Press.

– 1964. *One-Dimensional Man: Studies in the Ideology of Advanced Industrial Society*. Boston: Beacon Press.

– 1972. *Counter-Revolution and Revolt*. Boston: Beacon Press.

Marshman, Sophia. 2008. "Bauman on Genocide – Modernity and Mass Murder: From Classification to Annihilation?" In *The Sociology of Zygmunt*

Bauman: Challenges and Critique, edited by Michael Hviid Jacobsen and Poul Poder, 75–94. Aldershot, UK: Ashgate.

Marx, Karl, and Friedrich Engels. (1932) 1970. *The German Ideology, Part One and Selections from Parts Two and Three and Supplementary Texts*. Edited by Christopher John Arthur. New York: International Publishers.

Maslow, Abraham. 1943. "A Theory of Human Motivation." *Psychological Review* 50(4): 370–96.

– 1962. *Toward a Psychology of Being*. Princeton, NJ: D. Van Nostrand.

Mills, Charles Wright. 1959. *The Sociological Imagination*. Oxford: Oxford University Press.

Mokrzycki, Edmund. 1964. "Uwagi o pojęciu kultury." *Studia Socjologiczne* 4:241–8.

Morawski, Stefan. 1998. "Bauman's Ways of Seeing the World." *Theory, Culture & Society* 1:29–38.

– 1999. *Niewdzięczne rysowanie mapy... O postmodernie(izmie) i kryzysie kultury*. Toruń, Poland: Wydawnictwo UMK.

More, Thomas. (1516) 2014. *Utopia*. Translated by Clarence H. Miller. New Haven, CT: Yale University Press.

Muggleton, David. 2000. *Inside Subculture: The Postmodern Meaning of Style*. Oxford: Berg.

Niemeyer, Katharina, ed. (2014). *Media and Nostalgia: Yearning for the Past, Present and Future*. Basingstoke, UK: Palgrave Macmillan.

Norris, Pippa, and Ronald Inglehart. 2019. *Cultural Backlash: Trump, Brexit and Authoritarian Populism*. Cambridge: Cambridge University Press.

Offe, Claus. 1996. *Modernity and the State: East, West*. Cambridge, MA: MIT Press.

Ossowski, Stanisław. (1956) 2016. "Taktyka i kultura." In *Stanisław Ossowski w pełnym blasku. Suplement do Dzieł*, edited by Antoni Sułek, 181–92. Warsaw: Wydawnictwo Naukowe Scholar.

– 1962. *O osobliwościach nauk społecznych*. Warsaw: Państwowe Wydawnictwo Naukowe.

– 1998. "The Researcher's Duty: Obedience in Thinking and Social Duty of a Scientist." *Polish Sociological Review* 2:93–4.

Palmer, Jack. Forthcoming. *Bauman and the West: Exile, Culture, Dialogue*. Montreal: McGill-Queen's University Press.

Palmer, Jack, and Dariusz Brzeziński. 2022a. "Editors' Introduction: Through the Window Again; Revisiting *Modernity and the Holocaust*." In *Revisiting*

Modernity and the Holocaust: Heritage, Dilemmas, Extensions, edited by Jack Palmer and Dariusz Brzeziński, 1–21. Abingdon, UK: Routledge.

– eds. 2022b. *Revisiting Modernity and the Holocaust: Heritage, Dilemmas, Extensions*. Abingdon, UK: Routledge.

Palmer, Jack, Dariusz Brzezinski, and Tom Campbell. 2020. "Sixty-Three Years of Thinking Sociologically: Compiling the Bibliography of Zygmunt Bauman." *Thesis Eleven* 156, no. 1: 118–33.

Parsons, Talcott. (1951) 1991. *The Social System*. London: Routledge.

– 1972. "Culture and Social System Revisited." *Social Science Quarterly* 53, no. 2: 253–66.

Peel, John David Yeadon. 1987. "History, Culture, and the Comparative Method: A West African Puzzle." In *Comparative Anthropology*, edited by Ladislav Holy, 88–118. Oxford: Basil Blackwell.

Poder, Poul. 2007. "Relatively Liquid Interpersonal Relationships in Flexible Work Life." In *The Contemporary Bauman*, edited by Anthony Elliott, 136–53. London: Routledge.

Pollock, Griselda. 2022. "Reading *Modernity and the Holocaust* with and against *Winter in the Morning*." In *Revisiting Modernity and the Holocaust: Heritage, Dilemmas, Extensions*, edited by Jack Palmer and Dariusz Brzeziński, 177–96. Abingdon, UK: Routledge.

Popper, Karl. (1945) 2011. *The Open Society and Its Enemies*. London: Routledge.

Porter, Patrick. 2020. *The False Promise of Liberal Order: Nostalgia, Delusion, and the Rise of Trump*. Cambridge: Polity Press.

Prazmowska, Anita. 2016. *Wladyslaw Gomulka: A Biography*. London: I.B. Tauris.

Přibáň, Jirí, ed. 2007. *Liquid Society and Its Law*. London: Routledge.

Rattansi, Ali. 2017. *Bauman and Contemporary Sociology: A Critical Analysis*. Manchester, UK: Manchester University Press.

Ray, Larry. 2022. "Modernity or Decivilisation? Reflections on *Modernity and the Holocaust* Today." In *Revisiting Modernity and the Holocaust: Heritage, Dilemmas, Extensions*, edited by Jack Palmer and Dariusz Brzeziński, 25–38. Abingdon, UK: Routledge.

Reynolds, Simon. 2010. *Retromania: Pop Culture's Addiction to Its Own Past*. New York: Farrar, Straus & Giroux.

Ricoeur, Paul. (1969) 1974. *The Conflict of Interpretations: Essays in Hermeneutics*. Edited by Don Ihde. Translated by Kathleen McLaughlin, Robert Sweeney, Willis Domingo, Peter McCormick, Denis Savage, and Charles Freilich. Evanston, IL: Northwestern University Press.

Ritzer, George. 2010. "'Płynna globalizacja': Zastosowanie i krytyka pojęcia płynności Zygmunta Baumana." Translated into Polish by Michał Bogdan and Maciej Przybylski. In *Zrozumieć nowoczesność. Księga Jubileuszowa Zygmunta Baumana*, edited by Andrzej Chrzanowski, Wiesław Godzic, and Anna Zeidler-Janiszewska, 221–41. Warsaw: Wydawnictwo Officyna.

Rubenstein, Richard L. 1978. *The Cunning of History: The Holocaust and the American Future*. New York: HarperColllins.

Salmose, Niklas. 2019. *Contemporary Nostalgia*. Basel: Mdpi AG.

Sargent, Lyman Tower. 2010. *Utopianism: A Very Short Introduction*. Oxford: Oxford University Press.

Sartre, Jean-Paul. (1943) 2001. *Being and Nothingness: An Essay on Phenomenological Ontology*. Translated by Hazel E. Barnes. New York: Citadel.

Sayers, Janet. 2007. "Liquid Love: Psychoanalising Mania." In *The Contemporary Bauman*, edited by Anthony Elliott, 154–67. London: Routledge.

Sennett, Richard. 1998. *Corrosion of Character: The Personal Consequences of Work in the New Capitalism*. New York: Norton.

Sewell, William H., Jr. (1999) 2005. *Logics of History: Social Theory and Social Transformation*. Chicago: University of Chicago Press.

Simmel, George. (1908) 1921. "The Sociological Significance of the 'Stranger.'" In *Introduction to the Science of Sociology*, edited by Robert Ezra Park and Ernest W. Burgess, 322–7. Chicago: University of Chicago Press.

Smith, Dennis. 1999. *Zygmunt Bauman: Prophet of Postmodernity*. Cambridge: Polity Press.

Snyder, Timothy. 1997. *Nationalism, Marxism, and Modern Central Europe: A Biography of Kazimierz Kelles-Krauz (1872–1905)*. Cambridge, MA: Harvard Ukrainian Research Institute.

Standing, Guy. 2011. *The Precariat: The New Dangerous Class*. London: Bloomsbury Academic.

Steward, Julian H. 1955. *Theory of Culture Change: The Methodology of Multilinear Evolution*. Urbana: University of Illinois Press.

Stola, Dariusz. 2006. "Anti-Zionism as Multipurpose Policy Instrument: The Anti-Zionist Campaign in Poland, 1967–1968." *Journal of Israeli History* 1:175–201.

– 2017. "Jewish Emigration from Communist Poland: The Decline of Polish Jewry in the Aftermath of the Holocaust." *East European Jewish Affairs* 2–3:169–88.

Swidler, Ann. 1986. "Culture in Action: Symbols and Strategies." *American Sociological Review* 51:273–86.

Tarkowska, Elżbieta. 1995a. "Koniec i początek, czyli próba antropologii społeczeństwa polskiego." In *Powroty i kontynuacje. Zygmuntowi Baumanowi w darze*, edited by Elżbieta Tarkowska, 9–21. Warsaw: Wydawnictwo IFiS PAN.

– ed. 1995b. *Powroty i kontynuacje. Zygmuntowi Baumanowi w darze*. Warsaw: Wydawnictwo IFiS PAN.

– 2010. "*Homo sacer* Zygmunta Baumana." In *Zrozumieć nowoczesność. Księga Jubileuszowa Zygmunta Baumana*, edited by Andrzej Chrzanowski, Wiesław Godzic, and Anna Zeidler-Janiszewska, 255–64. Warsaw: Wydawnictwo Officyna.

Tester, Keith. 2002. "Paths in Zygmunt Bauman's Social Thought." *Thesis Eleven* 70:55–71.

– 2004. *The Social Thought of Zygmunt Bauman*. Basingstoke, UK: Palgrave Macmillan.

– 2006. "Intellectual Immigration and the English Idiom (Or, A Tale of Bustards and Eagles)." *Polish Sociological Review* 3:275–91.

Tester, Keith, and Michael Hviid Jacobsen. 2005. *Bauman before Postmodernity: Invitation, Conversations and Annotated Bibliography, 1953–1989*. Aalborg, Denmark: Aalborg University Press.

Tokarska-Bakir, Joanna. 2022. "The Sociology of Modernity, the Ethnography of the Holocaust: What Zygmunt Bauman Knew." In *Revisiting Modernity and the Holocaust: Heritage, Dilemmas, Extensions*, edited by Jack Palmer and Dariusz Brzeziński, 39–55. Abingdon, UK: Routledge.

Trueman, Carl R. 2020. *The Rise and Triumph of the Modern Self: Cultural Amnesia, Expressive Individualism, and the Road to Sexual Revolution*. Wheaton, IL: Crossway.

Turner, Jonathan. 1974. *The Structure of Sociological Theory*. Homewood, IL: Dorsey Press.

Turner, Victor. 1967. *The Forest of Symbols: Aspects of Ndembu Ritual*. Ithaca, NY: Cornell University Press.

Tylor, Edward Burnett. 1871. *Primitive Culture: Researches into the Development of Mythology, Philosophy, Religion, Art, and Custom*. London: John Murray.

Vaisey, Stephen. 2010. "From Contradiction to Coherence: Theory Building in the Sociology of Culture." SocArXiv. Accessed 31 January 2022. https://osf.io/preprints/socarxiv/9mwfc/

Venuti, Lawrence, ed. 2000. *The Translation Studies Reader*. London: Routledge.

Vermeulen, Timotheus, and Robin van den Akker. 2010. "Notes on Metamodernism." *Journal of Aesthetics & Culture* 2:1–14.

Vetlesen, Arne Johan. 2005. *Evil and Human Agency: Understanding Collective Evildoing*. Cambridge: Cambridge University Press.

– 2022. "Reassessing *Modernity and the Holocaust* in the Light of Genocide in Bosnia." In *Revisiting Modernity and the Holocaust: Heritage, Dilemmas, Extensions*, edited by Jack Palmer and Dariusz Brzeziński, 111–24. Abingdon, UK: Routledge.

Virilio, Paul. (1977) 1986. *Speed and Politics: An Essay on Dromology*. Translated by Mark Polizzotti. New York: Columbia University Press.

– (1998) 2005. *The Information Bomb*. Translated by Chris Turner. London: Verso.

Wagner, Izabela. 2020. *Bauman: A Biography*. Cambridge: Polity Press.

– 2022. "Janina and Zygmunt Bauman: A Case Study of Inspiring Collaboration." In *Revisiting Modernity and the Holocaust: Heritage, Dilemmas, Extensions*, edited by Jack Palmer and Dariusz Brzeziński, 156–76. Abingdon, UK: Routledge.

Walicki, Andrzej. 1997. *Marxism and the Leap to the Kingdom of Freedom: The Rise and Fall of the Communist Utopia*. Stanford, CA: Stanford University Press.

Warf, Barney, and Santa Arias, eds. 2009. *The Spatial Turn: Interdisciplinary Perspectives*. London: Routledge.

Weber, Max. (1905) 1930. *The Protestant Ethic and the Spirit of Capitalism*. Translated by Talcott Parsons. London: Unwin University Books.

– (1917–19) 2004. *The Vocation Lectures: "Science as a Vocation," "Politics as a Vocation."* Edited and with an introduction by David Owen and Tracy B. Strong. Translated by Rodney Livingstone. Indianapolis, IN: Hackett.

– (1922) 1968. *Economy and Society: An Outline of Interpretative Sociology*. Vols. 1–3. Edited by Guenther Roth and Claus Wittich. Translated by Ephraim Fischoff. New York: Bedminster Press.

White, Leslie A. 1959. *The Evolution of Culture: The Development of Civilization to the Fall of Rome*. New York: McGraw-Hill.

Williams, Raymond. 1966. *Modern Tragedy*. London: Chatto & Windus.

Wolf, Eric. 1982. *Europe and the People without History*. Berkeley: University of California Press.

Wrong, Dennis. 1961. "The Oversocialized Conception of Man in Modern Sociology." *American Sociological Review* 26, no. 2: 183–93.

Znaniecki, Florian. 1919. *Cultural Reality*. Chicago: University of Chicago Press.
– 1952. *Cultural Sciences: Their Origin and Development*, Urbana: University of Illinois Press.
Zuboff, Shochana. 2019. *The Age of Surveillance Capitalism: The Fight for a Human Future at the New Frontier of Power*. New York: Public Affairs.

Index